ORGANIZING AT
THE MARGINS

ORGANIZING AT THE MARGINS

The Symbolic Politics of Labor in
South Korea and the United States

Jennifer Jihye Chun

ILR PRESS

AN IMPRINT OF

CORNELL UNIVERSITY PRESS   **ITHACA AND LONDON**

Korea Foundation
한국국제교류재단

The Korea Foundation has provided financial assistance for the undertaking of this publication project.

First published 2009 by Cornell University Press
Printed in the United States of America

Librarians: A CIP catalog record for this book is available from the Library of Congress.

ISBN 978-0-8014-4711-2 (cloth : alk. paper)

Cornell University Press strives to use environmentally responsible suppliers and materials to the fullest extent possible in the publishing of its books. Such materials include vegetable-based, low-VOC inks and acid-free papers that are recycled, totally chlorine-free, or partly composed of nonwood fibers. For further information, visit our website at www.cornellpress.cornell.edu.

Cloth printing   10   9   8   7   6   5   4   3   2   1

To my parents

Contents

Preface

In the summer of 1998, I left Berkeley, California, and arrived in Seoul, Korea. I was immediately swept up in a wave of union protests organized by the Korean Confederation of Trade Unions (KCTU)—the militant democratic wing of the labor movement. With raised fists and indignant voices, hundreds of thousands of unionists participated in mass rallies, marches, and strikes to express their opposition to structural adjustment reforms by the International Monetary Fund (IMF).[1] While the Korean government insisted that privatization, labor market deregulation, and flexible labor law revisions were all necessary for the country to overcome the so-called IMF crisis, the nation's highly militant workforce rejected the assault on their wages and livelihoods. From the huge banners that were prominently displayed at public demonstrations to the synchronized chants of protesting unionists, the terms of their opposition were clear: "Eradicate Unilateral Economic Restructuring! Guarantee Job Security! Defend Workers' Right to Live!" There would be no national economic recovery off the backs of workers.

The mass opposition of Korean workers to the "flexible" prescriptions of neoliberal globalization was exactly what led my ethnographic pursuits from one of Silicon Valley's high-tech shop floors to the contentious streets of downtown Seoul. My previous research examining low-paid assembly work, and much of the literature on the fate of trade unions under globalization, indicated that workers had little, if any, power to challenge the flexible imperatives of today's highly competitive global economy. While touted for its "win-win" advantages for both workers and managers alike, the drive for flexibility was more than a business strategy to boost profits and efficiency; it constituted a powerful disciplinary force upon workers, whose very livelihoods had become subordinated to a dizzying array of performance indicators, quality-control measures, and market forecasts (Chun 2001). The militant struggles of Korean unionists, however, seemed to defy the universalizing laws of the new global marketplace. Rather than accept its inevitability, the Korean labor movement was mounting a full-scale effort to challenge neoliberal restructuring and its flexible prescriptions. While the IMF's structural adjustment loan conditionalities were virulently criticized, the Korean government's attempt to operationalize its universalizing mandates were also harshly censured. The mass-based, politically charged defiance of Korean unionists, I speculated, could signal the beginnings of a potential shift in the international geography of working-class power. Although workers and trade unions in the advanced industrialized core of the Global North had submitted to the logic of flexibility, however unwillingly at first, perhaps the workers and trade unions of the rapidly industrializing peripheries of the Global South could chart an alternative course.[2]

In a few short months, however, I would encounter the first of several violated expectations in the messy world of ethnography. Rather than lead a dynamic worker-based movement against the flexible prescriptions of global neoliberalism, the Korean labor movement seemed to be imploding. In August 1998, the leadership of one of the most militant of KCTU's member unions, the Hyundai Motors Union in Ulsan, consented to the mass layoffs under the rationale of "necessary business restructuring," igniting a chain of events that began undermining the strength and legitimacy of organized labor, especially militant forms of unionism (see chapter 2). Skyrocketing layoffs, unprecedented unemployment, and mass social dislocation followed the state deregulation of the labor market and the privatization of public industries. The criminalization of union militancy recommenced under the guise of shepherding national economic recovery. As the national economic crisis unfolded, the seduction of mass labor militancy gave way to a more sobering look at the internal schisms playing out among workers and their collective organizations, not only in Korea but also around the world. As more and more workers faced downward pressures on their wages and working conditions, clear fault lines began to emerge. Unions representing more privileged sectors of the industrial workforce increasingly prioritized the job security and interests of their members at the expense of more disadvantaged groups of workers, thereby exacerbating capital's divide-and-conquer strategies. Whereas in the United States, dividing lines cut across race, immigration status, and gender, in South Korea, they primarily cut across gender (see chapter 3). "Women fired first" seemed to be the overarching principle of mass layoffs, especially at the height of Korea's financial crisis, and some male-dominated unions were accused of using women workers as a buffer to mitigate the damaging effects of workplace restructuring on male members.

I left South Korea after fifteen months of fieldwork in an ethnographic haze. Instead of documenting the vibrancy of industrial unionism, my notes told a story of a militant, yet highly divided and conflict-ridden labor movement. While I had not anticipated writing another account of organized labor's defeats at the hands of global capital and neoliberal states, the Korean labor movement seemed to be heading on the same downward spiral as labor movements in the Global North, left only to try to slow down the erosion and decay.

To my surprise, the year 2000 threw up another violated expectation. After decades of exclusion, the Executive Committee of the American Federation of Labor and Congress of Industrial Organizations (AFL-CIO) issued a historic reversal of its anti-immigrant stance. Not only did the AFL-CIO Executive Council publicly declare that it "stands proudly on the side of immigrant workers," but it also called for sweeping protections of undocumented workers, including the repeal of employer sanctions, unconditional amnesty for undocumented immigrants and laws that provide full workplace rights for immigrant workers.[3] Likewise, in South Korea, in response to the exclusionary tendencies of big enterprise unions, the KCTU elected a new president in 2000 who passionately reaffirmed the KCTU's commitment to act as the "the genuine representative of all working people, including those workers in non-standard employment, the unemployed, and the vast array of workers in small enterprises."[4] In addition, the independent KCTU and the historically government-linked, more politically moderate Federation of Korean Trade Unions (FKTU), once starkly opposed, began uniting under the cause of "abolishing irregular employment" (*pijŏng'gyujik ch'ŏlpye*).

This unexpected convergence became the new starting point for my project. Previously stigmatized as "unorganizable," the ranks of unorganized workers in low-paid, insecure jobs represent the new *cause célèbre* of labor movements in two very different countries—South Korea and the United States (see chapter 4). Although the embrace of historically excluded sectors of the workforce in both countries is partial and contested, the relative successes of local organizing cases waged by marginalized workers are redefining the priorities and the vocabularies of crisis-ridden labor movements. In the United States, low-wage service workers in highly insecure, precarious jobs—many of whom are immigrants and women—have won historic victories in their fight to secure more just living and working conditions. By challenging the institutional policies and cultural values that permit workers and their families to live in a chronic state of poverty, immigrant janitors, hotel workers, home care workers, and others are paving the way for the renewal of the U.S. labor movement. In South Korea as well, low-paid workers in luxury hotels, country clubs, cafeterias, and other service sectors—many of whom are women—have begun challenging the deterioration of their wages and working conditions under more insecure forms of irregular employment. Given the harsh climate of antiunionism that has followed the Asian debt crisis (1997–1998), the unexpected militancy of irregularly employed women workers is injecting renewed vitality into the Korean labor movement.[5]

The gains made by these groups of workers are still relatively minor with respect to the deepening crises plaguing organized labor movements in today's global economy. However, they are part of a growing effort by unions, community organizations, social justice organizations, immigrant rights advocates, and labor activists, among others, to prioritize the struggles of workers that have been historically relegated to the bottom of national labor market hierarchies (see chapter 4). What might the striking convergence in the trajectories of the South Korean and U.S. labor movements mean for the dynamics of change taking place for labor on a global scale? To what extent does the embrace of marginalized groups of workers such as immigrants and women by previously exclusionary labor movements signal the development of more inclusive and democratic forms of labor politics? How can workers subject to overlapping forms of social, economic, and political marginality actually transform the unequal relations of power and domination that underpin downgraded forms of employment?

The answers to these questions constitute the heart of this book. What unfolds is a story about a sea change in the dynamics of labor politics and organization. South Korea and the United States have two different paths of industrial development, histories of class formation, and positions in the larger world economic system, yet both labor movements are experiencing profound shifts in who the "working class" is and how to build collective power under processes of globalization. Through a comparative historical analysis of the changing dynamics of the Korean and U.S. labor movements, the first part of the book reveals that global economic transformations are reshaping the balance of power among capital, labor, and the state in strikingly similar ways. While each labor movement previously built its base of power on the capacity of some of the most powerful workers in the labor market to extract concessions from capital and the state, the reconfiguration of national terrains of unionism under processes of globalization has begun shifting organized labor's attention to some of the most vulnerable groups of workers, especially the growing ranks of (im)migrant and women workers employed in low-paid, insecure service jobs. This shift has revived the importance of social movement–inspired forms of unionism that seek to challenge the overlapping conditions of economic and social marginalization.

Through a comparative analysis of ethnographic case studies of labor organizing, the second half of the book illustrates exactly how and under what conditions marginalized groups of workers can challenge the downward pressures on their wages and working conditions. In particular, I focus on two groups of workers in low-paid, service jobs: subcontracted university janitors and independently contracted personal service workers. Rather than rely solely on conventional tactics such as the labor strike, which harness workers' power at the point of production, these workers are cultivating an alternative form of leverage based on symbolic politics; that is, "symbolic leverage." By waging dramatic, morally charged struggles against the injustice of their living and working conditions, janitors, home care workers, and golf caddies are seeking to transform the relations of power and inequality that underpin downgraded forms of low-paid, service work. As I elaborate in chapters 5 and 6, "symbolic leverage" roots the source of worker power in the contested arena of culture and public debates about values. By shifting the focus of their struggles away from narrowly defined labor disputes, symbolic leverage aims to undermine official sources of authority such as the law and demand alternative applications of social justice.

By emphasizing how processes of globalization are reconfiguring national terrains of unionism in unexpected ways, this book attempts to provide a systematic account of the shifting balance of power among labor, capital, and the state and its implications for how workers and their collective organizations are refashioning their politics and practices. My aim is not to write a comparative history of trade union renewal, nor is it to produce a "best practices" guide that weighs the benefits and disadvantages of various organizing strategies. It is, rather, to convey an account of "what might be called a conjuncture, a turning point, a break, a rupture" (Cooper 1987, xii). The story at the heart of this book is about exposing the limitations of old ways of organizing the workforce, based on historical relationships among labor, capital, and the state, and uncovering new ways of strengthening the basis of worker power, especially when approached from the perspective of workers on the bottom of social and economic hierarchies. In a global economy that feeds on and profits from social inequalities, rooting worker power in the contested politics of justice is central to any effort to produce more emancipatory possibilities for future generations.

Please note that all Korean words have been Romanized according to the McCune-Reischauer system; exceptions are published Korean authors and well-known Korean names and events using a different spelling in English.

Acknowledgments

The process of writing this book has brought me into contact with many exceptional people. I want to begin by thanking the workers, activists, students, and teachers in Korea who embraced me into their worlds of activism and shared their joys, hopes, heartaches, and passions with me. I owe special thanks to Maria Chol Soon Rhie who welcomed me into the Korean Women Workers Associations United (KWWAU) and gave me so many opportunities to learn from the wisdom and experience of activists like herself and others. Jinyoung Park with the KWWAU has not only been an invaluable researcher but a wonderful friend and confidante. I am also thankful to Jinkyoung Bae, Sanglim Choi, Soonim Choi, Jeehyeon Kim, Juhwan Kim, Namhee Park, Insoon Wang, and the rest of the staff at the Korean Women Workers Association and the Korean Women's Trade Union. Whether it was scouring their archives, spending late nights at the office, tagging along on their workshops and membership retreats, or perpetually asking questions, I learned as much from their generosity as I did from their courage and perseverance in trying to create a more just and compassionate world. I am also deeply indebted to the staff at the KCTU Seoul Regional Center, the KCTU Central Office, and the Korean Health and Medical Workers Union. They greeted my eagerness to learn with much patience, kindness, and generosity, bringing me to strikes, protests, marches, meetings, and postmeeting *dwipuri* sessions. Witnessing the intensity, stamina, and sheer bodily deprivation required to fill their shoes was both humbling and inspiring. Sangyun Bak's passing was a great shock to many, and I will miss his endless teasing, irreverent humor, and unflinching commitment to irregular workers and class liberation. I am particularly grateful to Soonkyoung Cho, Kyungsook Choi, Bonghee Chu, Hyewon Chung, Jooyeon Jeong, Myoung Joon Kim, Yoon-joo Lee, and Aelim Yoon for helping me make sense of the inspiring history and complex politics of the Korean labor movement.

I also want to thank the workers and the staff at the SEIU locals in Boston and Los Angeles where I visited. I am grateful to every worker, union organizer, and student activist who took the time out of their tremendously busy schedules to talk to me about the specific cases I was interested in. Special thanks to Sujin Lee for introducing me to the USC case and putting me in touch with her friends and former coworkers.

At Berkeley, I owe a tremendous debt of gratitude to Michael Burawoy. His constant encouragement and unwavering expectations instilled me with the confidence to see this work to completion, challenging me to take my ideas to the next level and reminding me of the bigger picture (that we drew so many times on the white board in his office). From my brief and early days as a shop-floor ethnographer to my later years as a participant observer in the Korean labor movement, my forays into the world of ethnography were inspired by his rigorous pursuit of the linkages between everyday life and the broader historical and structural forces that shape them. Kim Voss has been an insightful teacher and wonderful friend, always willing to lend a constructive ear and sound advice when I needed it the most. Peter Evans, Gillian Hart, John Lie, and Michael Omi provided sound advice, constructive feedback, and enthusiastic support throughout this project. I am privileged to have benefited from their astute and rigorous insights about the workings of politics, power, inequality, and capitalism.

While at Berkeley, I was fortunate to have the support of a wide community of friends and fellow students. I am especially grateful for the strength, humor, and intelligence of Robyn Rodriguez and Michelle Williams both of whom I have learned so much from as scholars and human beings. Lynnéa Stephen was a wonderful office mate and good friend, and she is dearly missed. I am also thankful for the input and support of Hwa-Jen Liu, Josh Page, Gretchen Purser, Jeff Sallaz, Youyenn Teo, Elsa Tranter, and Chris Wetzel. Outside my academic life, I am thankful to the members of my drumming group, *Jamaesori*, and the members and staff at Asian Immigrant Women Advocates in the Oakland and San Jose offices. I also appreciate the friendship and support of Sarah Eunkyung Chee, Helen Kim, Mimi Kim, Sujin Lee, Shruti Mehta, Young Shin, Shin Yi Tsai, and Eliza Wee.

Many people generously provided valuable insights and feedback as I began to turn my research into a book. I want to thank my colleagues at the University of British Columbia who graciously read parts of the manuscript and offered constructive feedback: Neil Gross, Amy Hanser, Tom Kemple, Renisa Mawani, Wendy Roth, and Rima Wilkes. I want to thank Ruth Milkman for her enthusiastic support for the project and her close reading of the entire manuscript. Hagen Koo also offered insightful comments and suggestions for how to improve the manuscript. I also benefited from comments I received after talks I gave at the UBC Centre for Women's and Gender Studies, the UBC Centre for Korean Research, the UBC Inter-Faculty Initiative on Migration Studies, and the University of Toronto Institute for Asian Studies. I am particularly grateful to Rina Agarwala, Yunshik Chang, Gillian Creese, Nam-lin Hur, Ching Kwan Lee, Hyun Ok Park, Becki Ross, Jesook Song, and Henry Yu. The UBC Centre for Korean Research provided invaluable support to help me revise and finish the manuscript. I thank Sage Publications for permission to reprint portions of an article published in 2005 as "Public Dramas and the Politics of Justice: Comparison of Janitors' Union Struggles in South Korea and the United States," *Work and Occupations* 32 (4): 486–503.

As I prepared the final version, I had the good fortune of benefiting from the editorial assistance of UBC undergraduate, Tamara Ibrahim. I also thank the staff at Cornell University Press, especially Susan Specter for her fantastic manuscript editing and Fran Benson for her enthusiasm, commitment, and patience. All errors, of course, are mine alone.

Last but not least are the thanks I owe to my family for weathering the ups and downs of the seemingly never-ending process of writing and rewriting. I am deeply grateful for the love, support, and companionship of Ju Hui Judy Han. She has gone above and beyond to help me complete this milestone, from challenging me to sharpen and deepen my ideas to easing my bouts of stress and anxiety to making sure that Puca, George, and I did not go hungry. My steadfast and beloved friendship with Joanne Chang helped me keep the most important things in life in perspective. My sister, Joanne, has always been my rock, lending her unconditional love and support to everything I do. My brother, David, has brought humor and a healthy dose of perspective to all my endeavors. My greatest debt of gratitude is owed to my parents, Yang Kog and Kyung Ja Chun. My father instilled me with a love of books and writing; my mother instilled me with a passion and curiosity about the world around me. Without their unfailing faith and support, I would not be where I am today. It is to them that I dedicate this book.

Abbreviations

ACORN	Associations of Community Organizations for Reform NOW
AFL-CIO	American Federation of Labor and Congress of Industrial Organizations
BLS	U.S. Bureau of Labor Statistics
CIO	Congress of Industrial Organizations
ERAP	Economic Research and Action Project
88CC	88 Country Club
FLSA	Fair Labor Standards Act (US)
FKTU	Federation of Korean Trade Unions
GDP	Gross Domestic Product
GM	General Motors
HCECP	Harvard Committee of Employment and Contracting Procedures
HERE	Hotel Employees and Restaurant Employees
HPLM	Harvard Progressive Labor Movement
ICE	Immigration and Customs Enforcement
IHSS	In-Home Supportive Service System
ILO	International Labor Organization
IMF	International Monetary Fund
INS	Immigration and Naturalization Services
IWWA	Incheon Women Workers Association
JforJ	"Justice for Janitors"
KCTU	Korean Confederation of Trade Unions

KLI	Korea Labor Institute
KSPW	Korean Solidarity against Precarious Work
KT	Korea Telecom
KWWA	Korean Women Workers Association
KWWAU	Korean Women Workers Associations United
KWTU	Korean Women's Trade Union
LSA	Labor Standards Act (South Korea)
NACLA	North American Congress on Latin America
NFWA	National Farm Workers Association
NGO	Nongovernmental organization
NICs	Newly Industrializing Countries
NLRA	National Labor Relations Act
NLRB	National Labor Relations Board
OECD	Organization for Economic Co-Operation and Development
PATCO	Professional Air Traffic Controllers Organization
PASC	Personal Assistance Services Council
PD	"Participatory Democracy"
PICIS	Policy and Information Center of Internal Solidarity
PSSP	People's Solidarity for Social Progress
PWC	Power of the Working Class
ROK	Republic of Korea
SCALE	Student Coalition Against Labor Exploitation
SDS	Students for a Democratic Society
SNU	Seoul National University
SEIU	Service Employees International Union
SWTU	Seoul Women's Trade Union
TAN	Transnational advocacy network
UAW	United Auto Workers
UFCW	United Food and Commercial Workers
UFW	United Farm Workers
UFCW	United Food and Commercial Workers
USAS	United Students Against Sweatshops
USC	University of Southern California

ORGANIZING AT THE MARGINS

THE SYMBOLIC LEVERAGE OF LABOR

SEIU gets their moral center from the janitors.... We are the campaign that people in the public look at and gives SEIU its glamour and identity. People say all the time that janitors are the "urban farmworkers." They have that kind of moral cause that people are really able to unite around.... We put janitors forward as examples of what's wrong—economic injustice. But they are not victims of it, because people are standing up and fighting militant actions in the street. The personal stories that we put out there [about the hardships of health care workers, immigrants, and mothers]... in my opinion, that's really where public support comes from.

—Service Employees International Union (SEIU) organizer

When I see middle-aged or elderly women [*ajumma*] find a way through labor unions to show off the abilities and skills they have had all these years, it is moving and inspirational. I see how all their energies and capacities were repressed, all because they were women, working at the lowest rungs of the social hierarchy, earning minimum wages, as lowly janitors and irregular [*pijŏng'gyujik*] workers. These people meet women's movements and women's labor unions and they just blossom and come to life. There are some amazing orators and great leaders, and that's because their stories are rooted in life experiences. Sixty-something union members saying they can now live with pride.... It's only when the majority of the public participates that we'll see meaningful change.

—Korean Women's Trade Union (KWTU) organizer

The struggles of janitors as well as other low-paid service workers—many of whom are immigrants, people of color, and women—demonstrate that building power from the margins is not only possible but *pivotal* to the future of workers and their collective organizations in the twenty-first century. The unexpected makeover of one of the most unglamorous segments of the U.S. workforce speaks to the transformative potential of marginality. By rendering the injustice of poverty wages and social inequality both intimate and public, SEIU has refashioned the identity of janitors from one of the most undervalued and demeaned segments of society into the "moral center" of the most rapidly growing union in the United States. The use of tactics and vocabularies from civil rights–inspired unions such as the United Farm Workers (UFW) in the 1960s and 1970s has also garnered rare public support for unpopular trade unions. As the etymological origin of the word janitors to the two-headed Roman god Janus suggests, the role of janitors as doorkeepers or, more specifically, guards to the gates of heaven, makes the figure of the janitor a powerful catalyst of transitions and new beginnings.[1] Since the SEIU launched its morally charged "Justice for Janitors" (JforJ) campaign in 1985, one hundred thousand new janitors as well as many other low-paid service workers such as home care workers, nursing care workers, and security guards have joined the union's ranks. While its dynamic growth and aggressive organizing campaigns have created schisms and conflicts, the SEIU has led one of the most decisive shifts in the contemporary U.S. labor movement.

Likewise, in South Korea the growing ranks of *pijŏng'gyujik* (hereafter translated as "irregular" or "nonstandard") workers—many of whom are women employed in low-paid and insecure jobs—are redefining the landscape of unionism. By "irregular" workers, I refer to those workers employed outside the boundaries of full-time work under a single employer, including part-time, temporary, subcontracted, independently contracted, and daily workers among others, and thus, often denied basic rights entitled to fully employed workers such as paid sick and vacation leave, employer-paid health care, unemployment compensation, and seniority. No longer willing to accept the stigma and chronic poverty associated with work on the "lowest rungs of the social hierarchy," a new generation is rising up against the rampant cost-cutting and discrimination associated with the post-IMF deregulated labor relations climate. While "elderly women" and "lowly janitors" do not represent the "typical" image of a militant and male trade unionist, they too are joining unions and taking to the streets. Women's movement organizations and newly formed independent women's unions provide an important vehicle to empower "sixty-something union members" to live with pride and dignity, according to the KWTU organizer quoted above. For those who never imagined wearing a union vest or participating in a "demo" (*taemo*), a colloquial term for mass protests, the experience of speaking out against the unjust terms of irregular employment is both uplifting and transformative not only for individual workers but also for the broader labor movement. In addition to striking workers in the auto and steel factories, shipbuilding and transportation, telecommunications and other white-collar sectors, images of union struggles now include the primarily female workforce of golf game assistants and home study tutors misclassified as independent contractors; hotel room cleaners, school cafeteria workers, and train attendants employed under outsourced and often negligent third parties; and telephone operators and retail cashiers employed under highly insecure and unregulated short-term contracts.

The upsurge of labor unrest by atypical and vulnerable segments of the workforce in South Korea and the United States as well as around the world is reviving interest in the transformation of trade unions and labor movements, more broadly (Clawson 2003; Cornfield and McCammon 2003; Fantasia and Voss 2004; Milkman 2006; Moody 1997; Munck and Waterman 1999; Voss and Sherman 2000; Turner and Hurd 2001). Despite widespread consensus from both sides of the political spectrum that trade unions have become obsolete in a globalizing world, many are beginning to deliver optimistic forecasts for the future. The development of new organizational strategies and forms that can outsmart anti-union employers (e.g., comprehensive organizing campaigns), outmaneuver transnational corporations (e.g., consumer-student boycotts, transnational labor coalitions, cross-border organizing), and overcome overlapping forms of social, economic, and political disadvantage (e.g., community unionism, labor-community coalitions) represent hopeful signs of change amidst a backdrop of dwindling union density, deepening income polarization, and deteriorating labor standards.[2] While labor scholars and practitioners debate the pros and cons of different strategies and organizing models, most agree that the narrow, self-interested unionism of the post-1945 era has reached its limits. What we find, in particular, is renewed interest in the role of labor as a dynamic social movement, replete with contentious politics and collective mobilization (Clawson 2003; Fantasia and Voss 2004; Lopez 2004; Moody 1997; Turner and Hurd 2001).

The proliferation of vibrant forms of collective action that go beyond organized labor's traditional weapon—the strike—and mobilize the broader public alongside unions calls attention to the significance of the *symbolic* as a key site of contestation in contemporary labor struggles. The fight against economic injustice invariably includes another conception of justice that is rooted in the cultural or symbolic. The overlapping nature of such struggles is particularly salient for workers situated at the bottom of the socioeconomic and symbolic order. Challenging economic marginalization often entails overcoming "institutionalized patterns of cultural value that constitute some actors as inferior, excluded, wholly other or simply invisible," thus intertwining what Nancy

Fraser calls "struggles for recognition" with "struggles for redistribution" (1995, 70–71; 1997).

The entanglement of the material and symbolic also foregrounds the importance of the *public,* or perhaps more fittingly, "counterpublics" as driving forces of change (see Fraser 1996; Warner 2002). While the physical gathering of a broad array of individuals during a public protest is crucial for demonstrating strength in numbers, the morally charged language that is circulated on protest signs and in protest chants as well as in the media evokes a longer history of discursively mediated struggles on behalf of the poor, the excluded, and the marginalized. Using the signs, slogans, and vocabularies of past social movement legacies to revalue the identities and contributions of devalued members of society is crucial to reconfiguring the hierarchies that underpin and reproduce relations of economic domination and subordination. In other words, influencing how people think and act in relation to each other is about more than just the art of communication. The symbolic battleground of contemporary workers' struggles are reflective of, in Pierre Bourdieu's words, broader "political struggles…for the power to impose the legitimate vision of the social world…and the direction in which it is going and should go" (Bourdieu 2000, 185).

To better understand the potential leverage that derives from the symbolic and public dimensions of workers' struggles, we need to eschew the tendency to treat struggles over meaning and values as separate and unrelated to struggles over the distribution of power and resources.[3] Too often, the colorful and dramatic aspects of public protests are dismissed as attention-grabbing tactics with little staying power over the long term. We see this in the thinking of union organizers and researchers that deem public sentiment as an important but ultimately fleeting and intangible source of support. While it is certainly true that appealing to the public can have limited and even detrimental effects, neglecting to examine the interplay between the cultural and structural basis of worker power leaves some crucial questions unanswered: Why have the struggles of some of the most vulnerable, as opposed to most powerful, workers become such a revitalizing force for crisis-ridden labor movements in today's global economy? What is the significance of the symbolic and public dimensions of struggles for marginalized groups of workers? How do these struggles help change the unequal balance of power between workers and those entities that use and benefit from their labor? In other words, what exactly are the mechanics of converting social and economic marginality into a concrete form of leverage?

Building Power from the Margins:
A Comparative Study

To answer the questions above, I compare the struggles of workers employed at the bottom of labor market hierarchies in two distinct national contexts: South Korea and the United States. In both countries, this stratum of ·the workforce disproportionately represents historically disadvantaged groups that have faced and continue to face barriers to obtaining higher-paid and higher-skilled employment. Racialized groups of immigrants and women in the United States and socially disadvantaged women in South Korea are a predominant part of the marginalized workforce in each country, though other kinds of workers (e.g., youth, the elderly, the disabled, ex-offenders, former welfare recipients, and those with low education levels) also can be found in the low-paid, service workforce. The growth of flexible employment relationships such as part-time, temporary, independently contracted, subcontracted, and daily work (Cranford and Vosko 2006; Gonos 1998; Gottfried 1992; Houseman and Polivka 2000; Kelleberg, Reskin, and Hudson 2000) has rendered marginalized workers particularly susceptible to precarious and unfavorable wage bargains. Although there are certainly exceptions, in comparison to workers in full-time, permanent jobs, workers in flexible employment relationships usually receive fewer benefits and statutory entitlements, are subject to a greater risk of employer abuse, and are less likely to be unionized.

To understand how and under what conditions marginalized workers are attempting to overcome downgraded forms of flexible employment, I analyze the dynamics of workers' struggles on multiple scales—from the local and national to the global. While studies of labor movement revitalization in the United States provide the most concrete understanding of how unions are organizing new sectors of the workforce, there have been limited attempts to interrogate their "connections with dynamics at play in other places, and in wider regional, national and transnational arenas" (Hart 2002, 14). We know little about how labor movements in other national contexts are responding to similar conditions of crises associated with global economic restructuring and labor market deregulation. We also know little about the relationship of their struggles with respect to each another. To bring a much needed cross-national lens to the study of labor revitalization, I focus on the dynamics of change in South Korea and the United States.

On the surface, these two countries seem an unlikely pair for comparison; they represent two places with asymmetrical trajectories of economic development and divergent histories of trade unionism. South Korea is studied primarily as a developing nation or a newly industrializing country; whereas, the United States is studied as an industrialized or advanced capitalist nation. Korean unions are recognized as one of the world's most militant and mobilized labor movements, taking radical political stands against authoritarian regimes, free trade agendas, and neoliberal economic policies. By contrast, U.S. unions are characterized as highly bureaucratized and conservative organizations that are oriented primarily toward servicing its members' narrow economic interests. South Korea is also one of the few countries in the world in which enterprise unionism is dominant. Unlike the occupation- and industry-based unionism in the United States, Korean workers have historically affiliated with unions at the enterprise level. While this structure is conducive for strengthening solidarity among workers and management at the company level, in South Korea successive military dictatorships have historically used it to suppress independent labor militancy and prevent the broader consolidation of worker power at the industry and regional levels (Suh 2003). Given these differences, the U.S. labor movement is typically compared to other industrialized countries in the Global North (Fairbrother and Yates 2003; Griffin, McCammon, and Botsko 1990; Western 1997), while the Korean labor movement is conventionally compared to other newly industrialized countries (NICs) in the Global South, formerly referred to as the Third World, and the East Asian region (Deyo 1989).

The compressed nature of Korea's industrialization over the past three decades, however, requires that we traverse the conventional divides that have defined comparative research. Rather than mismatched opponents, the United States and South Korea face each other as economic competitors at century's end. The United States remains the largest world economy with a gross domestic product (GDP) of $10.4 trillion and a per capita GDP of $37,600 (2002), but its growth rates have stagnated in the context of heightened global competition and market liberalization. After two decades of stunning economic growth, South Korea ranks as the twelfth largest economy in the world with a GDP of $477 billion and a per capita GDP of $19,600 (2001) and has joined the ranks of wealthier nations in the OECD (Organization for Economic Co-Operation and Development). However, since the 1980s, Korea has faced intense pressure to liberalize its markets and open its borders to foreign investment and goods. Manufacturing workers in Korea, who led an upsurge in labor unrest in the late 1980s and secured significant wage and benefit gains, are now confronted with similar forces of capital mobility and industrial restructuring that U.S. workers faced a decade prior. Widespread insecurity in the form of nonstandard employment arrangements, weakened labor protections, and reduced social wages also beleaguers the rapidly growing workforce of low-paid service workers in Korea and the United States. In both countries deepening institutional crises related to global economic restructuring and labor market deregulation have created pressures for national labor movements to redefine their priorities, including a parallel emphasis on organizing the rapidly growing ranks of nonunion workers. While different histories inform the significance of each labor movement's changing priorities, they reflect striking similarities in the way crisis-ridden unions are attempting to adapt to the changing world of work and politics.

Given the stark disparities that once characterized the South Korean and the U.S. labor movements, what explains their converging trajectories? How are increasingly crisis-ridden unions concretely challenging their eroding base of power in a context of intensified global competition, capital mobility, industry transformations, and labor market deregulation? What do these dilemmas illuminate about how workers and their collective organizations can build power in today's global economy?

The Shifting Basis of Worker Power under Globalization

This book's central contention is that profound shifts in the balance of power among labor, capital, and the state have redefined how workers and their collective organizations can generate leverage during the course of a labor dispute, placing increased significance in the symbolic dimensions of labor's leverage. While colorful, dramatic, and public actions are common characteristics of protest politics, symbolic leverage is about more than tactics and strategies; it recognizes that the social exchange of labor for a wage is grounded as much in moral and cultural understandings as in economic calculations about profit and efficiency. It also recognizes when conventional forms of worker power such as the right to form unions and the capacity to strike have been severely eroded, workers can still exercise potentially potent forms of leverage by drawing upon the contested arena of culture and public debates about values. For workers located at the margins of the economy and society, this often entails drawing on recognized and legitimate forms of social injustice that have not only gained meaning and social influence during previous historical struggles but also continue to resonate in new historical settings.

Two factors have fueled the shift toward symbolic leverage. First, transnational flows of capital, labor, ideas, and goods across national borders have introduced new dilemmas for national labor movements, not just for manufacturing workers but also for service workers. While the age of industrialization strengthened the muscle of the mass strike and the powerful trade unions that carried them out, the transition to service-based economies in a rapidly globalizing economy is shifting the basis of worker power to historically unorganized and disadvantaged workers employed in low-paid, insecure service jobs. For national labor movements that historically built their base of power on more powerful segments of the workforce in manufacturing, construction, and transportation, this means figuring out how to rebuild the basis of worker power from a position of relative weakness as opposed to relative strength. Ironically, the very processes that have rendered historically disadvantaged workers such as immigrants, women, and people of color the targets of cost-cutting employer practices have also laid the groundwork for the resurgence of social movement–inspired forms of unionism that seek to overcome the social and cultural as well as economic conditions of worker exploitation. The state is an active force of intervention in reconfiguring national labor markets along existing and new lines of inequality, emphasizing the state's continued importance in mediating and directing the global forces of change.

Second, the reconfiguration of employment relationships along flexible and fragmented lines requires different approaches to unionism. Subcontracting, independent contracting, temporary agency employment, and other forms of triangulated employment exacerbate structural ambiguities over what constitutes a "worker" and an "employer" (Cobble and Vosko 2000; Gottfried 1992). As such, the legality of workers' representational organizations and their right to negotiate bargaining agreements is often discredited by employers or the state (or both) from the onset of a collective dispute. To overcome such legal barriers, marginalized workers are attempting to redefine the nature of employer-employee relationships in the eyes of the public, as opposed to the narrow confines of legal and contractual interpretation. While demands for social justice must navigate institutionally and historically sedimented relations of power and difference that have included some while excluding others, the organizational and cultural repertoires of past movement struggles provide marginalized workers with a distinct array of strategies and vocabularies that can undermine official sources of authority such as the law and justify alternative applications of justice. Social movement legacies also provide ongoing moral repertoires that can revalue the identities and contributions of devalued groups in the context of chronic poverty and intensifying inequality.

The following sections seek to reconceptualize national specificities in relation to global processes of change, as well as rethink labor politics and organization in new ways. First, I emphasize the importance of evaluating the shifting basis of worker power in the context of local, national, and global dynamics of change. Beverly Silver's analysis (2003) of workers' movements on a world-scale is crucial to my discussion, though I argue that she neglects to examine the central dynamics of struggle when it comes to some of the most vulnerable, as opposed to most powerful, groups of workers. Second, I draw on Pierre Bourdieu's concept of symbolic struggles (1989, 1991, 2000), and classification struggles (1984) more specifically, to develop an analytic of symbolic leverage. Although his work in this area is commonly applied to explain the struggles of the elite, it provides crucial insight into how workers and their collective organizations can convert seemingly negative forms of marginality into concrete sources of leverage. However, putting Bourdieu's ideas to work for those on the margins requires radically rethinking the dynamics of symbolic struggles when waged from below.

Labor's Leverage: Rebuilding Workers' Associational Power

Whether it is coined the age of "empire" (Hardt and Negri 2000), "millennial capitalism" (Comaroff and Comaroff 2000), or a new mode of capitalist domination under "flexible accumulation" (Harvey 1989), scholars across disciplinary boundaries agree that the contemporary period of global capitalism and its associated practices of labor deregulation, privatization, and flexibility are synonymous with the deterioration of working-class organizations on a global scale. The erosion of the nation-state and its capacity to control global flows is implicated in downward pressures on workers and their collective organizations (Tilly 1995). Gone is the old system of bargaining in which workers and employers negotiate over wages and working conditions. Gone is the system of stable employment under Fordist mass production, which provided industrial welfare for privileged sectors of the working class. Instead, future generations of labor increasingly represent traditionally disadvantaged workers—women, immigrants, and other socially marginalized groups—that are employed under lower-paid and more insecure forms of flexible employment, particularly in expanding sectors of the service-producing economy (Sassen 1998, 137–151). While many call for the creation of new social imaginaries that capture the changing demographics of the global working class, few provide concrete insight into how those incorporated into new capitalist work arrangements can transform the inequality and polarization that are endemic to them. Rather, scholars such as Michael Hardt and Antonio Negri (2004) coin provocative but superficial categories such as the "multitude" to illustrate how the isolated and localized struggles of the disenfranchised, landless, and urban poor can somehow join together and catalyze systemic transformation at the global level.

Part of the lack of depth regarding alternative class politics can be attributed to the failure to investigate the interplay between workers' struggles at the local and national level and broader global economic shifts. It can also be attributed to the inability to specify exactly how the shifting balance of power among labor, capital, and the state under processes of globalization is producing new conditions of struggle for workers and their collective organizations. By *globalization*, I refer to a set of contradictory processes on multiple scales that seek to reorganize relations of power and difference according to the profit-driven pursuits of capital over the values of sustainable human and ecological life (see McMichael 2005). Beverly Silver's (2003) influential study of the long-term, world-scale patterning of labor unrest is an important intervention into this debate. Through her rigorous empirical investigation of the "relational processes among 'cases' (workers and workers' movements located in different states/regions) on a world scale across both time and space," Silver provides key analytical tools for identifying the development of new forms of worker power under world historical capitalist transformation.

The theoretical foundation of Silver's analysis is the recognition that workers cultivate different and interrelated forms of power to secure economic and political concessions from employers and the state. Building on Erik Olin Wright's conceptual categories (2000, 962), Silver (2003, 13) distinguishes *structural power*, which stems from workers' location in the economic system, from *associational power*, which derives from workers' self-organization into trade unions, political parties, and other collective organizations. Structural power, which is most commonly associated with the economic leverage a strike yields, is most effective during the early phases of industrial development, when capital and the state are most vulnerable to the withdrawal of labor at the point of production and thus most willing to make concessions to workers and their collective organizations. However, as capitalists relocate production to lower-waged regions to weaken organized labor's hold on wages and working conditions, workers face heightened competition as well as more repressive state controls against labor militancy, which hamper the effectiveness of previously successful methods such as the mass strike. In the latter cases, workers can compensate for weaker levels of structural power by strengthening the basis of their *associational power*. Although Silver (2003, 14) narrowly defines associational power in terms of state legal frameworks regarding how unions can be established and what they can bargain about collectively with employers, her empirical discussion of Indian and Chinese textile workers in the early part of the twentieth century and of South African, Brazilian, and Korean automobile workers in the latter part of the century shows that workers relied on extralegal sources such as multiclass political alliances with national democracy movements to strengthen the basis of their associational power (Silver 2003, 90–91, 94–97; also see Koo 2001; Seidman 1994).

Silver's relational analysis not only highlights the significance of a diverse array of strategies and organizational forms—beyond the strike and trade union frameworks—that can underpin the basis of workers' associational power, but it also highlights the increased significance of associational power itself. This is particularly important for previously manufacturing-based labor movements that are grappling with the challenges of how to rebuild their collective organizations in the context of heightened competition, transnational capital mobility, and global economic restructuring. As capital shifts the site of its domestic investment into a new array of service-producing sectors, nontraditional working-class actors (women, people of color, and immigrants) are increasingly recruited to fill the growing ranks of low-paid service work, groups with whom existing unions have little to no linkages (Arrighi 1990). State deregulation of employment relationships and labor markets, which tilt the balance of power in favor of employers, also leave workers with little recourse against intensified wage cutting and employer abuse. Despite these obstacles, Silver (2003, 110) points to successful cases in the United States such as the "Justice for Janitors" campaign and local living wage movements to show that marginalized workers can effectively pressure employers whose image and profit is tied to a fixed location "by engaging in a strategic rethinking of how to leverage 'associational power.'"

To take Silver's claims about associational power seriously, however, we need to engage in a more nuanced discussion of how and under what conditions marginalized workers can leverage alternative sources of associational power. Silver's discussion of associational power is largely subordinated to her discussion of structural power, and what happens to workers' leverage as a result of global capital mobility in manufacturing industries. While she recognizes the significance of other factors such as national democracy movements and community-based organizing in strengthening the basis of workers' associational power, she fails to incorporate such insights into her theoretical discussion. In doing so, we have limited insight regarding how workers, particularly those employed on the bottom rungs of the labor market, can renew the basis of their associational power in the face of eroding labor rights and downgraded employment relationships. We also cannot account for how institutional structures of labor and employment regulation affect the ability of workers to exercise effective forms of associational power.

The establishment of national labor laws and trade union frameworks was pivotal in the expansion of industrialized labor movements. However, the codification of workers' rights under various national labor law frameworks had differential impacts on the character of workers' associational power. In the United States, workers fought vigorously for the freedom of association and the right to strike; however, fierce employer resistance to the passage of the National Labor Relations Act (NLRA) resulted in the transformation of militant industrial unions into highly bureaucratic and service-oriented unions that were narrowly focused on improving the living standards of their own members (Brody 1993; Lichtenstein 2002).

The uneasy relationship between worker protests and the labor laws can also be seen in post-1978 reform China (C. K. Lee 2007). By channeling labor protests into legally circumscribed grievance procedures, the Chinese state has been able to quell mounting worker discontent in China's rapidly expanding sunbelt. However, by imbuing the "rule of law" with contractual authority, the state has provided discontented workers with an unintended source of moral legitimacy. While the long-term implications of struggles over the law are difficult to assess, Ching Kwan Lee (2007, 238) emphasizes that what is important is not the codification of labor rights per se but the recognition that contested struggles over the "rule of law" directly shape the expression and efficacy of workers' associational power.

Struggles over the rule of the law and its moral and cultural underpinnings represent a crucial feature of the twenty-first century labor relations climate. This is due not only to heightened employer resistance to the existence of unions and their control over the price of labor under the banner of neoliberal globalization, but also to the proliferation of irregular forms of employment that complicate the ability of workers to exercise basic associational rights.

Irregular employment, also referred to as atypical, casual, contingent, nonstandard, and precarious employment, is essentially defined by what it is *not*: a stable, permanent job under a single employer that is regulated under protective labor law frameworks. Through a process of reclassification, irregular employment places workers in the "cracks" and "fissures" of formal employment—in what may be called a state of "legal liminality," that is, a state of institutional exception in which workers are neither fully protected by nor fully denied the rights of formal employment (see Rothenbuhler 1988). As such, labor struggles increasingly take the form of classification struggles aimed at redefining the terms and conditions of the employment contract (which I discuss in greater detail in the next section). Interestingly, these struggles are less about their official contractual expression under the rule of law than about what Emile Durkheim (1984, 316–320) calls the noncontractual elements of contracts: the principles of reciprocity and cooperation originating in the wills of consenting parties that underpin the foundational authority of all contracts, either verbal or written.

Given the difficulties of rebuilding the associational power of irregularly employed workers through existing institutional avenues such as labor law reform and formal grievance procedures, cases in South Korea and the United States reveal that marginalized workers are challenging the legitimacy of their employment contracts by highlighting the chronic poverty and material deprivation associated with structurally ambiguous employment. In other words workers are seeking to rebuild the basis of their associational power by rearticulating the moral norms and cultural values that underpin the social exchange of labor for a wage. This is particularly the case for marginalized workers such as immigrants and women in low-paid service work that have limited capacity to strengthen the legitimacy of their collective demands against employers and the state in the face of legal opposition and weak levels of structural power. To uncover the dynamics of this process, I turn to the insights of Pierre Bourdieu and his discussion of symbolic struggles.

The Symbolic Struggles of Labor

Symbolic power is one of the most fundamental mechanisms of change in the social world (Bourdieu (1984, 1989, 1991, 2000). Put simply, symbolic power is the power of naming. It is "in a sense a politics of perception aimed at making or subverting the order of things by transforming or conserving the categories through which it is perceived" (Bourdieu 2000, 185–186). Its power to influence stems from cognitive and cultural struggles waged by social actors competing for the "authority to impose legitimate knowledge of the sense of the social world, its present meaning, and the direction in which it is going and should go" (Bourdieu 2000, 185). Cognitive struggles are more than just battles over ideas, however, and cultural struggles are more than just battles over values. Winning the power to define the terms upon which the social world is perceived, evaluated, and acted on allows individuals and social groups to reorder material relations of domination and subordination. A key component of this process is the ability to convert various forms of capital, including symbolic capital, into economic capital—a conversion rate that Bourdieu (1984, 246; 1986) explains is "fought over at all times."

While most scholars, including Bourdieu, have deployed the concept of symbolic power to explain the dynamics of struggles among various fractions of the dominant classes, Bourdieu (1984, 483–484) recognizes that the "labour of categorization" is a "forgotten dimension of the class struggle." His emphasis on the importance of the symbolic in the dynamics of class struggles echoes contributions by prominent labor historians such as E. P. Thompson (1966) who critique structuralist interpretations of class and class formation. Like Thompson and the new social historians he inspired, Bourdieu points out that before a social group such as the "working class" can be said to exist, it must be concretely made. Forming unions, which have required a recognized social identity for advancing the collective interests of workers, represents a likely strategy for the working class. Yet what is important, according to Bourdieu, is not just the formation of a unified class identity or established institutions, but the ability to win recognition in the public arena as a legitimate political actor with the capacity to influence the distribution of power and resources in the broader society.

Various strategies can help subordinated groups such as the working class win a recognized place in the social order. Public spokespersons create visibility and coherence to the existence of a hitherto unrecognized social group by enabling separate individuals to act and speak as a group through a single leader (Bourdieu 1990, 248). Public mobilization validates the legitimacy of a group's leaders because the efficacy of their ideas is measured by the "number of different voices that assemble in a single place that can physically and historically verify the existence of a collective will" (Bourdieu 1990, 190–191). Alliances between social actors endowed with different forms of capital are particularly important for subordinated social groups. Although it can be a tenuous alliance, Bourdieu asserts that intellectuals play a strategic role in legitimating the symbolic struggles of the working class by offering the latter "explicit theory" and "institutionalized instruments of representation [such as] trade-unions, political parties, [and] social technologies of mobilization and demonstration." Thus, the power of the working-class's symbolic capital operates by "a sort of embezzlement of accumulated cultural capital [which provides the working class] the means of constituting objectively their vision of the world and the representation of their interests" (Bourdieu 1990, 245).

Despite his elaboration of the dynamics of labor's symbolic struggles, Bourdieu's emphasis on the role of leaders and intellectuals overshadows important dimensions of symbolic struggles when they are waged from below. His claims are historically, geographically, and autobiographically specific to late-twentieth-century France and Europe. However, in twenty-first-century Korea

and the United States, as well as around the world, intellectuals and labor leaders have declining relevance and therefore less ability to enhance the symbolic
capital of the working class.[4] However, rather than assume that the only forms
of symbolic capital to which workers have access are "borrowed," identifying
the forms of capital that workers already possess or can generate in relation
to other social groups during the course of a collective dispute should be the
subject of empirical inquiry. In other words, evaluating the dynamics of symbolic struggles from below entails foregrounding the concrete historical conditions under which subordinated groups such as workers are able to transform
a state of negative capital (i.e., overlapping conditions of economic, social, and
political marginality) into unexpected forms of leverage. An examination of
symbolic capital is particularly germane.

Unlike other species of capital (economic, cultural, and social), symbolic
capital has received relatively little empirical attention, especially in the analysis
of political struggles.[5] This is a notable gap, given that "his [Bourdieu's] whole
work may be read as a hunt for [symbolic capital's] varied forms and effects"
(Bourdieu and Wacquant 1992, 28). While it is certainly true that subordinated
groups are unequally equipped to verify their symbolic claims, workers do
have access to potentially potent forms of symbolic capital. Given that workers
possess multiple social identities and social locations, historical accounts reveal that racial and gender hierarchies have offered certain workers additional
symbolic capital, although it has often come at the expense of more vulnerable groups. For example, nineteenth-century male workers in England used
their privileged position in gender hierarchies to strengthen their opposition to
capitalist exploitation (Scott 1988). Patriarchy as well as racism served as potent
sources of moral legitimacy in nineteenth- and twentieth-century America. By
repudiating morally depraved Asian workers and dependent groups of slaves,
native Americans, and women who were deemed "unfit" to rule themselves,
white native male workers justified their demands for expanded citizenship
rights (Glenn 2002).

Forging "cultures of solidarity," as Rick Fantasia (1988) puts it, which rely
on the process of building and strengthening associational ties among workers,
has also constituted a potent source of symbolic capital for workers throughout
history. As "residents of society's bottoms, margins and cracks," workers have
engaged in collective actions "intend[ed] to do violence to the official culture
and its central structures" (Rothenbuhler 1988, 67; also see Piven and Cloward
1977, Tarrow 1998). Extralegal tactics such as mass protests, civil disobedience,
and media appeals have served as important vehicles for oppositional social
movements in publicly dramatizing their struggles. Participating in collective

protest activity not only helps forge shared meaning and purpose among dispa-
rate participants but also mobilizes an external base of support from churches,
community organizations, and other civic groups that can provide additional
resources and moral legitimacy to movements seeking to undermine existing
structures of power and authority (Jasper 1997; Morris 1983; Snow and Benford 1992; Zald and McCarthy 1980). An important component of "challenger"
movements, as social movement scholars often put it, is the ability to draw
upon signs, slogans, tactics, and moral vocabularies from previous struggles
and adapt them for use in future battles, emphasizing the ability of less authorized forms of symbolic capital to reproduce themselves over time. The dynamic nature of workers' symbolic capital is particularly vivid when looking
at the legacy of the Knights of Labor, the Wobblies (International Workers of
the World), 1930s Congress of Industrial Organizations (CIO) unionism, and
the 1960s civil rights movement in challenging discriminatory wages, working
conditions, and union practices as well as broader structures of racism, sexism,
and xenophobia (Cobble 2004; Dubofsky 2000; Gerteis 2007; MacLean 2006).

While struggles over meanings and values can help change uneven class relations, it is essential to recognize their contested dynamics (see Prezeworski
1985; Tarrow 1998). Like other forms of capital, the symbolic capital of workers is a mediated one; however, it is not accumulated and transmitted through
individuals and cultural objects. Its power to persuade and mobilize must be
continually renewed and reaffirmed in the face of contestation.

The literature on culture, politics, and social movements has generated
important insights about the meaning-making practices of subordinated social groups and their use of symbolic struggles to transform relationships of
power and inequality (Japser 1997; Johnston and Klandermas 1995; Morris
and Mueller 1992; Rose 1999; Snow and Benford 1992; Snow et al. 1986; Swidler
1995; Tarrow 1998; Williams 1995, 2004). Of particular interest is the contested
nature of symbolic or cultural struggles because "part of every public political
struggle is the battle over whose 'framing' of an issue is authoritative" (Williams
1995, 127). Since exactly *what* constitutes the "public good" and *whose* public
good is being promoted is a "matter of political contention" (Williams 1995,
125), subordinated social actors and groups have often resorted to contentious
politics—in the form of mass protests, symbolic actions, and morally laden
vocabularies—to change the balance of power against more powerful opponents. Given their lack of economic and political resources, contentious collective action, according to Sidney Tarrow (1998, 3), "is the main and often the
only recourse that ordinary people possess against better-equipped opponents
or powerful states."

Organizations also play a crucial role in shifting the balance of power during the course of a symbolic struggle. In addition to providing tangible resources and public support (see McCarthy and Zald 1977), organizations also serve as sources of values and meanings—or in the words of Elisabeth Clemens (1993, 758; 1997, 57), "cultural rules about what sorts of people should or could master what sorts of organizational competence." For example, the use of familiar organizational models by unfamiliar actors helped win disadvantaged groups such as disenfranchised women in nineteenth-century America "recognition as public actors and transform the logics of appropriateness governing political participation" (Clemens 1997, 55). Thus, strengthening the symbolic claims of less powerful social actors and groups includes a broad array of cultural and organizational repertoires that can shift the balance of power between mismatched opponents during the course of a heated struggle.

Figure 1 outlines the mechanics involved in converting workers' symbolic struggles into potent forms of leverage. Symbolic leverage attempts to rebuild the basis of associational power for workers with weak levels of structural power and blocked access to exercising basic associational rights by winning public recognition and legitimacy for their struggles. To overcome the legal

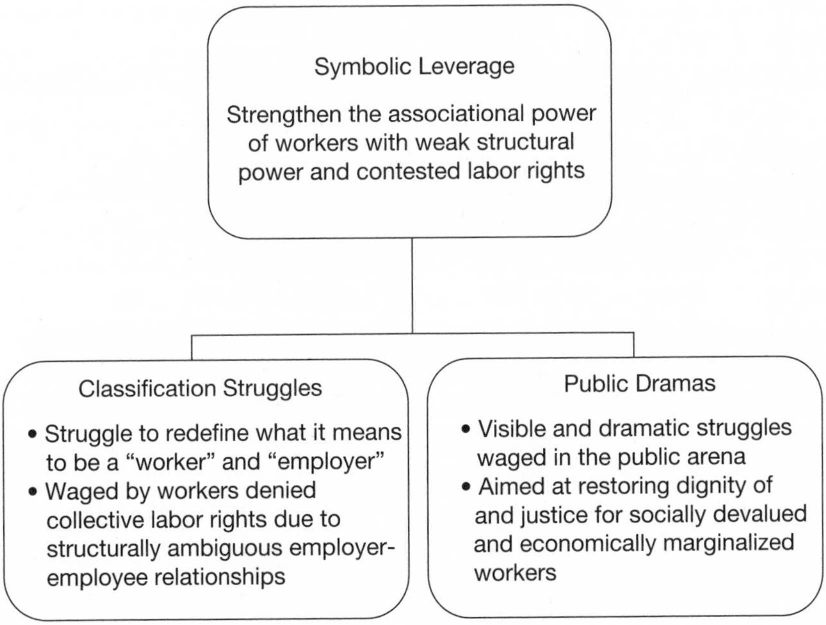

Symbolic Leverage

Strengthen the associational power of workers with weak structural power and contested labor rights

Classification Struggles

- Struggle to redefine what it means to be a "worker" and "employer"
- Waged by workers denied collective labor rights due to structurally ambiguous employer-employee relationships

Public Dramas

- Visible and dramatic struggles waged in the public arena
- Aimed at restoring dignity of and justice for socially devalued and economically marginalized workers

FIGURE 1. Two dimensions of symbolic leverage.

misrecognition associated with hybrid or inconsistent employment relationships, workers can wage *classification struggles* aimed at redefining what it
means to be a "worker" and an "employer" in the eyes of the public, rather
than the law (Goldberg 2005). This is partially attributed to the fact that many
marginalized workers are employed under ambiguous employer-employee arrangements that deny them access to labor rights and protections under existing labor law frameworks. Since workers' classification struggles depend on the
ability to win recognition in the face of opposition, using recognized symbols,
strategies, and slogans from existing political actors and past social movements
forges meaning and consensus about the legitimacy of their struggles, even if
employers and legal authorities do not recognize them as such. The state's own
discourses and practices around the rule of law can also supply workers with
salient forms of moral authority (C. K. Lee 2007, 238). The contradiction between *de jure* and *de facto* labor rights also generates powerful forms of moral
authority for discontent workers, as was the case under authoritarian state
regimes in South Korea (see chapter 2).

Grounding symbolic leverage in the temporal and spatial dynamics of *public
dramas* redirects narrow workplace disputes into full-scale "moral crises." Unlike their opponents who rely on official state classifications to produce a rec-
ognizable source of authority, marginalized workers must cultivate sources of
authority that circumvent existing rules and procedures, as well as the relations
of power and inequality that underpin them. While the targeted employer(s)
will attempt to restrict the boundaries of contention to legally circumscribed
contractual relationships, the public dramas of marginalized workers appeal to
historically and culturally contested notions of justice that have acquired moral
force during previous symbolic struggles (Chun 2005). This includes paying attention to the persuasiveness of rhetoric, symbols, and practices that construct
certain types of workers as "marginalized" and thus entitled to the intervention
of broader members of the public. At stake in public dramas are struggles to
overcome misrecognition in the arena of public life, that is, attempts to rebuild
the dignity and social worth of subordinated social actors who have been disenfranchised, devalued, and deemed inferior (Fraser 1995).

Engaging in morally driven struggles over the terms of justice is particularly
resonant in cases of verifiable social inequality and material deprivation. Eliciting firsthand testimonies of individuals who have been devalued, mistreated, or
deprived of acceptable standards of dignity and human welfare serve as potent
sources of verification. Generating recognition for the legitimacy of marginalized workers' claims is also particularly effective against institutions that are
susceptible to public opinion such as governments, brand-driven corporations,

and universities (as detailed in chapters 4, 5, and 6). For example, in cases when national governments or corporations are unresponsive to international women's rights, human rights, environmental solidarity, or cross-border solidarity campaigns, activists can mobilize a "politics of shame" to exert extralegal forms of pressure (Keck and Sikkink 1998; Armbruster-Sandoval 2004). Winning media attention also helps broaden the scope of public contention. However, it is important to note that all three cases—firsthand testimonies, publicly vulnerable institutional targets, and the media—are shaped by structures of power, dominance, and subordination that privilege the experiences of some over others.

Although the struggles of marginalized workers confront an uphill battle and a high likelihood of defeat, changes in the regulation of employer-employee relationships, particularly with respect to lower-paid, insecure service-sector work, are producing new conditions of struggle. The reclassification of employment relationships is a central mechanism of labor cost-cutting in today's global economy. While triangulated forms of employment such as subcontracting are one of the oldest forms of capitalist exploitation, they have become pervasive across manufacturing sectors as well as rapidly expanding service-producing sectors. The ability to define the legitimate divisions of the employer-employee relationship not only influences the distribution of rights and resources between workers and those who benefit from their labor under ambiguous and insecure forms of employment, but it can also subvert existing institutional channels for defining the meaning and application of the rule of law, especially when pertaining to subordinated social groups. As such, the classification struggles of labor may reflect an alternative mode of capital accumulation and conversion that foregrounds the centrality of the margins.

Global Ethnography of Labor's Leverage

This study investigates new forms of labor politics and organization among marginalized segments of the workforce. It takes an "old" subject—working-class struggles—and attempts to shine new light on its contemporary relevance. I analyze workers' struggles on multiple levels—from the local and national to the transnational—to dispel the notion that globalization is a totalizing, inexorable force that imposes itself on everyone everywhere in the same manner (Burawoy 2000). By exposing the contradictory and historically contingent dynamics that are part of global transformation, I attempt to uncover "the specificities and power relations obscured by the bland homogenization of global neoliberalism" (Burawoy 2000, 349). Reconceptualizing *place* as a central site in which struggles over power and resources occur is crucial to identifying the limits and possibilities of change. This "spatial point," in the words of Allan Pred and Michael Watts, "is simply that how things develop depends in part on where they develop, on what has been historically sedimented there, on the social and spatial structures that are already in place there."

To adapt ethnographic practices to studies of the "global," I utilize a two-pronged comparative historical and ethnographic approach. Part I engages in a comparative historical analysis of the interrelated dynamics of convergence and divergence for workers and their collective organizations in South Korea and the United States. Cross-national labor studies have typically sought to identify variation among cases with similar histories of industrialization to determine that which is distinct and unique among labor movements in different national contexts (Katznelson and Zolberg 1986). In my comparative historical account, I seek to move "away from [the study of] distinct cultural territorializations and to an analytic of interconnected spaces" (Gupta and Ferguson 1997). I employ Michael Burawoy's (1991) "extended case method" to develop a nuanced understanding of the similarities and differences between different cases of worker organizing in each country with respect to broader global transformations.

By analyzing the shifting balance of power among labor, capital, and the state in South Korea and the United States since 1945, my findings reveal a striking pattern of convergence in each country. Although trajectories of the Korean and U.S. labor movements up until the late 1980s reflected very different paths, chapter 2 demonstrates that processes of change associated with globalization are eroding the structural and associational base of power for privileged sectors of the unionized workforce in both countries, which, in turn, is undermining the effectiveness of previous strategies for exercising worker power. In the United States, core working classes, particularly unionized workers in heavy manufacturing and related strategic sectors, are no longer promised rising standards of living and increased consumer power in exchange for industrial peace. Overcoming stagnating profits and improving productivity mean dismantling the "costly" social compacts that previously included workers in the fruits of economic growth. The breakdown of social compacts among labor, capital, and the state in the United States has also weakened the claims of the burgeoning Korean labor movement. Rather than take advantage of the explosion of unionism in the late 1980s, representatives from the business and government sectors reason that if the world's most powerful workers have already consented to the deregulatory pressures of the global free market, then workers in developing countries have little grounds to justify their demands for increasing wages and enhanced labor protections. The rollback on union rights and protections have been particularly prominent in the aftermath of the 1997–1998 Asian debt crisis, as militant unions are blamed for jeopardizing national economic reforms.

Chapter 3 highlights the significance of historically sedimented inequalities in actively creating and reproducing a cheap labor force in expanding sectors of the low-paid, service economy. In the United States, a growing proportion of women and immigrants from Asia and Latin America are concentrated on the bottom rungs of urban service economies. These workers, who were previously barred from legal entry into the United States, now serve as "cheap labor" in the domestic labor market. Urban revitalization strategies, supported by local, state, and federal governments, have contributed to the flow of female and immigrant labor into low-paid, urban service jobs. In Korea, while there is a small and growing number of migrant workers recruited to fill peripheral jobs, native Korean women are the primary targets of cost-cutting labor strategies. The state has played an active role in the reproduction of a highly exploitable, predominantly female workforce. Discriminatory gendered practices by employers and male-dominated unions also exacerbate the marginalization of irregularly employed women workers.

Chapter 4 shows that, contrary to conventional wisdom, peripherally employed immigrants and women *can* challenge the intensification of discrimination and exploitation associated with downgraded employment. Distinct social movement legacies play a crucial role in providing cultural and organizational repertoires with which to organize historically disadvantaged groups of workers. In the United States, 1960s social movements, such as the civil rights and early New Left movements, influenced subsequent efforts to revitalize local unions and shift the priorities of the organized labor movement. In Korea, the 1970s and 1980s women workers' movement and student-led democratization movement also produced a generation of activists and social movement organizations that could support the struggles of exploited segments of society. When an explosion of grassroots labor unrest by irregular workers took place in the aftermath of extensive labor market deregulation in 1998, these activists and organizations played a key role in supporting their struggles, many of which were systematically ignored and even sabotaged by existing unions.

Chapters 5 and 6 attend to concrete cases of worker organizing (see table 1). I selected two groups of workers for my ethnographic comparison: (1) subcontracted university janitors and (2) independently contracted personal service workers. In the case of subcontracted workers, I examined the janitors' struggle at

Table 1.   Comparative Ethnographic Case Study Design

	UNITED STATES	SOUTH KOREA
Subcontracted workers	Janitors	Janitors
	USC (SEIU Local 399/1877)	Inha (KWTU Incheon branch union)
	Harvard (SEIU Local 254)	SNU (SNU Janitors' Union, affiliated with KCTU Seoul Regional Center)
Independently contracted workers	Home care workers (SEIU Local 434B)	Golf caddies (KWTU 88CC golf game assistants' branch union)

the University of Southern California (USC) in Los Angeles between 1996 and 1998 and at Harvard University (Harvard) in the Boston metropolitan region between 1999 and 2001. In South Korea, I examined the janitors' union struggle at Inha University (Inha) in Incheon between 1999 and 2001 and Seoul National University (SNU) in Seoul between 1999 and 2000. In the case of independently contracted personal service workers, I focused on the home care workers' union struggle in Los Angeles between 1987 and 2000 in the United States and the golf game assistants' union struggle in the Kyonggi-do region of South Korea between 1999 and 2002.

My ethnographic fieldwork began in South Korea and was conducted in three stages over twenty-two months between June 1998 and December 2002. During my first field visit, I immersed myself in the worlds of union activism with workers, trade unionists, labor leaders, women's movement activists, and students. I attended strikes, marches, public protests, after-protest debriefing meetings, public forums, and internal union meetings. I conducted additional site visits and interviews with unions and activists actively organizing regular workers. For each case, I constructed narratives that reveal the politics and strategies involved in organizing marginalized workers. I treat each of my cases as empirical puzzles, rather than best practices models, to uncover how a sequence of social actions and events relates to broader sociohistorical processes, as opposed to evaluating their abstract generalizability, regardless of time and place (Isaac 1997). For the U.S. cases, I rely heavily on internal union documents, newspapers, and secondary accounts. Since there has been an explosion of quality empirical case studies on local union organizing campaigns, I chose struggles that reflected trends in the national character of organizing that could be compared cross-nationally. The Justice for Janitors campaign is a well-known and documented case, but to streamline my comparison, I focused on struggles at two universities. For these cases, I also conducted site visits at local unions and interviews with union organizers in Los Angeles and Boston between April 2003 and April 2004.

Based on findings from my comparative ethnographic analysis, chapters 5 and 6 assert that new forms of employment exclusion require new forms of worker power. As more and more workers are incorporated into employment arrangements that place them outside the boundaries of basic labor protections, workers and their collective organizations are confronted with a central dilemma: how to legitimate their claims for basic associational rights. Chapter 5, "What Is an "Employer"? Organizing Subcontracted Janitors," explores how low-paid immigrant and women janitors in the United States and South Korea, respectively, are using classification struggles and public dramas to overcome structurally ambiguous subcontracting relations and to pressure building owners and cleaning contractors to uphold their moral responsibilities as "employers," whether or not they are legally bound under subcontracting agreements. Chapter 6, "What Is a "Worker"? Organizing Independently Contracted Home Care Workers and Golf Caddies," explores the struggles of two groups of peripherally employed personal service workers. I find that in both cases, local unions are redefining "independent contractors" as "legitimate workers" with the right to form unions and bargain collectively, whether or not they were technically eligible under existing labor laws. In chapters 5 and 6, alliances with students and other social movement actors are pivotal in strengthening the symbolic leverage of marginalized workers in both countries.

In the conclusion, I discuss the implications of symbolic leverage for labor politics and organization. Rather than focus solely on questions of strategy and scale, I discuss the significance of the margins in exposing the crossroads facing each labor movement. Each labor movement's crossroads highlight the persistence of social inequalities and hierarchies in impeding more genuine forms of change. They also emphasize the centrality of such legacies to organized labor's broader struggle against profit-driven forms of economic restructuring on a global scale. Rather than assuming that working-class struggles in the current global context must "think globally and act globally" or "think globally and act locally," union struggles in Korea and the United States reveal that efforts to transform the cultural logics and institutional practices of globalization take place on concrete historical and institutional terrains, each shaped by the production of different constellations of power among labor, capital, and the state.

2

EMPLOYER AND STATE OFFENSIVES AGAINST UNIONIZED WORKERS

While the balance of power between states and capital is the subject of continued debates in the contemporary world order (Evans 1997; Ohmae 1995; Ong 1999, 2006; Sassen 1996), the widespread decline of organized labor is rarely disputed. Over the past three decades, union density levels have declined across the industrialized world (Griffin, McCammon, and Botsko 1990; Tilly 1995; Western 1997). In countries with low levels of unionization such as the United States, the moral and material pressure of global market competition spelled early, rapid, and devastating defeats. Unions suffered massive losses as plants shut down and relocated to lower-waged, nonunion regions (Bluestone and Harrison 1982). In countries with relatively higher union density levels, such as those in Northern Europe, industrial workers confronted pressures to weaken institutionalized labor market protections and bring wage rates in line with transnationally depressed standards (Western 1997). Despite their higher levels of militancy and mass mobilization, neoliberal restructuring policies have also weakened the bargaining power of trade unions in countries such as Brazil, South Africa, and Korea (Webster and Buhlungu 2004).

Converging patterns of union decline across the industrialized and industrializing world are striking when seen through the comparative lens of South Korea and the United States (see figure 2). Although union density rates in the United States have been steadily declining since its peak at 35 percent in 1953, levels began steeply declining in the late 1970s. An unprecedented wave of plant closings, workforce reductions, and concessionary bargaining contributed to the loss of over four million union members during this period, and union

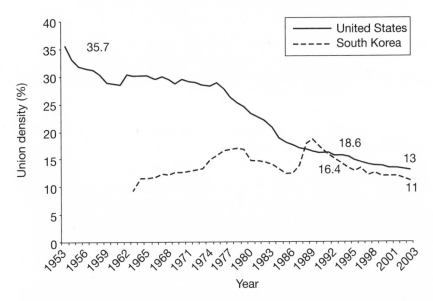

FIGURE 2. Union density levels in South Korea and the United States, 1955–2003. U.S. figures compiled from *Employment and Earnings,* Current Population Survey (CPS), U.S. Bureau of Labor Statistics, 1983–2003, and Historical Tables, U.S. Bureau of the Census, 1953–1982. Figures for South Korea compiled from *Korea Monthly Statistics,* National Statistics Office, 1963–2003.

density levels plummeted from 28.5 percent in 1975 to 16.9 percent in 1989. Over the next decade, union membership deteriorated by another 1.5 million persons with union density levels hovering around 12–13 percent in 2000.[1] In contrast to the United States, union density levels in South Korea rose and fell repeatedly during roughly the same period, corresponding mainly to the degree of state repression over labor militancy. Union density peaked in 1988 at 18.6 percent, with the unprecedented formation of over 3,500 new unions and a 70 percent increase in total union density in less than a single year (see Koo 2001, 159). The explosion of democratic unionism seemed more synonymous with the massive labor upsurge of U.S. unions in the 1930s than the stagnating business unionism of the 1980s. However, as South Korea faced mounting pressures to open its markets and bring them in line with the neoliberal mandates of global market expansion, this historic moment of possibility was eclipsed, and union density levels plunged throughout the 1990s. Of twenty-nine OECD countries, only three had union density rates below 15 percent in 2000: the United States (13%), Korea (11%), and France (10%).[2]

Why did labor movements headed on two very different trajectories up until the late 1980s experience strikingly similar levels of decline by the turn of the century? I begin this chapter by investigating the reconfiguration of power relationships between labor, capital, and the state in each country since 1945, paying close attention to the nature of employer and state offensives against unionized workers, especially those employed in more privileged sectors of the industrial economy. Although the timing and dynamics of industrial development resulted in asymmetrical trajectories, my comparative historical analysis reveals that employer and state offensives in each country were mediated by the institutional conditions that regulated how and under what conditions unions could use their structural power to strengthen the basis of their associational power. As I discussed in chapter 1, *structural power* represents the economic leverage that workers possess by virtue of their strategic position in key economic sectors; *associational power* represents the leverage that workers can exercise as a result of their organization into collective entities.

The relatively early incorporation of U.S. workers into manufacturing industries such as auto and steel and their location in the world's most powerful economy after 1945 resulted in a welfare-based system of industrial unionism. While this system resulted in higher standards of living, especially for workers located in strategic economic sectors, it channeled militant worker protests into a narrow and bureaucratic process for dispensing wage and benefit increases and job security guarantees. When heightened competition and stagnating company profits began threatening the global superiority of U.S. companies in the mid- to late-1970s, employers began revoking the terms of its social compacts with unionized workers, thwarting existing institutional channels for exercising workers' associational power. The U.S. state supported employer offensives by deregulating labor standards and actively intervening in labor disputes against striking workers, further weakening the associational power of unions.

In South Korea, employer and state offensives against organized labor took place in a more compressed and antagonistic fashion. Given the relatively late incorporation of Korean workers into global manufacturing industries, they first had to overcome the labor repression of authoritarian state regimes, which prevented workers from exercising their basic constitutional rights to form independent unions and wage lawful strikes. After the explosion of industrial unionism in the late 1980s helped usher the transition to democratic rule, the Korean labor movement was poised to convert their burgeoning structural power into more institutionalized forms of associational power. However, this moment also corresponded with the consolidation of neoliberal state regimes in the 1990s that linked the nation's economic competitiveness with organized labor's cooperation with dramatically weakened labor protections.

Forging Industrial Welfare in the United States

The end of the National War Labor Board and the no-strike pact after World War II opened the floodgates for another round of labor militancy and mobilization in the 1940s and 1950s. In response to skyrocketing inflation, layoffs, and wage cuts, 175,000 General Motors (GM) auto workers waged a 113-day walkout in 1945, which was followed by a strike of 175,000 steelworks in 1946. By the end of 1946, hundreds of thousands of rubber, meatpacking, oil-refining, and electrical appliance workers had joined the nationwide wave of strikes, "making 1946 the single most strike-torn year in American history" (Zieger 1995, 104). In a single year, 4,630 work stoppages involving 4.9 million workers resulted in the loss of 119.8 million days of production (Brody 1993, 158). According to labor intellectual, J. B. S. Hardman, the dynamism of labor militancy fueled a shift in organized labor's image both in the wider public and within its ranks: "American unions have become a social power in the nation and are conscious of their new import" (quoted in Brody 1997, 158).

To contain the upsurge of domestic labor unrest and its threat on industrial productivity, U.S. corporations began offering militant unions wage and benefit concessions in exchange for peace on the shop floor. In 1946, the United Mine Workers was the first union to obtain private pensions, and in 1949, after a bitter strike involving 480,000 workers, it won employer-funded health benefits for its members. By the end of 1948 the United Steelworkers signed over 300 agreements containing provisions for health and welfare benefits, covering almost 14 percent of its membership, and in 1949, it set a standard at Bethlehem Steel for full employer contribution to pensions and joint contribution to health insurance (Derickson 1994, 1347–1349). Initially, the acceptance of wage and benefit concessions by striking unionists was considered a temporary solution to intense class warfare. However, corporations began offering unionized workers economic concessions as a way to avoid the encroachment of union involvement in what they considered the "sacred" domain of management rights.

Perhaps the most decisive agreement for institutionalizing a system of workplace-based social welfare was the landmark five-year contract between the United Auto Workers (UAW) and General Motors (GM). Despite the insistence of militant CIO leaders such as Walter Reuther of UAW for expanded union influence in the sphere of management, GM successfully pressured the UAW into relinquishing influence over managerial decisions in exchange for social wage guarantees. GM brokered the first deal with union management in 1948 that provided employees automatic cost-of-living adjustments

(COLAs) in their wages and an annual improvement factor that automatically increased wages by 3 percent per year (Davis 1986, 111–112; Lichtenstein 2002, 123).[3] In 1950, the UAW negotiated an historic five-year contract with GM which guaranteed employees pensions, health insurance, and a 20 percent increase in real wages over the course of the contract. This landmark contract set a new standard for other unions that also began negotiating fringe benefits into their collective bargaining agreements (see Klein 2003). However, the UAW's acceptance of formula-setting wage and benefit mechanisms was considered a better "bargain" for GM, because it channeled union militancy into a narrow arena of collective bargaining. Exercising the associational power of unions become synonymous with securing contractual guarantees for improved wages and living conditions for more powerful segments of the industrial working class.

Under this system of industrial welfare, unionized workers benefited from rising real wages and improved standards of living under collective bargaining contracts, which were negotiated by union and company management on a firm-by-firm basis. However, unlike European welfare states where social wages represented a basic entitlement of social citizenship, in the United States, social wages were dependent on one's participation in the labor market. Individual employers, not public entities, provided individuals and their families retirement pensions, health and medical insurance, unemployment insurance, and sick and vacation pay (Klein 2003; Jacoby 1997).

Federal guidelines—or more specifically, the absence thereof—regarding the cost and dispensation of basic social welfare benefits made collective bargaining the primary institutional mechanism for improving working and living conditions. The Fair Labor Standards Act (FLSA), passed in 1938, established minimal restrictions regarding who could and could not participate in the wage labor market, including prohibitions around child labor, a minimum wage floor, and general guidelines about the maximum length of the work week and overtime pay, each of which have been amended at various points in history.[4] However, it did not establish any clear or formal guidelines regarding how to compensate or ensure the social reproduction of human labor. Rather, the FLSA addressed only what was considered "fair" in the realm of exchange for labor as a commodity in the market. The passage of key legislation in the postwar period continued to link worker welfare to active employment status as well as union membership. By offering tax-free incentives for employers who "voluntarily" provided job-dependent welfare benefits such as pensions and health insurance, the federal government created a mechanism that made increased welfare benefits for workers dependent on employer-based policies. Thus, when contestation arose over basic welfare provisions, the courts deemed it within the scope of private, firm-level bargaining processes, not within the jurisdiction of state or federal governments.

The dependence of workers on a localized collective bargaining process for social wage protections, however, was considered a victory for management not labor (Lichtenstein 2002; Klein 2003). While this decentralized system of industrial welfare did deliver steady improvements in living standards for more privileged sectors of the unionized workforce, it rendered them highly vulnerable to the resurgence of employers' offensives. First, the continuity of the employer-based system of social wage provision depended on a shared commitment between union and company management to tie wages to social welfare principles. This system would soon crumble as employers revoked the terms of their social compacts with organized labor.[5] Second, the expansion of a decentralized system of collective bargaining depended on the strength of big unions to secure steady increases in wages and welfare benefits. This system, commonly referred to as "pattern bargaining," established a kind of trickle-down effect for workers in less favorable positioned companies and industries. Downgrading standards for big unions would have ripple effects on the living and working conditions of the workforce at large. Third, the "employment-based welfare states" covered only more privileged sectors of the industrial unionized workforce. Millions of unorganized workers were excluded from the umbrella of industrial welfare. "As late as 1971, fully half of the labor force lay outside NLRA jurisdiction, while a quarter were not fully eligible for the minimum wage, unemployment insurance or workers' compensation. Moreover, the vast majority of the U.S. labor force who are in nonunion firms [had] absolutely no 'just cause' protection against arbitrary dismissal" (Davis 1986, 115–116). As more workers became employed outside the boundaries of regulatory labor protections, especially due to the growth of low-wage, nonunion service sector jobs, the limits of the industrial welfare system for guaranteeing the basic associational rights of workers would become increasingly evident.

Dismantling Industrial Welfare in the United States

Events in the 1970s began eroding the system of industrial welfare on which industrial unions had become dependent. The U.S. government's continued involvement in the Vietnam War contributed to rising inflation and an expanding trade deficit, which caused capital and the state to begin looking inward at labor market rigidities. The increased competitiveness of German and Japanese firms in the automobile industry also hampered growth rates and corporate profits for U.S. firms, exerting pressure on domestic businesses to streamline costs, especially labor costs. In response to stagnating profits and global market volatility, U.S. employers focused their attention on rising labor costs, buttressed by strong union influence over the price of labor. In the garment industry, firms began seeking out nonunion production sites, both in "right to work" states in the United States and newly industrializing regions abroad where they could count on government policies to depress wages and prohibit union activity.

In place-based domestic industries such as construction, firms began working together to break the "stranglehold" of unions over the wage bargain. Some of the world's largest construction companies and the world's largest corporations in the oil, chemical, metals, automobile, and rubber industries joined together to form the Construction Users Anti-Inflation Roundtable, which by 1972 became known as the Business Roundtable and included the membership of 120 of the world's largest firms (Linder 2000, 183–220). They engaged in joint lobbying efforts, such as efforts to repeal the 1932 Davis-Bacon Act, which mandated that the federal government pay a "prevailing wage" on all construction contracts. They also advocated the end of union-controlled workplaces and the expansion of the "open shop" in which employees were not required to join or pay dues to unions as a condition of employment.[6] Some local and municipal governments, plagued by deepening fiscal crises, also began withdrawing their support of public sector unions and reducing funds allocated for public welfare and education. Despite employer attacks against unionism in the labor-intensive manufacturing sector, construction, and the public sector, the impact on unionism was uneven. Union membership levels fluctuated throughout the decade, dropping from 18.1 million workers in 1973 to 17.4 million in 1976 and rising again to almost 21 million in 1979 (U.S. Bureau of the Census, 1973–1979).

The attacks against the nation's highest paid workforce in the auto and steel industries signaled a more decisive shift in the labor relations climate. In 1979, the UAW struck an unprecedented deal with the Chrysler Corporation that ushered in a new era of concessionary bargaining. Chrysler was facing the threat of bankruptcy, and the Carter administration had made union concessions a condition of a billion dollar corporate loan bailout. Rather than challenge the rollback on workers' welfare, UAW union leaders argued that adversarial industrial relations needed to be "sacrificed" for the economic solvency of the company and convinced its members to accept $602 million in wage and benefit concessions over the next three years.[7] Instead of setting high standards for other negotiations between union and company management, as in the case of pattern bargaining, the UAW's acceptance of contract concessions at Chrysler broke the terms of centralized bargaining for the Big Three in the auto industry. Unions at Ford and GM first agreed to reduced wages, benefits, and job security provisions and then consented to the early renegotiation of collective bargaining contracts before their scheduled date of expiration in 1982. Temporary concessions at all three companies led to the gradual elimination of automatic wage increases as well as pension, vacation, and seniority benefits (Katz 1985, 53–63).

While some union members fought bitterly against the rollback on wages and welfare benefits, the pervasive climate of labor insecurity severely eroded the associational basis of power for unions. The collective bargaining system, which had once secured the economic stability and social welfare of the nation's most strategically located industrial workers, had become a site of institutional disempowerment. After having traded away the right to exert influence over the managerial decisions of the company, big unions had little leverage to challenge unilateral decisions by corporations to shut down plants, even profitable ones; relocate to nonunion, lower-waged regions, including domestic regions in the South and the West; and automate production.

Despite initial claims that massive union concessions were a "temporary phenomenon that would end when business got better," by the mid-1980s, the *New York Times* described givebacks as "a fundamental change, a grim but necessary recognition that labor costs would have to be reduced if American businesses are to remain competitive and jobs preserved."[8] Once it was clear that the strongest companies could force the strongest unions to their knees, healthy firms also began to "demand that workers give back wages, benefits and work rules won in prosperous years" (Milkman 1997, 80). According to one management leader, "Just because we're making money again, why shouldn't we continue to seek to hold costs down by demanding givebacks? With labor in a weakened state, why not push for concessions?"[9] In March 1983, the United Steelworkers accepted a temporary 9 percent pay cut, rescinded COLAs, and reduced benefits such as vacation time, which represented the first time steelworkers gave back benefits won in previous contracts. Unions in the transportation industry also accepted wage and benefit concessions, including the acceptance of wage freezes by the Teamsters in March 1982, 45 percent wage reductions by rehired pilots at Eastern Airlines, and 7.8 percent pay cuts by Greyhound workers with the Amalgamated Transit Union.[10]

The state played a decisive role in dismantling the postwar industrial welfare system and establishing a more hostile labor-relations climate. During the

1970s economic crisis, the Nixon administration identified the negative influence of unions on wages and labor markets as an urgent national priority (Linder 2000, 233–234). The Carter administration acted on these assessments by passing the Motor Carrier Act of 1980, which "formally began the era of economic deregulation" (Belzer 2000, 29). In the transportation industry, this Act supported the efforts of nonunion carriers to cut wages and benefits among truckers and establish more competitive and flexible work arrangements. These changes had devastating consequences for truckers in the late 1970s and 1980s, one of the most heavily unionized industries according to the U.S. Department of Labor. At the beginning of the 1970s, Michael H. Belzer (2000, 21) stated that in 1977, 88 percent of truck drivers were union members and earned wages on par with auto and steel workers in the 1950s and 1960s. After state deregulation in the 1980s, they experienced a 30 percent earnings drop, a decline almost four times greater than the average annual earning decline among all manufacturing workers. The railroad and airlines industries were also deregulated, which destroyed labor-relations stability in the entire transport sector and cut unionization rates by one-third (Lichtenstein 2002, 236).

Active state intervention in the erosion of labor standards continued during the next presidential administration. In 1981, the Reagan administration used legal force to break up the Professional Air Traffic Controllers Organization's (PATCO) strike and replace striking air traffic controllers with nonunion counterparts. This decision set a precedent for direct state intervention in labor disputes during times of peace (Farber and Western 2002). Reagan also appointed new officials to the National Labor Relations Board (NLRB) who greatly weakened the scope of union rights. "NLRB provisions which establish[ed] collective rights as paramount to individual rights" were repealed, and the NLRB consistently ruled in favor of employers and their First Amendment right to interfere with union elections (Davis 1986, 139; also see Gross 1995).

The erosion of workers' associational power could not have happened without the state's prior role in weakening collective labor rights during the course of unionization. Under the Taft-Hartley Act, the state revised the Wagner Act to protect "freedom of speech" rights for employers during unionization campaigns, which institutionalized "a state of fictitious contractual equality between employers and individual workers" (Brody 1997, 76). This decision directly challenged the original intent of those who sponsored the Wagner Act, which established collective labor rights as a vehicle for addressing the unequal power relations between labor and management in the workplace. In the context of intensified capital mobility and globalized competition in the 1980s, employers began waging lengthy and resource-intensive campaigns to exercise their "freedom of speech" rights and prevent the formation of unions during the course of an NLRB election. These campaigns were aimed at eroding worker confidence in unions and undermining their legitimacy as institutions that genuinely operate on behalf of workers' interests. Aggressive anti-union campaigns were aided by the use of public relations firms and management lawyers who could turn the opinions of workers as well as the public at large against unions (see Clawson 2003, 41–42). Employers also became more emboldened throughout the decade and initiated a number of union decertification efforts as well, forcing unions to take a defensive posture and battle aggressive employers from workplace to workplace.

By the mid- to late 1980s, union membership had paid the price. Between 1979 and 1985, the UAW lost 38 percent of its membership, shrinking from 1,473,000 to 917,000. During the same period, the United Steelworkers lost 639,000 members (57%), the International Brotherhood of Teamsters lost 594,000 members (34%) and the International Ladies Garment Workers Union lost 302,000 members (67%) (U.S. Department of Labor 1969–1987). On the whole, union membership in manufacturing declined from 46.6 percent in 1964 to 20.5 percent in 1990, with the total loss of 2.88 million workers between 1979 and 1990 (U.S. Bureau of the Census 1979–1990). The overall decline in union membership coincided with a parallel decline in the number of workers that were covered under collective bargaining agreements with employers. Individual workers also suffered severe declines in their living and working conditions. From the mid-1970s onward real hourly and weekly earnings for workers stagnated and even declined for many. In 1989, the average production worker made twenty dollars less per hour in real dollars, in comparison to 1977, with steady declines continuing over the 1990s, despite steady increases in productivity as well as increased number of hours worked (Zieger and Gall 2002, 241). The absence of health insurance has also become a public health issue for working Americans. Today, the majority of the uninsured are employed, with over six out of ten (61%) uninsured adults under the age of sixty-five working full- or part time.

Strengthening Militant Democratic Unionism in South Korea

A defining feature of contemporary unionism in South Korea is the struggle by workers to infuse their formal labor rights with substantive meaning under the banner of democratic unionism (*minju nojo*). Unlike in the United States, where intense struggles among labor, capital, and the state resulted in the legalization of collective labor rights and the institutionalization of social wages for the unionized workforce, in theory, basic labor rights protections and social wage protections for all workers in South Korea existed from the nation's founding years. The 1948 Constitution of the Republic of Korea (ROK), which outlined the governing structure of the newly formed liberal democratic nation, guaranteed the three basic associational rights of labor: the freedom to form collective associations, wage collective actions, and engage in collective bargaining.[11] The nation's first labor law, the Labor Standards Act (LSA) of 1953, strengthened labor protections by guaranteeing workers basic social wage protections, which effectively decommodified the basis of their labor power. Based on the rationale that "all people have the right to maintain the minimum standards of wholesome and cultured living,"[12] the LSA contained detailed clauses for the maintenance and reproduction of workers as human beings, including fixed standards for wage remuneration, hours of rest, compensation for workplace accidents, severance, and retirement.[13]

Despite the existence of strong labor protections in the nation's founding documents, workers were not only denied their rights but, if they attempted to exercise them, subjected to harsh repression by three successive military dictatorships—the Rhee Syngman regime of 1948–1960, the Park Chung Hee regime of 1961–1979, and the Chun Doo Hwan regime of 1980–1988. Each authoritarian regime prioritized its own vision of nation-building over the existing rule of law. Each also utilized the National Security Law to arrest and torture anyone suspected of being communist, which allowed the state to suppress all forms of independent unionism. As the only legal official representative body for unions at the time, the Federation of Korean Trade Unions (FKTU) served more as an institution of state repression against any and all forms of independent union activity than as a genuine worker organization.

The extreme disconnect between de jure and de facto labor rights was largely attributed to the continual threat that worker militancy posed both to U.S. geopolitical interests and the anti-Communist dictatorships it supported. In postliberation Korea, virtually the entire industrial workforce (approximately 600,000 workers) from a wide range of industries, from railroads and transportation to construction and mining, was organized into a single national organization, Chŏnp'yŏng (National Council of Korean Labor Unions).[14] Between August 1945 and March 1947, 2,388 labor protests involving over 600,000 workers broke out across the country, making it one of "the most violent periods in the history of the Korean labor movement" to-date (Koo 1993, 134). Although the Rhee regime violently suppressed the outburst of independent unionism in the mid- to late 1940s, Rhee's overthrow on April 19, 1960, by a student-led popular uprising unleashed another wave of labor militancy. During this brief period, 227 labor disputes broke out, 315 new unions were formed, and workers won 15 to 50 percent wage increases. However, like the previous insurgency, a military general, Park Chung Hee, violently suppressed the vibrancy of independent unionism by waging a coup d'etat on May 16, 1961, and seizing state power for the next eighteen years.

In addition to repressing all oppositional forces, the Park regime considered state-sponsored labor repression a necessary component of its new national development strategy: export-oriented industrialization. Because the Park regime had usurped power "through a complete exclusion of popular consensus and participation...anti-communism and industrial development became the coup leaders' raison d'être and state policy" (N. Lee 2001, 62). Park's strategy for securing legitimacy for his right to rule the nation without any popular base of support was an accelerated state-directed plan for national economic growth. In the introduction to his first Five Year Plan, Park stated, "This year we have launched the first Five Year Plan for Economic Development, to banish age old curses of poverty one after another and to prepare the groundwork for an industrialized modern State....To carry out our economic plans with more freedom and minimal planning is to realize a 'Miracle on the Han River' [and] is the only way to gain superiority over Communism" (C. H. Park 1970, viii).

From the early 1960s to the late 1970s, a system of national economic development based on popular sacrifice and state repression fostered the principle of industrial growth before social welfare. During this period, rapid economic growth supported the development of the nation's infrastructure as well, with significant advances in electricity, transportation, and communication. However, improvements in the standard of living, especially for workers who directly contributed to the expansion of the export industry, did not keep pace with these rates. Wage levels remained extremely low at $0.34 an hour in 1975 to $1.01 an hour in 1980 (Deyo 1989, 91). Constant overtime and grueling working conditions constituted an everyday feature of life in a Korean factory, particularly for the nation's predominantly female industrial workforce, who were repeatedly told that "disruptions in production are a help to our enemies and a blow to our national goals" (S. K. Kim 1997, 24–25; Ogle 1990, 56).

The disjunction between nationalist rhetoric and the everyday realities of workers' lives became the site of intense political struggle between the 1970s and 1980s. As more and more workers learned about the contradiction between their formal labor rights and repressive labor practices, they began forming independent democratic unions that directly challenged the legitimacy of

authoritarian regimes that deprived workers of their right to live with human-
ity and dignity in service of broader goals of national welfare and economic
development (Koo 2001). Women working in export-oriented manufacturing
industries led the struggle to form democratic unions in the 1970s, confronting
the harsh and often violent repression of male workers hired as company thugs
and state riot police (see S. Chun 2004; S. K. Kim 1997; Koo 2001). However,
their efforts were constrained by the weak bargaining power of workers incorporated into later stages of the labor-intensive manufacturing product cycle
and the state repression associated with more competitive market conditions.
The dominance of patriarchal ideologies and the role of masculine violence in
suppressing militant unionism led by women workers also undercut the continued dynamism of the women worker–led democratic labor movement. During
the next decade, the convergence of rapid industrialization in heavy industries
as well as the intensification of arbitrary repression under General Chun Doo
Hwan's military dictatorship enabled militant democratic unions to infuse their
moral demands for democracy with greater leverage and legitimacy.

Politically, Chun Doo Hwan's regime faced massive popular resistance, particularly due to its role in the reported massacre of thousands of civilians during the
1980 Gwangju democratic uprising (see N. H. Lee 2007, 44–55). "Not since the
Korean War had the civilian population been so brutally victimized by the military…[and] the Chun regime had to resort to direct military rule" (Choi 1993,
36). Radical students, in particular, began more actively supporting the struggle
for worker liberation, infiltrating workplaces, organizing independent labor
unions, and attempting to raise workers' consciousness about their rights (N. H.
Lee 2007).

Economically, the growing size and structural power of the industrial workforce made labor strikes, particularly in capital-intensive sectors, a greater threat
to the national economy. The state began to display hesitation in answering
employers' calls for immediate police intervention against striking unionists.
Employers who were all too accustomed to the immediate assistance of riot
police to quell labor militancy were increasingly pressured to meet union demands for higher wages and improved working conditions. Significant victories
in places such as the Daewoo Motors factory in Bupyong in 1985 contributed
to the subsequent explosion of political and labor unrest by industrial workers in mid-1987, often referred to as the "Great Workers Struggle." Between
July and September, an estimated 1.2 million workers participated in 3,311
labor protests and strikes across the nation. Democratic unions replaced existing company unions in manufacturing sectors such as textile and auto, and
new unions were created in white-collar workplaces such as hospitals, financial
institutions, and public companies.

Over the next two years, the size of the organized labor force nearly doubled, increasing from approximately 1.0 million to 1.9 million between 1987 and 1989. Wage levels also rose dramatically, as nominal wages increased from 15.5 to 21.1 percent between 1988 and 1989 (Suh 2003, 163). One of the most significant shifts was the growth of unionization among workers in capital-intensive industries such as auto, steel, and shipbuilding and the relative decline among workers in labor-intensive industries such as garment and textiles, shoes, and toys. While the textile workers federation was the largest union federation in 1975, the metal workers had become the largest federation by 1990 with 429,710 members representing a 580 percent growth over fifteen years (Lee and Choi 1998, 67).

The expansion of capital-intensive manufacturing industries and its growing centrality in the economy was poised to give protesting workers the leverage they needed to begin dismantling nearly three decades of political repression under authoritarian state regimes. However, intensified pressures, particularly by the increasingly protectionist trade policies of U.S. capital and the state, to reconfigure South Korean markets in line with the principles of neoliberal globalization intervened in this historical moment of possibility. Instead of expanding its influence in the governing structures of society, militant democratic unionism faced renewed attempts by employers and the state to undermine, not support the development of, workers' associational power.

Undermining Militant Unionism in South Korea

Although the downward pressures of globalized competition are commonly highlighted to explain the erosion of trade unionism in today's global economy, it is crucial to provide historical and geographic specificity to this claim when considering the case of South Korea. Unlike in labor-intensive manufacturing sectors where plant closings and capital flight resulted in the failure of 80 percent of trade unions in small and medium plants by 1990,[15] in more capital-intensive sectors where production was flourishing, the outright relocation of production to "union-free" worksites was less feasible. The state's post-1987 "hands-off" policy toward unions also pressured employers to deal more directly with the structural power of labor strikes (Koo 2000, 235). Rather than jeopardize production, *chaebols* (large family-owned conglomerates), which contributed over 60 percent of total domestic sales and two-thirds of total exports in key national industries such as auto, steel, shipbuilding, electronics, and public utilities, began granting more extensive union concessions in exchange for labor peace (Lee and Lee 2002, 3). During this time, unions began securing stronger guarantees for lifetime employment, seniority-based promotions, and welfare benefits.

Despite making significant wage and benefit concessions to trade unions in the workplace, signaling their willingness to engage in good-faith bargaining, employers also initiated a new round of policy initiatives aimed at weakening the institutional basis of workers' associational power. In December 1989, employers formed the Korean Association of Industrial Organizations and began actively lobbying for anti-labor legislation, including the passage of a "no work, no pay rule" that banned workers from receiving pay during the course of a strike action and called for the elimination of severance payments for dismissed workers. Employers also argued that the government needed to "modernize" its seniority-based wage payment system in line with the more competitive, performance-based wage system used by other industrialized nations. Many large firms also began restructuring their organizations to include personnel or human resource management departments that could implement more flexible wage policies, which had not existed prior to 1987 (Koo 2002, 192). To justify their demands for increased "labor flexibility," employers emphasized that the elimination of rigid rules and protections regulating labor was essential and necessary for the survival of businesses as South Korea came under greater pressure to liberalize its markets and survive in a highly competitive and volatile global economy.

The burgeoning labor movement was somewhat successful in preventing employer-driven efforts from rolling back existing labor rights, including the 1993 proposal for legalization of temporary agency work (*p'agyŏn*). However, the neoliberal policies of the next two presidents, both of whom, ironically, represented well-known pro-democracy activists during the authoritarian period, were pivotal in downgrading existing labor rights and protections. Under the banner of *sekyehwa* (loosely translated as globalization), which was aimed at dismantling the legacies of authoritarian dictatorships and catapulting Korea into "an advanced country active on the center stage of world affairs in the 21st century" (Bobrow and Na 1999, 182), President Kim Young Sam attempted to weaken the regulatory climate for labor by legalizing such practices as at-will dismissals and temporary agency employment. The mass mobilization of workers during the first nationwide General Strike, led by the Korean Confederation of Trade Unions (KCTU) in 1996–1997, which at its height reached one million protesters, was able to stall the legalization of Kim Young Sam's neoliberal labor reforms.[16] However, during the next administration under Kim Dae Jung, neoliberal labor reforms were successfully legalized.[17]

Conditionalities attached to the $57 million IMF bailout loan created the ideal conditions to implement neoliberal structural adjustment policies; however, "the IMF had an enthusiastic partner in President-elect Kim Dae Jung who asserted that the full liberalization of Korea's economy and society was both necessary and inevitable for resolving the national crisis and securing its future prosperity" (Crotty and Lee 2006, 4). In his "Second Nation Building" plan, President Kim emphasized the importance of "sharing the burden" in a new society that could advance the principles of market liberalization, structural reforms, and democratization:

> Amid such rapid changes, no single nation, wherever it is in the world, can develop and run its own economy without being inextricably linked with the rest of the countries. . . . Even the smallest Korean rural village will have to compete with farmers across the globe. A small factory in a back alley will have to engage in competition with same types of plants in every corner of the world. We will advance into the world, and the world will move into our country. Both competition and cooperation will take place simultaneously. It is a path we cannot avoid.[18]

For Kim Dae Jung, the full compliance of organized labor to neoliberal restructuring was both essential and inevitable to the future security and prosperity of the nation.[19] In particular, Kim Dae Jung was intent on removing existing job security protections. Unlike in the United States, Korean employers were not legally allowed to fire workers at will. Regularly employed workers, typically full-time, male workers in large firms, enjoyed a system of lifetime employment, based on the Japanese system. The proposed labor law revisions were aimed at making Korean employment standards in line with eroded U.S. standards.

Up until this point, the KCTU had pursued a somewhat multifaceted program for strengthening the basis of the democratic labor movement, including a concerted effort to transform the enterprise-level system of unionism—which was installed by authoritarian leaders to suppress the political activity of independent unions—to an industrial level system of unionism, to promote greater solidarity among unionists across companies and occupations. During the crisis, the KCTU represented the independent workers' movement in the first Tripartite Commission, which discussed issues of trade union and labor policy with representatives from labor (FKTU), government, and the business sector.[20] The possibility for engaging in more participatory involvement in industrial relations, however, was short-lived. Although there is considerable debate regarding KCTU's consent to the legalization of flexible labor policies in the Tripartite Commission, a subsequent amendment to the Labor Standards

Law, passed in February 1998, allowed employers to legally lay off workers due to corporate restructuring and rehire them through temporary agencies.[21]

With organized labor's *perceived* consent to the reduction of social protections for workers, employers, starting with the Hyundai Motors Company in Ulsan, also began to dismiss workers en masse. During the early months of the Asian debt crisis, an estimated ten thousand workers a day lost their jobs, with a disproportionate number of women and migrant workers "fired first." Although the government agreed to ensure that employers take "every effort to avoid dismissals" and engage in "sincere consultations" with unions before engaging in mass layoffs, it took no measures to prevent the reckless abuse of the mass dismissal law by employers. The lack of government enforcement of amended labor law provisions fueled a climate of rampant labor abuse. Employers justified blatantly illegal employment practices by deeming them necessary for the survival of firms during times of economic duress. By the end of July 1998, there were 873 cases of unfair dismissals reported involving 1,610 workers, a 450 percent increase over the same period in the previous year. Cases involving the failure to pay back-wages also escalated during this period (KCTU 1999).

The government was a major force behind mass layoffs, mandating as high as 30 percent workforce reductions, regardless of the firm's economic condition. The state justified the deregulation and privatization of public-sector industries that were not experiencing financial strains by emphasizing the need to implement greater labor flexibility. The state also cracked down on unionists who opposed mass dismissals, privatization, and other components of the state's neoliberal restructuring program. Militant labor struggles in sectors undergoing economic restructuring (such as *chaebol*-dominated heavy industries and state-controlled financial, banking, and public utilities) were repeatedly broken up by state intervention, including the violent crackdown on Hyundai Motors Union's strike and the Mando Machinery union strike in 1998, both of which represented some of the first strike actions by protesting unionists against legalized mass dismissals (KCTU 1998).

In response to intensified employer abuse against workers and trade unions, the KCTU has attempted to re-escalate militant opposition to the deregulation of the labor market. However, its initial concessions helped lay the basis for a new political climate for labor. Although some unions continue to maintain a voice in managerial decisions, most unions have little to no influence over employer's use of irregular employment. According to Jooyeon Jeong (2005, 53), "[union] consent is not required for either massive discharges or hiring subcontracted employees in place of ordinary union members." In addition, the sale of Korean firms to foreign firms has also curbed or eliminated union influence. Union compliance with flexible labor practices is viewed as a critical component of the nation's broader project of economic reform and recovery, while union opposition, particularly militant opposition, is considered a threat to national security and prosperity. The KCTU's repeated calls for international solidarity against increased police violence and government repression against striking unionists highlights the consequences of this new political climate. Almost every strike action by KCTU unionists has resulted in escalating clashes between militant workers and nonreceptive employers. To resolve these heated standoffs, the government has intervened with penal force against striking unionists to restore a favorable business environment. Employers have further imposed punitive actions by filing onerous civil suits against striking unionists for loss of profits and the provisional seizure of property during strike actions—a tactic that has led desperate unionists such as the branch president of Hanjin Heavy Industries, Kim Joo-ik, to immolate themselves in protest of the excessive fines that force workers as well as their friends and family into bankruptcy (KCTU 2005).

The consolidation of neoliberal regimes in the post-IMF era has significantly hampered the traditional source of power for the democratic labor movement—union militancy in the workplace and on the streets. Contrary to conventional explanations that identify *neoliberalism* simply as "an economic doctrine with a negative relation to state power," in South Korea, as in other Asian countries, explains Aihwa Ong (2006, 3–4), neoliberalism has provided newly democratic regimes with techniques to manage and regulate their citizens according to the "infiltration of market-driven truths and calculations into the domain of politics." Whereas direct confrontation against repressive employers and the state once revealed the injustice of state repression under a formal democracy, especially for striking workers demanding the enforcement of their formal labor rights, union militancy no longer exposes a contradiction between de jure and de facto rights. Even when democratic administrations invoke repressive labor practices akin to the authoritarian regimes of the past, militant unionists are rarely able to generate public support for their struggles. Media outlets routinely characterize militant union struggles as "selfish" and "shortsighted" with respect to national economic goals. Passersby to militant union protests also rarely view public disruptions on city streets as vehicles for fighting injustice and oppression. Instead, the tactics used by militant unions to disrupt everyday life on the streets of Seoul are increasingly seen as impediments to moving the nation forward and restoring levels of prosperity and economic growth that were characteristic of the "pre-IMF" era. The legalization of neoliberal values in the regulation of employment and labor markets, thus, can be seen as the victory of employers and the state over labor in redefining the priorities necessary for Korea to compete in an increasingly competitive and volatile global economy.

Conclusion: Weakening the Structural and Associational Power of Unionized Workers

Comparing the dynamics of change for organized labor in South Korea and the United States reveals that workers and the unions representing them experienced similar patterns of decline by the end of the twentieth century. This convergence is especially striking given the divergent trajectories of each labor movement from the 1950s to the 1980s. Unlike the U.S. labor movement, which had already been ensconced in a slow and steady path of decline, the Korean labor movement was exploding in the late 1980s, highlighting the emergence of a new site of labor unrest in the non-Western, developing world. However, this moment proved to be short-lived in the context of global economic shifts associated with deregulation, privatization, and economic restructuring. A close examination of the way in which union decline took place, however, highlights the significance of concrete historical and institutional factors in mediating and directing the global dynamics of change.

In the United States, employers and the state weakened the associational power of unions by dismantling the postwar system of industrial welfare—a system that depended on the structural power of privileged sectors of the workforce to secure increased social wages and job security through collective bargaining agreements. This meant that the "unmaking" of organized labor in the United States largely took place within the boundaries of formal institutional processes, although the resurgence of employer offensives against unionized workers certainly utilized contested and questionable legal practices. Nonetheless, because many industrial workers traded union influence over managerial decisions for job security, welfare benefits, and cost of living increments, they had limited means to contest the erosion of their living and working conditions as a result of such managerial decisions as plant relocations, workforce reductions, and concessionary bargaining. Once unions accepted the "inevitability" of such processes, the balance of power shifted decisively in favor of capital in the context of heightened global competition and market volatility.

In contrast, in South Korea, although industrial workers had relatively high levels of structural power during the period of employer offensives against unionized workers in the early 1990s, the associational power of their unions was severely undermined by systematic employer and state offensives against militant unionism. Independent unions that had secured significant gains in wage and welfare benefits for workers were fiercely resistant to rollbacks in the context of "globalization." They were also deeply skeptical of state and capital discourses about the necessity of implementing welfare-depriving policies such as labor market flexibility, privatization, and neoliberal economic restructuring. However, the sudden and unexpected collapse of the national currency market in 1997 and 1998 shifted the balance of power decisively to the side of capital. Under intense ideological pressure, militant democratic unions temporarily accepted the "necessity" of labor peace during the national economic crisis, including the erosion of basic labor standards that protected workers against arbitrary dismissal and more exploitative forms of flexible work. When the costs of union concessions became apparent in the context of escalating state repression against protesting workers, militant unions quickly recommenced opposition against employers and the state. However, the new institutional and political climate regulating labor had profound effects on more militant forms of unionism, paving the way for capital and the state to redefine the terms upon which workers could build legitimate forms of associational power. These changes would have profound consequences on attempts to rebuild the moral and material legitimacy of unions.

In chapter 3, I discuss how the decline of unionism among more privileged sectors of the unionized workforce coincided with the creation of a more exploitable and socially vulnerable workforce in rapidly expanding sectors of the service-producing economy—a shift that would have profound consequences for the way national labor movements could rebuild the basis of worker power in the face of deepening crises.

3

RECONSTRUCTING THE
MARGINALIZED WORKFORCE

As privileged segments of the unionized workforce experienced severe roll-backs in union gains in declining industrial sectors from the 1970s onward, the more vulnerable segments also confronted downward pressures on wages and deteriorating employment standards. While much attention has been paid to the recruitment of young, single, third-world women into transnational production circuits, where the wages and working conditions are reminiscent of nineteenth-century industrial sweatshops (Fernandez-Kelly 1983; Fröbel, Heinrichs, and Kreye 1980; Fuentes and Ehrenreich 1984; S. K. Kim 1997; Lim 1983; Salzinger 2003), less attention has been paid to the production of a "third world within"—that is, immigrants, racial-ethnic minorities, and women recruited to work at the bottom of the labor market hierarchies of advanced industrialized economies (Chang 2000). In particular, few have analyzed the connections between global economic restructuring and the concentration of historically disadvantaged workers along gender, race, and immigration status in expanding sectors of the low-paid service economy.

The resegmentation of urban labor markets, according to leading globalization scholar Saskia Sassen (2000, 1998), is a key feature of the changing capitalist world economy. As major cities like Los Angeles and Seoul are reconfigured into "command centers" of transnationally dispersed and globally integrated economic activities (what Sassen calls "global cities"), urban service economies are afflicted by deepening levels of polarization. On the one hand, the expansion of specialized business and trade services has increased the number of high-skilled, high-paying jobs in industries such as finance, banking, marketing, advertising, and information technology. On the other hand, there has been a corresponding increase in demand for lower-skilled, lower-paid workers to clean corporate buildings, luxury hotels, and universities, and also to attend to the personal and domestic needs of urban professional elites. Historically sedimented inequalities along race, gender, immigration status, and other axes of social difference provide a rich topography for the intensification of economic marginalization along more flexible and informal lines.

The intensification of polarization and inequality in urban labor markets highlights the renewed significance of labor market segmentation. Historical accounts of labor market segmentation have posited that socially stratifying systems such as patriarchy (Hartmann 1976), internal colonialism (Blauner 1972), and white settler nativism (Bonacich 1972) serve to produce and maintain separate and distinct labor market "tiers," each regulated by its own characteristics and behavior rules (Reich, Gordon, and Edwards 1973, 359). While workers in the upper tier enjoy the possibility of higher wages, promotion, and job security, workers in the lower tier or secondary markets are confined to low-wage, low-skilled, and dead-end jobs. Whether confronting capital's divide-and-conquer strategies (Reich, Gordon, and Edwards 1973), white working-class racism (Bonacich 1976), or male domination (Hartmann 1976), workers in the lower tier have historically faced multiple barriers to improving their working and living conditions through job mobility and career advancement.

However, we must recognize the key difference between the labor market segmentation of the past and that of the present-day: The boundaries between the upper- and lower tiers of the working class are not as immutable as they once were. As I discussed in chapter 2, privileged sectors of the unionized workforce no longer benefit from job protections and automatic wage increases. Rather, they face what Jamie Peck and Nik Theodore (2009) aptly call a "downward gravitational drag" on wage and employment conditions. Thus, instead of two different labor markets with distinct characteristics, workers across both tiers face conditions typically associated with the lower tier: declining wages, worsening employment conditions, and a more pervasive state of precariousness (see also Vosko and Cranford 2006, 45–46).

Expansion of the "Lower Tier"

The shift to a service-based economy is contributing to the reconstruction of the marginalized workforce in the "lower tier" of both the South Korean and the U.S. labor markets. In the case of South Korea, gender as well as age and class are primary determinants of one's likelihood to be employed in the growing sector of low-paid, insecure, and socially devalued forms of service work. In the case of the United States, race and immigration status as well as gender and class are salient characteristics of the low-paid, service workforce.

In both national contexts, marginalized workers in the lower tiers of the service sector are likely to hold precarious and irregular jobs, which have been largely created by employers and the state to depress wages, working conditions, and labor standards. *Precarious employment,* also referred to as casual and contingent employment, encompasses downgraded forms of work characterized by low wages, pervasive job insecurity, limited employer-based benefits, weak regulatory protections, few opportunities for job mobility, and little control over work schedules and the labor process (Cranford and Vosko 2006). *Irregular employment,* also referred to as atypical and non-standard employment, includes forms of work that deviate from full-time, paid employment under a single employer with access to job security, employer-based benefits, labor protections, upward job mobility, and some voice in controlling one's schedule and working conditions. Examples of irregular employment include part-time, temporary, short-term, daily, and on-call work as well as self-employment, independent-contracting, and triangulated forms of employment due to business practices such as outsourcing.

United States

The overall expansion of precarious employment in the United States is clear when looking at the growth of the service-producing sector. Between 1970 and 2000, the service-producing sector contributed 58.3 million new jobs, which represented 96 percent of all (net) jobs created (U.S. Bureau of Labor Statistics [BLS] 1970–2000). By contrast, employment in the manufacturing sector declined 0.96 percent, the mining sector declined 0.13 percent, and the construction sector grew by a mere 5.15 percent (see table 2). With the shift toward the service sector came a downward trend in average wages. In terms of hourly compensation, in 2001, service jobs had the lowest hourly compensation ($19.74) compared with mining ($31.44), manufacturing ($24.30), construction ($24.08), and government jobs ($30.64) (Mishel, Bernstein, and Boushey 2003, 176).

Although the service sector does include higher-paying jobs in the finance, business, and government subsectors, low-wage work is a significant component of the service sector. "Low-wage workers" are often defined as such in terms of their proximity to the government's official "poverty line," which is the

Table 2. U.S. Employment Growth by Industry, 1970–2000

SECTOR	NEW JOBS CREATED (IN THOUSANDS)		1970–2000 CHANGE (IN THOUSANDS)	NET GROWTH (%)
	1970	2000		
Goods-producing	22,179	24,649	2,470	4.1
Mining	677	599	−78	−0.1
Manufacturing	17,848	17,263	−585	−1.0
Construction	3,654	6,787	3,133	5.1
Service-producing	48,827	107,136	58,309	**95.9**
Trade, transportation, and utilities	14,144	26,225	12,081	19.9
Information	2,041	3631	1,590	2.6
Financial activities	3,532	7687	4,155	6.8
Professional and business services	5,267	16,666	11,399	18.8
Education and Health	4,577	15,109	10,532	17.3
Leisure and Hospitality	4,789	11,862	7,073	11.6
Other services	1,789	5,168	3,379	5.6
Government	1,268	2,079	811	1.3
Total	71,006	131,785	60,779	

Sources: Current Population Survey (CPS), U.S. Bureau of Labor Statistics, 1970 and 2000.

minimum income thought to be necessary to satisfy basic needs (measured in terms of food subsistence), based on family size. Average 1999 hourly earnings (in 2000 dollars) in the two largest service subsectors, retail trade and services (including personal services, restaurants and hospitality, health services), were only slightly above the official poverty wage ($8.19) at $9.08 and $13.36, respectively (Hatch and Clinton 2000, 14). The BLS predicts that between 2000 and 2010, jobs paying less than $18,490 annually will constitute half of the top ten fastest growing occupations. Another two of those ten fastest growing occupations will pay less than $25,760 annually. These seven low-paying occupations are all in the service sector: food preparation and service workers, customer service representatives, retail salespersons, cashiers, office clerks, security guards, and waiters and waitresses.

One reason why service workers are poorly remunerated is that, historically, only a small proportion of them have been unionized. With the exception of protective service workers, such as police officers, in 1993, 9.5 percent of service workers were members of unions and their weekly pay rates were 173 percent higher than their nonunion counterparts. By 2006, the proportion of unionized service workers had fallen to 7.8 percent, and the union premium dropped to 160 percent more per week (U.S. Bureau of Labor Statistics 1993, 2006). In 2003, unions also increased the wages of members with earnings in the lowest and second-lowest quartiles by 27.9 percent and 16.2 percent, respectively (Mishel, Bernstein, and Boushey 2003, 189–195). For unionized women, the pervasive gender wage gap between themselves and their male counterparts is partially mitigated. Most significant, however, is their advantage over other women who are employed in occupations with low union density. Unionized women workers, on average, earned 133 percent more than nonunion women workers (U.S. Bureau of Labor Statistics 2003; also see Milkman 2007).

At the peak of the anti-union fervor of the 1980s, wage trends revealed an overall "downward shift" in the wage structure, which had a disproportionate impact on women and racial-ethnic minorities (Mishel, Bernstein, and Boushey 2003, 136). Although the overall proportion of women earning poverty-level wages decreased slightly during the 1980s, women are overrepresented in the lowest-paying jobs. In an analysis of 2003 and 2004 Current Popular Survey data, conducted by Vicky Lovell, Heidi Hartmann, and Misha Werschkul (2007) (see figure 3), women were found to comprise 60.9 percent of workers in the twenty-five low-wage jobs studied ($8.75 hourly median wage). Of those twenty-five low-wage occupations, twelve were dominated by women, including personal and home care aides ($8.00 hourly median wage), child care workers ($8.00), and maids and housekeeping cleaners ($8.22). In gender-integrated service occupations such as restaurant service, retail sales, and commercial and office cleaners, women also received lower median hourly wages than their male counterparts (Lovell, Hartmann, and Werschkul 2007, 38–40).

Race and ethnicity are also significant factors in determining low-wage work. Of the twenty-five low-wage jobs surveyed by Lovell, Hartmann, and Werschkul (2007, 38–40), African Americans and Hispanics were disproportionately represented as personal and home care aides, maids and housekeeping cleaners, and child care workers. Among male-dominated low-wage jobs, Hispanics comprised an overwhelming 46.8 percent of agricultural workers and 43.2 percent of groundskeepers; African Americans comprised 27.9 percent of security guards. In more gender-integrated low-wage jobs, Hispanics are overrepresented as janitors, cooks, food-preparation workers; packers and packagers; and dining room, cafeteria, and bar workers. This pattern of racialized job polarization is consistent with the findings of Lawrence Mishel, Jared Bernstein, and Heather Boushey (2003). They found that in 2000, 31.8 percent of all black workers and 42.5 percent of all Hispanic workers earned poverty-level wages. Women of color were also disproportionately represented in low-paying jobs: 36.5 percent of black women and 49.3 percent of Hispanic women were found to earn poverty wages.

The race and gender dynamics of low-wage work reflect a broader pattern of racial polarization in the workforce at large. Erik Wright and Rachel Dwyer

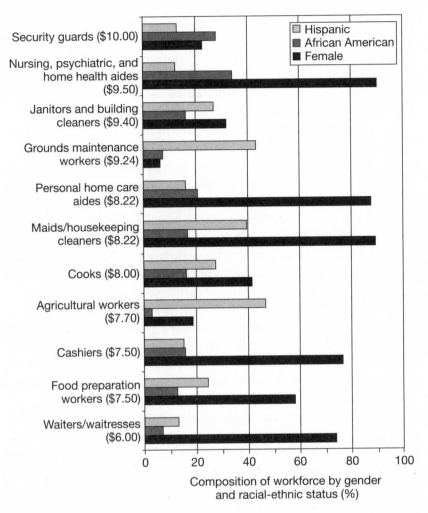

FIGURE 3. Low-wage jobs by gender and race/ethnicity in the United States. Adapted from Lovell, Hartmann, and Wershkul, 2007, 38–40 (table 2.2).

(2000, 22–23) explain that the period between the 1960s and 1990s can be characterized as one defined by "racially polarized job expansion." At the top of the employment distribution, white men experienced 62 percent of the net job expansion, and white women experienced nearly 90 percent. For all nonwhite workers, job expansion was concentrated at the bottom of the job distribution. Hispanic women accounted for 50 percent of the net job expansion, and Hispanic men for 35 percent. Black women accounted for 28 percent of net job expansion, and black men for 25 percent (as opposed to white women for 15% and white men for 4%) (Wright and Dwyer 2000, 24).

Although official statistics rarely aggregate workers by immigrant group, many low-wage service jobs in the United States are held by immigrants from non-Western countries. Many immigrants who arrived after 1965 have settled in urban centers and their surrounding areas, where job polarization and inequality are at their most extreme. In contrast to the 1960s, the foreign-born population is currently more likely to reside in Los Angeles, New York, Miami, San Francisco, and Chicago than in the former urban manufacturing hubs of the Midwest (Waldinger and Lee 2001). Of these major immigrant-receiving metropolitan areas, Los Angeles and New York represent "two mega-immigrant regions," containing almost 40 percent of the total immigrant population. California as a whole is also a major destination for immigrants. Between 1970 and 1996, California's total workforce more than doubled, growing from six million to thirteen million. There was a 500 percent increase in the Latino workforce and an 800 percent increase in the Asian workforce (Lopez and Feliciano 2000, 32). Immigrants have also become the preferred workforce in less-urban areas in the Midwest, Atlantic Northeast, and Pacific Northwest. Given the tremendous expansion of the post-1965 immigrant population and the vast linguistic, cultural, and educational differences among the groups, it is difficult to make sweeping generalizations about the "immigrant population." That said, a significant proportion of the workers currently employed in low-skill, low-pay service and manufacturing jobs are immigrants, especially in these immigrant dense urban areas.

Temporary, part-time, and home-based work arrangements are common in low-wage service work. However, the impact of such irregular or nonstandard work arrangements is difficult to assess in the United States [hereafter, I use the terms irregular and nonstandard interchangeably]. According to the BLS (2005), only between 1.8 percent and 4.1 percent of all employment was considered nonstandard (contingent). Nonstandard work arrangements are not necessarily "bad jobs." For highly skilled workers, such arrangements can allow for greater flexibility and room for growth. For the majority of low-wage, lower-tier workers, nonstandard work arrangements have some very undesirable features. When faced with the choice between temporary and permanent employment, the BLS (1999) found that the majority of temporary workers (53%) prefer to be employed as permanent, regular workers. There is also considerable evidence that employers use nonstandard employment as a cost-cutting and anti-union strategy. Nonstandard workers, on average, receive lower wages and fewer benefits and labor protections (Gonos 1998; Houseman and Polivka 2000; Kalleberg, Reskin, and Hudson 2000; Vosko, Zukewich, and Cranford 2003). In a report by the National Alliance for Fair Employment, about 29 percent of firms that underwent restructuring in 1999 replaced fired workers with lower-paid, temporary workers.[1] Furthermore, traditionally disadvantaged workers, such as women and racial-ethnic minorities, have tended to be overrepresented in nonstandard jobs. In 2001, women represented 46.9 percent of all workers but held 55.8 percent of all nonstandard employment. African American and Hispanic workers also were disproportionately represented (Mishel, Bernstein, and Boushey 2003, 255–257).

South Korea

When we examine the changing composition of employment in South Korea, we also see a distinct pattern of growth in the service sector and a relative decline in manufacturing and other goods-producing sectors. Between 1981 and 1999, of the total employment growth (4.062 million jobs), manufacturing jobs contributed 50.5 percent of the new jobs, and service sector jobs added 76.6 percent. During the next decade, the composition of employment growth significantly changed. Between 1990 and 2000, of the 2.976 million jobs created, manufacturing lost 667,000 jobs (net loss of 22.41%), and the service sector gained 4,422,000 jobs (net increase of 148.59%) (Korean National Statistics Office 1990, 2000) (see table 3). However, it is important to note that the manufacturing sector still comprises a much greater share of overall employment in South Korea than it does in the United States. In 2000, the Korean manufacturing sector accounted for 20.15 percent of all employment; the service sector accounted for 61.08 percent. By contrast, the U.S. manufacturing sector contributed 13.1 percent of total jobs in 2000, while the service sector contributed 81.3 percent (U.S. Bureau of Labor Statistics 2000).

Table 3.   Employment Growth by Industry, 1981–2000, Korea

SECTOR	NEW JOBS CREATED (IN THOUSANDS)			1990–2000 CHANGE (IN THOUSANDS)	NET GROWTH (%)
	1981	1990	2000		
Agriculture	4,801	3,237	2,288	−949	−31.89
Industry	3,891	6,406	5,908	−498	−16.73
Manufacturing	2,859	4,911	4,244	−667	−22.41
Service	5,331	8,442	12,864	4,422	**148.59**
Total	14,023	18,085	21,061	2,976	

Source: National Statistics Office, South Korea, 1981, 1990, 2000.

When looking at employment growth by occupation between 1993 and 2000, service and sales (54.5%) grew the most, followed by technicians (49%), and professionals (12.3%) (Ahn 2002a). As in the United States, there are significant wage differentials in the service sector. In 2000, the average monthly wage for service workers (1,011,927 Won) and sales workers (988,856 Won) was significantly lower than for all occupations (1,313,910 Won) (Ahn 2002a). Annual fringe benefits (legal retirement allowance, bonuses, and overtime), which are a significant part of the overall legal wage calculation in Korea, were also significantly lower in services and sales.[2]

To better understand the extent of downward wage and employment pressures in the Korean labor market, it is necessary to situate the growth of service-producing sectors in the context of the rise of irregular or nonstandard employment. Joyup Ahn (2002b, 3), a Research Fellow at the Korea Labor Institute, explains, "while the 1980s were marked by an increase in the proportion of paid [wage and salary] workers among the total workforce from 47.2% in 1980 to 60.5% in 1990, the 1990s were characterized by the rapid growth in the ratio of contingent workers (daily and temporary workers) among all paid workers." The category "contingent workers" refers to two basic criteria used by the Korean National Statistics Office to classify workers in non-standard employment: 1) job tenure (less than one year) and (2) entitlement to fringe benefits.[3] Between 1993 and 2000, the number of regular (permanent) workers decreased by 309,000 workers, while the number of nonstandard ones, as defined by their contingent status, increased by 2.025 million. In 1999, the proportion of nonstandard workers (51.7%) surpassed permanent workers (48.3%) (Ahn 2002b). Despite the fact that the majority of Korean workers are nonstandard, only 3.2 percent are unionized (N. Park 2006, 492).

Every industrial sector (except mining) has experienced a significant expansion in lower-paid, nonstandard jobs, but this growth is particularly pronounced in the service sector, which is the national economy's only growth sector. In the service sector, the percentage of workers who are full-time has steadily decreased from 35.7 percent in 1993 to 28.7 percent in 2000 (Ahn 2002b, 9). The robust association between nonstandard employment and service work has become clear in the aftermath of the 1997–1998 Asian debt crisis. In 1999 when over one million workers lost their jobs, there was a stark decline in the percentage of regularly employed manufacturing and mining workers. However, the rates of standard employment have recovered since 2000, with 57.7 percent and 74 percent of manufacturing and mining workers, respectively, in regular employment. By contrast, service sector workers maintain one of the highest proportions of nonstandard workers with 76.3 percent in retail, wholesale, hospitality, and food services. This gap is even more apparent when comparing employment status by occupation. In 2000, 81.2 percent of service and sales workers were nonstandard versus 34.3 percent of plant and machine operators and assemblers (Ahn 2002a, 12–13).

By 2000, the pervasiveness of nonstandard employment drove the National Statistics Office to develop a more precise data collection method in order to properly measure it. That year, the National Statistics Office created a "Special Supplement to the Economically Active Population Survey" to distinguish workers according to the nature of their employment arrangements. "Indirect arrangements'" include workers employed by subcontracted companies and temporary employment agencies. "Special employment arrangements" include wage-earning and salaried "independent contractors" as well as on-call workers. These arrangements represent a small fraction of the entire paid workforce, but they are prevalent in lower-paying service work. Indirect employment grew from 2.4 percent (444,000) to 4.0 percent (548,000) of the wage and salary workforce between 2000 and 2005 (Ahn 2002b 23; 2006, 9). Subcontracted agency employment is increasingly prevalent among janitors, hotel room cleaners, cafeteria workers, and other low-paid service workers. The number of workers employed as independent contractors increased from 553,000 to 633,000 workers between 2000 and 2005, but their percentage has remained relatively stable at around 4.2% of the paid workforce (Ahn 2002b, 24; 2006, 11). Independent contracting is particularly prevalent for those working in the educational service industry as home-based tutors for elementary school students, in the finance and insurance industry as insurance salespersons, and in the wholesale and retail industry as golf game assistants.

Unlike in the United States, nonstandard employment in South Korea is highly correlated to lower wages, fewer benefits, and heightened job insecurity. In 2001, the average monthly wage for nonstandard employees was only 52.45 percent (877,000 Won) of that of regularly employed workers (1,672,000 Won) (Ahn 2006, 23).[4] The earnings gap between standard and nonstandard workers is more clear when you look at hourly wage levels. Compared with 2001 hourly wages for standard workers (8,130 Won), nonstandard workers received 4,833 Won (59.4%). For workers subject to multiple forms of irregularity such as those employed by temporary agencies or engaged in home-based employment, hourly wages were as low as to 3,864 Won (47.5%) and 3,165 Won (38.9%), respectively (Ahn 2006, 24). Social insurance coverage and fringe benefits were also significantly lower for nonstandard workers, particularly those in temporary agencies and independently contracted or on-call work (Ahn 2006, 27).

Women have historically been disadvantaged in the Korean workforce. Due to the male-dominated social and economic structure, the female workforce participation rate has been historically low and highly concentrated in certain occupations such as agriculture, low-wage factory work, clerical work, personal service, and sales (Nam 1991, 646). However, since the 1970s, women's workforce participation has increased almost fourteen points to 41 percent within twenty-five years. In 2005, there were 8.71 million women in the total economically active population (21.06 million). This growth is significant, especially given relatively stable levels of male workforce participation during this same period.

Although women's employment has grown significantly, South Korea's rate of female workforce participation is relatively low compared to other OECD countries. The OECD Economic Survey of Korea (2005) predicts that gender labor force participation will not reach parity until as late as 2050. The gendered impact of labor market restructurings is increasingly apparent in the context of the shift toward service work and nonstandard employment. Since 1988, when the proportion of manufacturing workers who were women peaked at approximately 29 percent, women have increasingly become employed in service sectors. The drastic decline in the number of women employed in forestry, agriculture, and fishing has served to redirect women into the service sector (Korean Women Workers Associations United 1994, 6). Compared with men, a higher proportion of women workers have also joined the burgeoning nonstandard workforce. Despite the overall growth of temporary employment throughout much of the 1990s, the proportion of temporary employees who are male actually decreased to 43.53 percent. The proportion of female temporary employees increased to 56.47 percent during that time. Women also hold the majority of lower-paid, insecure work. In 2005, women held 56.85 percent of jobs in independent contracting, including 90 percent of home-based jobs and 63.6 percent of jobs through contract agencies, which are not subject to the law (Ahn 2006, 9, 11). A Report by the Korean Women Workers Associations United (KWWAU; 2000) also found that educational attainment and age have little influence on temporary or daily work; women across occupations and skill levels were overrepresented in nonstandard employment.

The persistent gender wage differential between male and female workers underscores the cost advantage employers can extract by hiring female workers. Although the gender wage gap did narrow from 48.1 percent to 61 percent between 1985 and 2005, the gender wage gap in South Korea is higher than in any other of the twenty-one OECD countries.[5] The gap is significantly greater in certain nonstandard employment arrangements. For example, employers who hire irregular female workers pay them only 42.7 percent of the average wage for that job, resulting in a wage savings of almost 60 percent. This is the case in every category of employment. In South Korea, to hire a female worker is often to reduce labor costs by anywhere from one-third to over two-thirds (S. H. Lee 2001) (see table 4).

Low levels of unionization also make women a more vulnerable workforce. In 2005, out of 15 million wage and salary workers, 11.8 percent (1.76 million) were union members. Women composed 23.86 percent (420,000 members) of the unionized workforce but just 6.7 percent of the all unionized workers (Park 2006, 492). The female unionization rate has also sharply declined since 1987 when it peaked at 11 percent. The gender ratio of unionized workers is also skewed in favor of men, who compose approximately 19 percent of the total male workforce.

The role of firm size is also significant. If you look at union density in large enterprises (more than 299 employees), union membership increased from 60 percent in 1989 to an all-time high of 70.9 percent in 2000. In contrast, union density in small enterprises (with less than 100 employees) decreased from 9.5 percent in 1989 to 1.1 percent in 2000 (Lee and Choi 1998, 64; Lee and Lee 2002, 15). These figures reveal stark disparities between workers in small and large firms, especially in light of the former's group's much larger share of the labor market. In 2000, small enterprises accounted for 78.3 percent

Table 4. Average Monthly Income by Employment Status and Gender, Korea

CLASSIFICATION	TOTAL	WAGE RATIO (%)	FEMALE	TOTAL WAGE (%)[a]	MALE COUNTERPART WAGE (%)
Regular wage worker	1,693,973	100.0	1,243,000	73.4	66.9
Irregular wage worker	891,105	52.6	722,699	42.7	67.6
Temporary	911,354	53.8	753,984	44.5	70.4
Regular part-time	895,416	52.9	804,446	47.5	71.8
Temporary part-time	468,273	27.6	434,396	25.6	78.3
On call	691,294	40.8	468,501	27.7	57.3
Contractor	1,094,136	64.6	917,404	54.2	68.1
Dispatch	1,006,421	59.4	628,450	37.1	71.5
Subcontracted	785,114	46.3	628,450	37.1	71.5
Work at home	497,888	29.4	373,620	22.1	31.2

Source: Adapted from table 13, Lee Sang Hak, KCTU Report, raw data from August 2001, Supplemental Research on Economically Active Population Census.

[a] Calculation based on percentage of monthly income of regular wage worker, in Won.

of the workforce versus 8.7 percent for large enterprises (Jeong 2005, 46). Few women (18.8%) are employed in firms with more than one hundred employees. In fact, approximately 44 percent of women workers are concentrated in work-places with fewer than ten employees, which have the lowest wages of all (Park 2006, 492).

Creating and Reproducing the Lower Tier

In both the United States and South Korea, a cheap labor force did not just exist; it had to be actively created and reproduced. Historical and structural conditions have shaped how and under what conditions traditionally disad-vantaged workers came to be overrepresented in the lower tier of both national labor markets. Structural shifts, along with discriminatory employer hiring and firing strategies, facilitated the ongoing concentration of racialized immigrants, including women, in the United States and native women in Korea in down-graded forms of service work. The state has played an active role in producing a cheap workforce in each country.

U.S. Immigration, Racialization, and Low-Paid Work

Between 1924 and 1965, U.S. federal immigration policies restricted the entry of racialized immigrants, particularly from Asia, though some may trace the roots of race-based immigration policy as far back as the 1882 Chinese Exclu-sion Act.[6] Anti-immigration policies were supported primarily by white, native male workers who condemned the influx of cheap Asian labor. According to the American Federation of Labor, "If the products of our mills and factories are to be protected by a tariff on articles manufactured abroad, then by the same token, labor should be protected against an unreasonable competition from a stimulated and excessive immigration" (quoted in Reimers 1998, 20; also see Ngai 2004).[7]

While much has been written about the effects of discriminatory immigra-tion policies, very little scholarly work has addressed the relationship between race-based immigrant exclusion and the growth of the organized labor move-ment. According to Edna Bonacich (1972), the organized labor's promotion of race-based immigrant exclusion from the 1880s to the 1920s was linked to its desire to restrict wage competition and the threat of declining wages by lower-paid, racial-ethnic groups. By excluding the entry of racialized work-ers or confining them to lower-tier employment, native, male workers could protect their jobs and their wage levels. It is perhaps no coincidence that the tremendous expansion of the U.S. labor movement in the 1930s and 1940s followed by massive union gains in the 1950s and 1960s took place with a backdrop of four decades of federal immigration exclusion.

Cold War anti-communist foreign policies helped dismantle decades of anti-immigrant union protectionism. The 1952 McCarran-Walter Act was the first of such policies. Passed during the Korean War, this act allowed Asian immigrants to become naturalized citizens for the first time, and it increased the annual quota of immigrants from the Asia-Pacific region from 100 to 2,000.[8] The United States' prolonged entanglement in the Cold War coupled with the domestic civil rights movement at home provided further impetus for the U.S. government to address federal immigration policies. The passage of the 1965 Hart-Celler Act officially ended four decades of racially motivated immigration restrictions.[9] Although exemptions were built into the system to limit the entry of non-European immigrants (then still a major concern), precisely the opposite happened. Immigration skyrocketed. In the late 1940s, an average of 250,000 persons immigrated annually. By the 1990s, annual immigration reached historic levels at 929,000. Almost two million immigrants arrived in 1991 alone. While before 1960, over two-thirds of all immigrants came from Europe, by the mid-1980s, the proportion of European immigrants dropped below 10 percent. Immigrants from Asia, the Caribbean, and Latin America have dominated post-1965 immigration flows.

Despite popular claims that "push factors" are primarily responsible for outward migration from poverty-stricken third-world countries, demographic particularities reveal the importance of structural factors as well: "As the United States has become more deeply involved in the world, the world has become more deeply involved in America" (Rumbaut 1994, 588). The U.S. military has been and continues to be heavily involved in Asia, which has influenced the character and growth of Asian immigration (Sassen 1998). The arrival of free trade zones and direct foreign investment has also created structural migration pathways that first stimulated rural-to-urban migration, especially of young single women in the Caribbean and Asia, to factories in the city, which then facilitated transnational migration from these urban areas to the United States (Sassen 1998).

The role of U.S. state intervention in recruiting cheap labor from Mexico also highlights the structural conditions involved in producing an exploitable, racialized workforce within U.S. borders. During World War II, the legal exclusion of all Asian immigrants, combined with rapid urbanization and industrialization, resulted in a shortage of domestic workers willing to endure the harsh conditions of low-paid agricultural work. The *Bracero Program,* a tempo-rary contract labor program jointly operated by the U.S. Departments of State, Labor, and Justice from 1942 to 1964, was the government's answer to pressure from the U.S. agricultural industry. The *Bracero Program* not only set a prec-edent for active state involvement in recruiting, regulating, and reproducing a cheap immigrant workforce, but it also contributed to the marked expansion of an "illegal" migrant workforce. Recruitment of rural Mexican farmwork-ers far outstripped demand for their labor; thus, hundreds of thousands of Mexican migrants were left in search of work. In the mid-1950s, political pres-sure to curb Mexican migration resulted in the increasing militarization of the U.S.–Mexico border and the active apprehension and deportation of Mexican workers by the Immigration and Naturalization Services (INS), now known as Immigration and Customs Enforcement (ICE) (Massey, Durand, and Ma-lone 2002, 33–37; also see Ngai 2004). The 1964 Immigration Act put in place further restrictions of Mexican immigration and increased the population of unauthorized Mexican immigrants.

Today, immigration from Mexico constitutes the largest immigration flow to the United States. Before 1970, Mexicans accounted for 22 percent of the total foreign-born population and 26 percent of all immigrants to the United States. Today, there are over 15 million migrants from Mexico. As shown in the previ-ous section, Mexicans as well as other workers from Central and Latin America are overrepresented in a variety of low-skilled, manual labor—"the very jobs that were once key strongholds of union organization" (Milkman 2000, 1). In the context of southern California, Milkman (2006, 7) emphasizes that the in-flux of immigrants into such jobs as janitors, "drywallers," truck drivers, and garment workers came about *after* the exodus of native-born workers from these increasingly low-wage jobs, not before it. Despite the widely held belief that immigrant workers drove down wages and displaced native-born workers from these kinds of jobs, evidence suggests that they were actually replacing the workers who had already left those jobs in the context of declining wages, widespread deunionization, and employment restructuring.

U.S. Urban Revitalization, Neoliberal Restructuring, and Low-Wage Service Workers

The transformation of the U.S. employment structure in the 1980s fueled a con-tinued stream of immigrant labor into low-wage, urban labor markets. Cities, plagued by job destruction, reduced business tax revenue, and suburban flight attempted to reorganize their economies to attract businesses back to urban centers. Municipal governments created "domestic economic zones," which are similar to offshore free trade zones, to provide a more hospitable business climate for urban development projects. They offered subsidies, tax incentives, and relaxed environmental and zoning restrictions, all of which businesses argued were necessary for them to operate in urban areas. Among the financial incentives offered in such urban enterprise zones, which were actively and unsurprisingly supported by the Reagan administration, were relaxed minimum wage laws for firms in "designated distressed areas." By the 1990s, enterprise zones, or what the Clinton administration called "empowerment zones," were a widely practiced form of urban economic development.[10] Government and business justified incentive packages by pointing to their long-term benefits in economically depressed urban neighborhoods.

Business-first strategies, however, have not simply failed to address the problems of urban poverty. They have exacerbated them. Few, if any, municipal governments require businesses receiving subsidy packages to designate a certain number of jobs to low-income residents. Urban enterprise zones and their corresponding financial incentives also create a "race-to-the-bottom" dynamic in the labor market. Cities that created urban development policies later had a more difficult time competing for business investment, which compelled them to offer more tax breaks and weaker labor protections (Pollin and Luce 1998, 58). Downward pressures on wages, as well as job polarization, inequality, and poverty are apparent in major cities where downtown businesses are booming.

The creation of "urban frontiers" that replicate the pro-business, anti-labor policies of third-world free trade zones has aggravated urban poverty. Between 1979 and 1992, the U.S. poverty rate increased from 11.7 percent to 14.8 percent. Poverty rates in central-city regions increased from 15.7 percent to 21.5 percent during the same period. As of 1996, more than 16 million people and 20 percent of the urban population lived in poverty (Pollin and Luce 1998, 54). Poverty levels are also increasing for recent immigrant cohorts, women, and people of color. These groups are not only historically disadvantaged in the labor market but also historically overrepresented in the kinds of socially reproductive labor (cleaning, care, and food-related work) that are a rapidly growing part of the urban service economy.

The federal dismantling of public assistance has also intensified the economic vulnerability of traditionally disadvantaged workers. The 1996 Personal Responsibility and Work Opportunity Reconciliation Act, which effectively

ended sixty years of cash assistance to poor families with children, is one notable example. As the figures from the previous section show, more women,
especially single mothers, have shifted into lower-wage jobs since the 1980s.
Workfare policies have not only eroded basic social safety nets for the poor but
they have also driven the poor to accept low-paid jobs in order to maintain
eligibility to partial forms of public assistance. As such, workfare policies have
created an institutionalized pathway for the expansion of a more vulnerable
and exploitative workforce. Restrictions on public assistance to immigrants,
which began under the 1986 Immigration Reform and Control Act and expanded under the 1996 Personal Responsibility Act, have rendered immigrant
women of color particularly vulnerable to gendered forms of low-paid service
work (Chang 2000).

The erosion of basic employment and welfare protections for socially and
economically vulnerable workers has had a profound impact on the dynamics
of urban labor markets. Under protective regulatory frameworks established
during the 1930s New Deal period, which legalized the associational rights of
workers (NLRA 1935) and created state welfare assistance for the poor, the elderly, and dependent social groups such as women and children (Social Security Act of 1935), the regulatory environment for labor established in the 1980s
can be described as a neoliberal mode of labor regulation. Jamie Peck and Nik
Theodore (2009, 19) explain:

> [Under New Deal frameworks,] minimum wage legislation and wel-
> fare provisions constituted a "floor" in the job market, which was then
> gradually ratcheted up; core workers achieved significant employ-
> ment security, expanded the legitimate scope of union activities, and
> secured an institutionalized system of cost-of-living raises....This
> institutional complex has been gradually pulled apart over the past
> three decades, a process actively assisted by a plethora of corporate and
> government initiatives, so these anti-gravitational forces were at first
> stalled and subsequently reversed. In the regressive regulatory climate
> established in its wake, the (admittedly partial) upward pull of pro-
> gressive labor and welfare standards has been overcome by a downward
> gravitational drag.

One of the most decisive changes under the neoliberal mode of labor regulation, thus, is the downward pull on wage and livelihood standards, which
places minimum levels of dignity and welfare for vulnerable social and economic groups at risk.

Labor Market Deregulation and Gender Inequality, South Korea

Since Korea's rapid development under authoritarian rule, the state has been centrally involved in the creation, regulation, and reproduction of a cheap labor force, especially along gendered lines. As I mentioned in chapter 2, the state and employers directly targeted women as a source of cheap labor in export-oriented industries in the 1970s. When the state shifted its economic priorities in the 1980s and 1990s, it also became actively involved in channeling women into precarious and irregular forms of service work. During the 1980s and early 1990s, shifting state priorities in national economic development as well as the successful unionization of Korean women workers in export-oriented labor-intensive industries (see Cho 1985) resulted in the decline of female-dominated manufacturing industries. Under the Sixth Economic Development Plan (1987–1991), the Roh Tae Woo administration redirected state financial and tax subsidies to promote overseas investment in female-dominated, labor-intensive manufacturing sectors. It also promoted automation and technological advancements in domestic production. Between 1987 and 1988, over 40,000 women factory workers producing toys, textiles, garments, and simple electronics lost their jobs. Over the next several years, tens of thousands more workers lost their jobs as well. Industries nearly collapsed in the Masan Free Trade Zone, where foreign investments were concentrated, and in Daegu, where textile industry was concentrated; Pusan, where much of the shoe industry was based, collapsed (KWWA 1991, 3).

Industrial restructuring also resulted in deteriorating wages and working conditions as well as a general shift to temporary and outsourced work. Starting in 1988, more women were employed in temporary and daily work than in permanent, full-time work. The Korean Women Workers Association (KWWA) reported that the hiring of nonstandard workers was a strategy for reducing wages and undermining unionism. Because "temporary" workers do not enjoy the right to participate in collective bargaining through unions and are not entitled to the other legal benefits of permanent employment, employers have a double incentive to hire them: their wages are lower and they can be discharged at will (KWWA 1991, 6–7). KWWA also reported that the government and employers' federations "began actively encouraging the recruitment of married women and older people for temporary jobs" as a means of redirecting retrenched women workers into nonstandard employment. This was justified on the basis of patriarchal ideology dictating that men are the "breadwinners" and women are "secondary" household earners.

Although the passage of the 1987 Equal Employment Act slowly began eliminating overt and blatant forms, gender discrimination persisted in employment practices and state labor policies.[11] For example, before 1987, there was an explicit practice of exclusively hiring women for clerical positions in the financial sector. After 1987, financial companies replaced this blatant practice with a more covert form in which they mapped existing gender discrimination onto new human resource systems that allowed them to maintain a cheap workforce. By dividing the workforce into "variable" and "standard" positions, a practice developed in the Japanese financial industry in the 1980s, companies could partition workers into two groups and systemically withhold advancement opportunities from one. Workers in variable positions were eligible for promotions; workers in standard positions, which were almost predominantly women, were not. Workers in standard positions also tended to be confined to lower-skilled, repetitive jobs (Moon 2006).

The state has also taken an active role in downgrading wage and employment standards by institutionalizing demands for increased labor flexibility. While the erosion of job security protections did not occur until 1998 for privileged sectors of the workforce, employers were successful in increasing the flexibility of more vulnerable jobs from the early 1990s onward. Employers' groups introduced a 1991 labor law revision proposal, which passed in January 1992, to exclude part-time workers from receiving basic welfare benefits such as a paid day off per month, annual personal leaves, pregnancy leaves, and other benefits (KWWAU 2000, 35). According to the KWWA, the government had long focused on ways to encourage part-time and other forms of irregular work among workers. In the 1992 "White Paper on Labor," the Ministry of Labor stated that "women are limited by family life and skills and therefore more suited to hourly work than regular employment" (KWWA 1991, 38). The subsequent passage of the 1994 Standard Plan on the Welfare of Women Workers institutionalized the state's gendered ideology. The intent of this Plan was to devise a comprehensive policy on women's employment security, maternity protection, and welfare. However, under this plan, the state took measures to direct women into temporary agency employment by reauthorizing temporary agency work, which was banned in 1987 as an authoritarian labor practice.

The South Korean government also created a foreign industrial trainee system in November 1991 in response to pressure from employers in small- and medium-sized manufacturing companies. Migrant workers were classified as "trainees," which allowed employers to legally hire them in the "3D" (dirty, dangerous, and difficult) manufacturing industries at less than half the average wages of native Korean workers. While employers' organizations have advocated the increased use of migrant labor, its use, thus far, has been restricted to downgraded manufacturing industries and subject to a rigid set of guidelines. Ethnic Koreans from China, who also work as migrant labor in Korea, are concentrated in construction, restaurant, and domestic work. The industrial trainee system spurned intense protest from migrant workers, religious groups, and social movement activists. This pressure to eliminate the system's abusive and discriminatory conditions resulted in its transformation into the 2003 Employee Permit System. However, as a temporary contract labor program, the movement of migrant workers across workplaces is severely restricted. Ethnic Koreans from China (as well as the former Soviet Union) have been excluded from the 1998 Overseas Korean Act on Entry and Exit and Legal Rights, which provides overseas Koreans with work visas among other economic benefits. According to Hyun Ok Park (2008, 9), the exclusion of this population stems directly from the government's concern that the "number of ethnic Korean migrant laborers would increase unemployment [...] from 664,000 in 2003 to up to about one million."

Persistent gender discrimination in employer and state labor market practices intensified the vulnerability of women to unstable and insecure employment during and after the Asian debt crisis.[12] Many have noted that significantly more women than men were retrenched from the labor market in 1998. Women were also disproportionately impacted by the shift to lower-paid, insecure nonstandard employment. The Korea Labor Institute reported that six months after the acceptance of the IMF economic bailout loan in December 1997, only 7.8 percent of newly hired women workers were employed under regular conditions. The remaining 92.2 percent were employed as nonstandard workers. If you consider just the financial sector, over 90 percent of new hires in the financial sector were employed on a temporary basis, and 82 percent of those hired were women (Korea Labor Institute 2000).

The practice of "voluntary resignations" also exacerbated the impact of gendered labor discrimination. Instead of directly firing workers, employers pressured more vulnerable workers, such as those near the legal retirement age and women, to voluntary resign. This was particularly prevalent in the banking sector where a highly gendered division of labor already existed; male employees, who were primarily responsible for central business operations, were retained, while female employees, who worked as bank tellers and in customer service, were "asked" to resign. "Voluntary resignations" usually came with a financial incentive package, but it was a subtle form of employer coercion. "What [voluntary resignation] means is that banks selected a number of people to be removed in accordance with their own lay-off criteria and informed the workers of the fact that they would be forcefully removed if they tried to remain at work" (Moon 2006, 6).

One particularly revealing case involved the dismissal practice at Nonghyup Bank, the National Agricultural Cooperative Federation, in 1999. In the context of state-mandated economic restructuring, Nonghyup Bank, along with many other banks, began immediate workforce reductions by issuing requests for "voluntary resignations." Kyoung-Hee Moon (2006), who conducted a study on gender discrimination in Korea during the Asian debt crisis, explained, "In the process of Nonghyup's downsizing in January 1999, the employers explicitly forced married women with husbands working in the same bank to resign their jobs. The female workers were threatened that their husbands would be suspended from their work by force unless they made a voluntary retirement" (Moon 2006, 7). Among the 762 couples that worked at the bank, 752 couples accepted the voluntary dismissal of one partner and 688 of such cases involved the voluntary dismissal of the female partner. Demands for resignation, however, were not motivated by the need to eliminate certain jobs or reduce the absolute number of workers the bank needed to operate. After accepting workers' resignations, the bank proceeded to rehire the majority of the workers as nonstandard workers. Women were rehired for the same tasks as their previous ones but on fixed-term contracts or in other forms of nonstandard employment (Moon 2006; also see Cho 2000).

The feminization of labor under state-mandated labor market flexibility has exacerbated labor market segmentation and contributed to downward pressures on wages and working conditions. Yoonsook Moh, the head of the Incheon Women Workers Association, articulated the links between flexible restructuring policies and the feminization of labor:

> Under the current economic crisis, many companies have discriminated against women and forced regular female workers to become irregular workers under the pretense of necessary restructuring.... Regular women workers are dismissed and/or victims of the closure of their women-concentrated departments and then re-employed through temporary employment agencies. In addition, companies usually terminate female workers who attempt to resist these unfair labor practices. Since companies target female workers first and concentrate on women for unfair labor practices, the irregular employment of women workers has rapidly increased.[13]

Irregular Employment as Mechanism of Labor Cost-Cutting in Korea

Using irregular employment as a vehicle for downgrading wages and employment security was not limited to women, although as Guy Standing points out (1999), the differential impact on women points to the significance of feminization as a mechanism for labor cost-cutting under flexible employment. As I explained in the previous chapter, the state's legalization of employment deregulation contributed to a pervasive climate of labor cost-cutting. Studies show that after the 1998 economic crisis, many employers prefer to hire irregular over regular workers as a way to reduce labor costs (Kim and Park 2006; Lee 2004). Wage disparities between regular and irregular workers indicate that employers can hire irregular workers at almost half the price as regular workers, emphasizing the cost advantage of hiring irregular workers.

Hiring workers under short-term contracted employment, temporary agency employment, part-time employment and "special employment," a category similar to status as an independent contractor, allows employers to hire workers under virtually the same working conditions as regular employees (i.e. working hours, workplace supervision), except with no job security and little to no benefits such as paid overtime and paid sick and vacation leave. According to the KCTU, "the employment 'status' of a 'part-time' worker becomes the grounds for differentiated treatment in employee rights and welfare by the management," not real differentiations in the conditions of employment (KCTU 2004). A 2004 newspaper article in the *Korea Central Daily* (confirmed the KCTU's finding: "They [non-standard workers] do the same job during the same hours as regular workers, but for far less pay. Legally, it's not discriminatory because these employees are classified as non-regular, meaning they have been hired on a temporary basis or on contract. In the efforts to cut costs, companies are free to adopt a two-tier wage system."[14]

The perceived threat of labor cost-cutting and job displacement has exacerbated tensions among regularly employed workers and their irregularly employed counterparts. In their study of relations between regular and contract workers, Byoung-Hoon Lee and Stephen J. Frenckel (2004) find that contract workers feel stigmatized and demoralized by the exclusionary behavior and attitudes of regular workers, who exclude contract workers from social activities, blame them for taking jobs at such low pay, and deny them resources and protections on the job. A study evaluating union attitudes by regular workers toward contingent or irregular workers, based on a 2002 survey conducted by the Korea Labor Institute (KLI), confirms these findings, highlighting that the majority of union members and leaders are not willing to act in genuine solidarity with irregular workers, especially if supporting the latter brings about a loss of their own interests (J. Park et al. 2004). While some union members and leaders expressed that they are willing to address some work-related grievances related to irregular workers, they are much less willing to allow irregular workers to join their organizations as equal members (Park et al. 2004, 8–9). The persistence of negative attitudes of regular union members toward irregular workers is especially telling given the strong tendency of employers to hire contingent workers in establishments where the rate of union membership is high and the influence of unions is strong. This finding supports the argument that employers tend to hire irregular workers to cut labor costs and to weaken the constraints imposed by unions on managerial authority.

Conclusion: Eroding Wage and Livelihood Standards for Workers in the Lower Tier

Although the specific conditions vary in each country, parallel shifts in the United States and South Korea have occurred in the creation and reproduction of a cheap labor force. With the conclusion of four decades of race-based immigrant exclusion in 1965, U.S. borders reopened to legal (and illegal) immigration from Asia and Latin America. The state's involvement in creating and regulating migrant labor from Mexico contributed to the tremendous expansion of a low-paid immigrant workforce. At the municipal level, urban economic revitalization programs directed the flow of traditionally disadvantaged workers into expanding sectors of the low-wage urban service economy.

In South Korea, the marginalized workforce consists primarily of native Korean women who are overrepresented on the bottom rungs of the expanding service sector. A small but growing number of migrant workers have been recruited to fill low-paid, peripheral jobs, and they have since been largely confined to jobs in declining manufacturing sectors with the exception of ethnic Koreans from China who are increasingly employed in low-paid service jobs in small restaurants and businesses. The South Korean state has played an active role in downgrading wage and employment standards, especially for more vulnerable sectors of the female workforce, justified on the basis that they were "secondary wage earners" to men. Employers have also capitalized on gendered ideologies about women wage earners through discriminatory policies such as the pursuit of "voluntary resignations" by women first, when possible.

The reconstruction of a marginalized workforce along overlapping dimensions of social, economic, and institutional vulnerability has coincided with downward pressures on wage and livelihood standards for workers under neoliberal employment regimes. Socially devalued workers are highly susceptible to the proliferation of low-paid, precarious, and deregulated forms of employment. Despite the intensification of employer and state abuse and discrimination, organized labor in both South Korea and the United States has offered minimal support to marginalized workers. It is in this context that a new constellation of social actors and institutions emerged since the 1960s in the United States and since the late 1980s in South Korea to protect and organize highly vulnerable sectors of the marginalized workforce.

4

SOCIAL MOVEMENT LEGACIES AND ORGANIZING THE MARGINALIZED

Employer and state offensives against privileged workers in traditional union strongholds, alongside the concentration of historically disadvantaged workers in expanding sectors of the low-paid service economy, have contributed to deepening crises for labor movements in both South Korea and the United States. Faced with downward pressures on union membership, wage and benefit levels, job security, and employment standards, the labor movement in these two countries is embarking on surprisingly similar avenues of change. Instead of engaging in exclusionary forms of unionism against more vulnerable workers to prevent further wage degradation and job loss, as Edna Bonacich (1972, 1976, 1980) argued in her seminal work on split labor markets, organized labor movements are attempting to develop more inclusive practices, albeit in partial and contested ways.

In 1995, the newly elected president of the American Federation of Labor and Congress of Industrial Organizations (AFL-CIO), John Sweeney issued a "do-or-die warning" to "organize the unorganized." He argued that organizing all workers, including the many invisible workers employed in "thankless jobs" was essential to the AFL-CIO's survival if it hoped to "continue to exist as a viable institution" and have any relevant impact on political, economic, and social issues.[1] Discontent with the pace and scale of change under Sweeney's reform agenda, the Service Employees International Union (SEIU) and the International Brotherhood of Teamsters (Teamsters)—two of the AFL-CIO's largest affiliates—along with five other unions, disaffiliated from the AFL-CIO in 2005 and formed the Change to Win Federation (CTW), resulting in the loss of 5.4 million workers and over $40 million dollars from the AFL-CIO's annual operating budget.[2] According to CTW leaders, its goal was not to divide the U.S. labor movement but to rebuild it through an infusion of resources and hope. SEIU president Andrew Stern explained, "We have to do everything in our power to help workers. But when you're going down a road and it's headed in the wrong direction, and you know where the road ends, you got to get off the road and walk in a new direction where there is hope."[3] For Stern and other CTW leaders, this new direction pointed toward the millions of workers such as janitors, cashiers, nursing home aides, and security guards whose jobs could not be moved overseas or replaced by machines.

Similarly, in South Korea, the 2000 election of Korean Confederation of Trade Unions (KCTU) president Dan Byung-ho challenged a narrowing tendency within the national labor confederation that increasingly privileged the few at the expense of the many. In his first address as KCTU president, Dan reaffirmed the KCTU's commitment to serve as the "the genuine representative of all working people, including those workers in irregular employment, the unemployed, and the vast array of workers in small enterprises."[4] Although many regularly employed workers refused to act in solidarity with irregularly employed workers, the continued "betrayal" of the latter by the former has provided new vitality and direction for an increasingly conflict-ridden movement. KCTU has waged mass rallies, petition campaigns, hunger strikes, and joint solidarity actions with the more politically moderate Federation of Korean Trade Unions (FKTU) to "abolish irregular employment." New organizational entities such as the Korean Women's Trade Union (KWTU) and the Korean Solidarity against Precarious Work (*puranchŏng ch'ŏlpaeyŏndae;* KSPW) were also created explicitly to organize the growing ranks of irregularly employed workers.

To better understand the converging priorities of national labor movement organizations in Korea and the United States, this chapter directs our lens to the historical conditions that facilitated these parallel shifts. More important than changes in leadership are the efforts of a new generation of grassroots actors to overcome the exclusionary unionism of the past and organize workers subject to multiple forms of discrimination and disadvantage. In each country, prior social movement legacies influenced the kinds of moral and organizational repertoires invoked. In the United States, a new activist generation drew on 1960s civil rights and early New Left student movements to challenge the intersect between economic subordination and racial discrimination. In South Korea, union activists invoked discourses and practices from the 1970s and 1980s women workers' and democratization movements to organize the growing ranks of irregularly employed workers, many of whom were women. While such efforts generally remained isolated from mainstream unions, they began framing certain groups of workers as "marginalized" and thus deserving of broader public intervention to change the conditions of their lives. These efforts were crucial not only for developing new strategies and vocabularies with which to organize the marginalized but also for laying the groundwork for subsequent shifts in the direction and priorities of crisis-ridden labor movements in each country.

Challenging Labor Exclusion in the United States, 1960s and 1970s

The 1960s and 1970s is commonly thought of as a reactionary and regressive time for organized labor. Major labor leaders and conservative unions became increasingly disconnected from the needs of their members and a diversifying working class, and they came to represent a major oppositional force against the dynamic social movements sweeping the country. While the civil rights movement exposed the injustice and inhumanity of racial segregation, many labor unions defended Jim Crow in the South and protected discriminatory hiring systems in the North. Then AFL-CIO President George Meany supported the ideals of racial equality and civil rights, but limited his support to state-sponsored reform. He refused to condone union participation in such mass mobilizations as the 1963 March on Washington, the 1965 Delano marches led by Cesar Chavez and the California farmworkers, and the 1968 Poor People's March. Meany also refused to address the persistence of racism and white supremacy within its own union structure and decision-making processes, rejecting a 1962 proposal submitted by A. Philip Randolph, who headed the Brotherhood of Sleeping Car Porters and later spearheaded the 1963 March on Washington, to expel union affiliates found guilty of discrimination from the merged AFL-CIO (Levy 1994, 244). Thus, despite the path-breaking struggles for economic and racial justice pioneered by black workers and unions during this era (see MacLean 2006), the AFL-CIO was largely unwilling to shed its exclusionary ways.

The AFL-CIO existing leadership's refusal to change was partially attributed to its skepticism in swaying the country's political direction. Both Meany and his successor, Lane Kirkland, opposed centralized organizing campaigns, such as those advocated by Walter Reuther and other CIO-affiliated union leaders, to challenge the spread of nonunion business practices in the South. They also refused to mobilize the AFL-CIO's base in solidarity strikes across industry; for example, protests against Reagan's decision to end the 1981 air traffic control-ler's strike (Aronowitz 1998, 15). For Meany, the "place to break new ground [was] in the field of labor-management relations...[and] the establishment and maintenance of industrial peace."[5] Only by promoting the prosperity of U.S. industry could the AFL-CIO ensure its members' needs would always be met. By championing federal legislation such as worker's compensation and social security, Meany believed the AFL-CIO could secure benefits for workers that could be "enjoyed equally" by the "unorganized as well as organized."[6]

Despite these and numerous other examples of organized labor's disconnec-tion and, often, direct confrontation with progressive movements for social change, a movement for change was brewing. According to Philip Levy, a new generation of "social activist unions" emerged during this period that "sought to revitalize a generally moribund labor movement" (Levy 1994, 6). Social activ-ist unions, a diverse group, believed that the solution to the labor movement's ideological conservatism and numerical decline rested in the progressive ideals and creative tactics of new social movements. Older CIO unions such as the United Auto Workers (UAW), the Packinghouse Workers, and the Amalgam-ated Clothing Workers union, among others, helped fund and support new efforts to challenge workplace discrimination, racialized poverty, and wide-spread unemployment. However, activists outside the labor movement largely represented the driving force of change.

Deeply critical of business unionism and armed with a critique of the U.S power structure, these activists sought to reform the labor movement. Awak-ened by southern blacks' grassroots struggle for racial equality, they sought to dismantle the linkages between racial oppression and labor exploitation. They focused their energies on the plights of the powerless, such as the urban poor, the unemployed, the unorganized, migrant farmworkers, and others. Grass-roots community organizations and student movement organizations pro-vided the resources, organizational structure, and manpower to spread the struggle to the North and the West. Although these activists and the organiza-tions they created had minimal impact in changing the priorities of the labor movement at the time, they contributed to new strategies and organizational forms that would be crucial to the subsequent period of union revitalization: (1) community-based unionism and (2) corporate campaigns.

Community Organizing and the United Farm Workers

Saul Alinksy's (1972) model emphasized colorful, confrontational, and David-and-Goliath-type strategies for community organizing. His emphasis on com-munity organizing was connected, in part, to his disillusionment with organized labor. Although his own history as an organizer was closely linked to the CIO's progressive spirit, he believed that bigoted union leaders had led the labor movement down a path of self-interest and moral bankruptcy. As early as 1945, Alinksy called for "complete change in the philosophy of the labor movement" and a new political organization for labor that could serve as a cutting-edge political force (Horwitt 1989, 169–170). In his groundbreaking text, *Reveille for Radicals,* Alinsky (1946) proposed that "People's Organizations" could reinvigorate the labor movement by offering an alternative to both monopolistic capitalism and organized labor. Modeled after the kind of community organizing that Alinksy helped cultivate in the industrial slums of 1930s Chicago, these People's Organizations were designed to build a broad-based movement that could "unite to conquer all those destructive forces which harass the worker and his family" (Horwitt 1989, 171). Organizers were a key component to building People's Organizations. Alinsky-trained organizers worked in a diverse range of organizational structures—from ethnic community service organizations to local religious support organizations—that could support poor peoples' efforts to improve their living and working conditions. Although Alinsky's top-down, centralized leadership and use of external community organizers was the target of much criticism, he became known for influencing a new generation of organizers who embodied the movement politics of the 1960s and 1970s and sought to implement their political visions into new organizing methods.

One such organizer was Cesar Chavez, the founder and charismatic leader of the United Farm Workers (UFW), perhaps the most inspiring example of community-based unionism in the 1960s. In 1952, while working in the apricot groves of San Jose, Chavez met Alinksy-trained organizer Fred Ross, who recruited him to work first as a volunteer and then as a full-time staff member of the Community Services Organization (CSO), California's first statewide Mexican American community organization. For ten years, Chavez organized local CSO chapters across the Central Valley, forging connections with farmworkers and their communities in hopes of eventually creating an independent farmworkers' union. After repeatedly failing to secure the CSO's support in establishing an independent farmworkers' union, Chavez, along with another Ross-trained organizer, Dolores Huerta, helped found the Farm Workers Association (FWA), which expanded into the National Farm Workers Association (NFWA) in 1964 and eventually into the United Farm Workers (UFW) in 1972.[7]

Although the charismatic leadership of Chavez and Huerta was responsible for the dynamic and creative style of community organizing that is characteristic of the UFW, the union's success was largely attributable to its vision of community-based unionism. From its inception, the UFW expanded its membership base through classic community-based tactics such as house meetings, which gathered workers in safe and familiar environments to talk about the benefits of a union. To build legitimacy during its early stages as the Farm Workers Association (1962–1964), the union provided basic social services, created a community credit union, and established ethnic language newspapers. Lacking financial resources and refusing philanthropic donations, the UFW relied on member and community support, including religious groups and civil rights organizations. This broad base of support was a vital source of material support and moral leverage in later campaigns targeting growers and the state, particularly the historic 1965 Delano Grape Strike.[8]

According to Marshall Ganz, a key organizer for and researcher of the UFW, NFWA's participation in the Delano Grape Strike signified the "first step in the birth of the farmworkers movement" (Ganz 2000, 1032). Under the NLRA, farmworkers were excluded from the right to form unions, wage strikes, and secure collective bargaining agreements. Rather than fight the terms of its exclusion in the legal arena, the NFWA used the strike as a symbolic weapon to demand union recognition. The purpose of the strike and its associated public demonstrations was clear: "If the law will not make grape growers bargain, the pickets and their supporters [hoped they could] by shutting off the sales of the growers' produce."[9] The grape workers' strike and boycott tapped into the social justice sentiments of the time by equating the struggles of exploited farmworkers with the pursuit of civil rights. This alignment shifted the arena of union struggle from narrow labor-management disputes to the public at large, and its use of popular civil rights strategies, such as mass boycotts, allowed people across the country to support farmworkers in California. Thus, while the leaders of the AFL-CIO refused to endorse the broad-based unionism of the UFW, those who were alienated from the political direction of organized labor became reconstituted into a "compelling social movement"—where justice for migrant farmworkers represented the key moral issue of the time.[10]

Community Organizing and the Early New Left

Student organizers associated with the early New Left and Students for a Democratic Society (SDS) also represented a force for social change within the organized labor movement. Although turmoil over the war in Vietnam had led to the early New Left's demise by the late 1960s, leaders in the early 1960s outlined an agenda for change—one which sought to infuse the principles of racial and economic justice into organizing the poor and unemployed, particularly in communities of color. The *Port Huron Statement*, one of SDS's most widely read documents, was named after the site of a historic union struggle. This self-described "political manifesto" of the New Left stated that the "seeds of rebirth" for a morally and organizationally defunct labor movement could be found in the "organizational crisis itself"—"the technologically unemployed, the unorganized white-collar men and women, the migrant and farm workers, the unprotected Negroes, the poor, all of whom are isolated not from the power structure of the economy, but who are the potential base for a broader and more forceful unionism."[11] SDS leader Richard Flacks reflected twenty-five years later: "The Port Huron hope was not that a mass movement would make a revolution, but that a coalition spearheaded by the revitalization of organized labor, morally impelled by the civil rights movement, and aided by…students and intellectuals, could emerge" (quoted in Levy 1994).

One of its major projects toward this end was the 1963 Economic Research and Action Project (ERAP). The UAW provided the seed money for the ERAP pilot project as well as the funds to create eleven different local chapters. ERAP chapters represented a nascent form of community unionism. Their model for mobilizing the poor and unemployed centered on cultivating horizontal organizational linkages with religious groups, unions, and other social justice organizations in a particular place. According to SDS leaders Carl Wittman and Tom Hayden, "it is through the careful selection and identification of these groups that [ERAPs] will find vital sources of new power and support" (Levy 1994, 30). ERAP organizers embodied the ideals of Alinksy-trained organizers—they lived, worked, and participated in the communities they sought to organize. Hundreds of organizers went to live in poor, urban neighborhoods in Baltimore, Boston, Cleveland, Chicago, Philadelphia, Trenton, and Newark, among other cities, and they organized communities to fight for fair housing, welfare, education, and employment. Although their efforts were short-lived, they influenced the formation of new organizations that prioritized community and union partnerships that were critical to paving a more imaginative and dynamic path of union revitalization such as the National Welfare Rights Organization, in 1966, which in 1970 spun off into the Associations of Community Organizations for Reform NOW (ACORN).[12]

New Left leaders and Alinksy-trained community organizers viewed corporations as "the very basis of power in the United States" and the main culprits in exacerbating racial inequality and oppression under U.S. capitalism (NACLA 1970, 14). In 1966, SDS joined in coalition with the National Council of Churches and Peace Corps volunteers to establish the North American Congress on Latin America (NACLA), which developed the first manual on how to conduct a corporate campaign—the *NACLA Research Methodology*

Guide. The NACLA Guide outlined an agenda for conducting power-structure research, which could identify

> the people and institutions which make our lives and the lives of so many others intolerable…[,] locate weak points in the system…to give us the leverage to challenge the system effectively…[,] take the information about power in this society, and turn it against that power in ways which weaken its stranglehold…[and] propel ourselves and others into a higher consciousness of where the nodes of power lie and how they function. (NACLA 1970, 3)

Generating leverage over corporations involved jeopardizing their relationships with strategic suppliers, community organizations, and religious organizations as well as publicly shaming them. In the same year that NACLA published its Guide, the National Council of Churches established the Interfaith Center for Corporate Responsibility, which mobilized religious communities to pursue the strategies and objectives set forth by NACLA (Manheim 2000, 9).

Birth of the Union Corporate Campaign

Architects of the corporate campaign became active participants in several union efforts to offset membership and job losses due to plant shutdowns and economic restructuring. The first union to launch a corporate campaign and hire an external activist to lead it was the Amalgamated Clothing Workers Union (ACWU) in 1972. At the time, many companies were relocating manufacturing operations to the South and Southwest where employers could capitalize on anti-union "right to work" policies and recruit a highly vulnerable Latino workforce, mainly from nearby Juárez, Mexico. In protest, the ACWU launched a corporate campaign against Farrah Manufacturing, a rapidly growing company based in El Paso, Texas. What began as a walk-out of 3,000 in an El Paso plant in May 1972 mushroomed into a twenty-two-month ordeal. The union's struggles led to consumer boycotts in New York and gained the support of prominent political, civic, and religious leaders including presidential candidate George McGovern, Senator Edward Kennedy, and Archbishop S. M. Metzger. Roy Rogers, son of union parents and former VISTA (Volunteers in Service to America) volunteer, identified himself as the guru of the corporate campaign, and was hired in 1973 to take it over. The struggle ended just three weeks after Rogers took over and confronted Farrah management (Manheim 2000, 49–57). Throughout the 1980s more unions hired organizers with previous experience in social activism to adapt the strategies and tactics of the corporate campaign for their own purposes.[13]

According to Charles Perry (1987), author of *Union Corporate Campaigns*, the increasingly hostile climate against unions shaped the unexpected emergence of corporate campaigns as a major union tactic. Conventional National Labor Relations Board (NLRB) methods for organizing workers into unions had become increasingly ineffective. Employers waged lengthy and resource-intensive anti-union campaigns during NLRB election periods, which eroded worker confidence in unions and led to declining rates of success for NLRB union certification elections. The corporate campaign's ability to "supplement or supplant government regulation as a basis for worker/union participation" became the lynchpin of its dynamism. By combining strategic pressure and conflict escalation, the corporate campaign sought to "seize the moral high ground" and engage in a kind of issue and conflict escalation usually beyond the traditional scope of collective bargaining. The central element of corporate campaigns was to "publicly paint the target company as a corporate outlaw or villain" and "cast union or unions in question in the role of good in the battle of good and evil" (Perry 1987, 19). Building coalitions with other social groups over such moral issues was also central to strengthening union capacity and its base of associational power.

Resource-intensive, morally charged, and publicly oriented corporate campaigns had minimal impact in challenging the power of capital mobility to displace its workforce, downgrade working and employment conditions, and recruit a predominantly immigrant, nonunion, and increasingly undocumented workforce. What is more, the dominant labor movement largely ignored and discredited activists like Roy Rogers who sought to transform the bureaucratic unionism of the day. Though the civil rights activists and organizations from the 1960s and 1970s continued to remain separate from the dominant labor movement, their movement legacies, particularly their commitment to and strategies for labor organizing, would later become the foundation of a steadily growing and increasingly influential Service Employees International Union (SEIU).

Challenging Labor Exclusion in Post-1987 Korea

For almost three decades, the independent labor movement and the pro-democracy student movement were focused on overthrowing authoritarian regimes and the labor repressive labor policies they espoused. After the establishment of an electoral democracy and the installation of a civilian administration in 1987, "the people's movement groups (*minjung undong tanch'e*)" struggled to "find a new identity and role" (S. Kim 2003, 86). Some activists became directly involved in formal politics as elected and appointed government officials. Many others found voice and purpose in new "citizen" organizations (*simin tanch'e*) addressing a wide range of issues from economic and environmental justice to electoral reform to women's, consumer, and disability rights. Although many highlight the chasm between the primarily middle-class reformist character of citizens' organizations and the people's movement groups of the previous decades (unions, radical students, peasant organizations, and urban poor groups), growing divisions also plagued the burgeoning labor movement after 1987, especially among radical student and labor activists as well as women worker activists.

Korean Left Activists in the 1990s

While many labor activists shifted their focus to the organizational and political consolidation of the democratic labor movement, including the formation of a unified national center, a national labor party, and industrial unions, others directed their energies toward furthering mass-based workers' struggles and engendering anti-capitalist transformation. In spite of their dwindling numbers, some radical students continued to work underground in factories with the aim of promoting the political consciousness and empowerment of a revolutionary workers' vanguard. Other students expected to join the ranks of the working class after graduation in solidarity with blue-collar workers in key manufacturing sectors such as automobile, shipbuilding, and steel industries. Known as the "shop-floor wing" (*hyŏnjangp'a*) or the "left wing" (*chwap'a*) of the democratic labor movement, these activists were ideological descendents of the "Participatory Democracy" (PD) tendency of the 1980s student movement. The PD tendency prioritized mass-based class struggle over reunification with North Korea as the road to national liberation, which reflected the other major student movement tendency known as the "National Liberation" (NL) tendency. NL activists supported worker-led plant occupations and militant protests in the streets throughout the 1990s, which were pivotal in winning economic and political gains for workers across the country. Although the relationship between students and workers was often uneasy, the efforts of student activists to promote the self-organization and grassroots leadership of rank-and-file workers partially contributed to the mass mobilization of KCTU's militant base during the 1996–1997 General Strike, which many saw as a "political declaration of the working class" in which "organized workers became conscious of their strategic political role in leading the masses" (I. Kim 2000).

Despite the ideological and tactical differences among them, different factions of the democratic labor movement largely worked together to build the political power of organized labor throughout the 1990s. This consensus changed in the context of the Asian debt crisis. While an in-depth analysis of internal divisions within the democratic labor movement is outside this book's scope, it is important to emphasize that internal dissent was pivotal to challenging the priorities and direction of the organized labor movement. Left wing activists were deeply critical of what they saw as the "reformist" tendencies of the existing KCTU leadership, which prioritized electoral and social democratic avenues for change. In particular, KCTU's participation in the 1998 Tripartite Commission, which eliminated basic job security protections, generated intense internal opposition (see chapter 2). Many of its fiercest critics on the left viewed the KCTU leadership's cooperation with the Kim Dae Jung's corporatist and neoliberal regime as a "crisis of leadership," and called for a new national organization that could "overcome Democratic Unionism through Democratic Unionism."[14] Although its numbers were relatively small—only two hundred founding members—the Power of the Working-Class (*nodongchaŭi him;* PWC) was established in August 1999 "to reinforce the development of the democratic tradition and the class character of the trade union movement."[15] As the gravity of criticism shifted toward the issue of abolishing irregular employment, PWC members became outspoken critics of regular worker-dominated unions "betraying" the principles of democratic unionism. PWC members have also actively supported the workplace struggles of irregularly employed workers since 2000 (discussed in greater detail later).

University students politicized in the 1990s also challenged the emphasis on reformism and social democracy within the leadership ranks as well as the growing trend toward economic unionism among KCTU's most powerful and privileged affiliate unions. In the tradition of PD student activism, they supported a mass-based, worker-led, and militant approach to political transformation. However, they had also become critical of the "workerist" politics of their elder PD comrades. This "New Left" asserted that the revolutionary struggle could no longer be waged as "one single confrontation against one single enemy."[16] Inspired by Marxism, the New Left articulated a theory of the *chinbo* (progressive) movement that identified multiple arenas including trade unions themselves as sites of revolutionary struggle. The People's Solidarity for Social Progress (*sahoechinboyŏndae;* PSSP), which served as the organizational representative of the New Left, actively promoted more diverse forms of social movement unionism within an anti-capitalist and Marxist framework. Through training and education sessions as well as public forums, PSSP has played an active role in supporting the grassroots struggles of irregularly employed workers. It has also participated in anti–free trade and global justice movements as one of neo-liberal globalization's most impassioned critics.

Korean Women Workers' Movement

While the Old and New Left waged an internal battle over the KCTU's priorities, women worker activists began strengthening the organizational basis of the women workers' movement. Women student activists who had worked underground in factories in Incheon, Busan, Masan, Seoul, and other cities joined women unionists from the 1970s and 1980s to form the Korean Women Workers Association (KWWA) in 1987. These activists viewed the development of a vibrant women workers' movement as an integral component of the broader struggle for democratic unionism. However, they were "particularly motivated to install independent women's labor organizations separate from male-dominated labor unions and male-centered labor organizations" (Nam 2000, 97).[17] In its inaugural statement, the KWWA stated:

> We women workers earn extremely low wages which are less than half of what men workers earn and work longer hours. Our health suffers under compulsory overtime work. In addition, we have to shoulder the household chores. We are often sexually harassed in the workplace and in times of strikes, we are even beaten up or suffer sexual torture. We are taught to obey and not to protest. Despite all this, we women workers have been fighting on the frontlines against all forms of oppression.... [However], many women, unable to recognize their self-dignity as women and self-confidence as workers, have been dropping out of the struggle, once they get married and have children. Because of this, we realize that unless women find a way out of their oppression and discrimination as women, they cannot actively take part in the labor movement.[18]

Because many male unionists and union leaders viewed the creation of separate and autonomous women-only groups as a potentially divisive force, the KWWA navigated possible tensions and conflicts by defining itself as an external support organization rather than a popular organization in direct competition with unions. The KWWA educated and trained women workers to become union leaders; supported the creation of new unions in female-dominated sectors, no matter how small; and organized workers' wives to support their union activism. The KWWA also pushed for the creation of independent women's departments within newly forming national labor movement organizations such as *Chŏnnohyŏp* (National Council of Trade Unions) and later the KCTU.

While the increasingly male-dominated leadership of the radical *Chŏnnohyŏp* focused its attention on fending off police repression and consolidating their organizational power, women worker activists devoted their attention to supporting the local and regional struggles of tens of thousands of women workers whose jobs and livelihoods were devastated by industrial retrenchment in light manufacturing. Women worker activists and associations became the lifeline for women workers—the majority of whom were older, married women—who bitterly struggled to defend their unions and secure just compensation in the midst of plant closures and capital flight. Although the majority of unions in this sector eventually collapsed, massive deunionization strengthened KWWA's organizational dynamism. Many fired union leaders continued their activism by joining the staff of the KWWA, either at its national office in Seoul or by establishing a regional branch. For example, in Incheon, a branch office was set up by women worker activists "who were banned from being employed and those who were not able to work after marriage," and they "hoped to set up a [place] where they could develop skill training, network systems for finding new jobs, and union activities."[19] By 1992, there were seven regional women worker associations across the country (Incheon, Bucheon, Sungnam, Kwangju, Pusan, Machang, Seoul).

To strengthen organizational infrastructure and capacity on a national level, in 1992, all seven regional women workers' associations consolidated into a single national network under the umbrella, the Korean Women Workers Associations United (hankuk yŏsŏng nodongchahoe hyŏŭihoe; KWWAU). During this time, women workers' associations began to function less as external support organizations and more as "mass-based, membership organizations, focusing on building a broad organizational base" (KWWAU 2007). Regional branch offices offered direct counseling, advocacy, and training at the grassroots level. As staff workers became intimately involved with the myriad grievances of women workers, especially older women working in small companies where they were excluded from existing labor law protection, KWWAU recognized the growing severity of highly insecure and low-paid irregular employment. Through their direct counseling and advocacy sessions, KWWAU staff also learned that demotion to part-time, short-term, and temporary work often involved arbitrary wage reductions, employer intimidation, and the loss of welfare benefits including paid maternity and menstruation leave and paid vacation.[20] In 1995, the KWWAU improved and expanded its grassroots counseling and advocacy services by establishing Equality Phone Counseling Centers, which provided information on how to address grievances that working women faced when employed outside the scope of standard labor law protections.

Given the pervasive climate of gender exploitation in Asia's free trade zones, the KWWAU led in sharing information about the struggles of Korean women workers with other women workers' organizations in Asia. Spearheaded by the vision and leadership of Maria Chol Soon Rhie, who became chairperson in 1996, the KWWAU began prioritizing the importance of international solidarity and exchange. As one of the first women worker activists in the 1970s and the first of her comrades to work abroad, Rhie was instrumental in expanding the scope and perspective of the KWWAU's work. Rhie explains, "While I was working at CAW [Committee for Asian Women in Hong Kong], I spent about 6 months of the year traveling....I was exposed to women workers from almost every country in Asia, and I learned how big the impact of globalization has been and realized that solidarity was so important because it would be impossible to succeed in organizing in one country alone" (quoted in Park 2005, 288–289).

Domestically, the KWWAU also endeavored to strengthen the labor movement's promotion and support of women-related activities through joint efforts with the KCTU, including a series of policy countermeasures to combat "flexible labor policies." This included the revision of the employment equality law, the passage of protective policies regarding employment security, the continued opposition to the legalization of dispatch agency employment, and the support of protective legislation for part-time and home-based workers. However, the KCTU consistently sidelined gender issues. For example, when the KCTU mobilized opposition against the clandestine passage of flexible labor law revisions through the National Assembly in 1996, which led to the KCTU-led General Strike, it neglected to acknowledge the disproportionately gendered impact of flexible labor policies, which the KWWAU had been vigorously emphasizing through its policy reform work. The KCTU's disregard of gender issues was also reflected in its organizational structure. Two years after its 1995 inauguration, the KCTU still had yet to establish a separate women's department. Sexual harassment also remained a serious problem among union members.[21] The KCTU itself reported that 67.1 percent of female union members had experienced sexual harassment in the workplace, and this figure was even higher for hospital workers, among whom were a high proportion of nurses (76.1%).

The need to address the specific character of gender exploitation and discrimination sparked internal debate within the women workers' movement. "Until now, the women's labor movement was focused on working to guarantee the legal rights of women with regular employment. However, the number of these women workers who have legal rights is decreasing every year."[22] The urgent question was figuring out exactly how to protect workers with little to no access to existing rights protections. As a nongovernmental organization (NGO) and not a union, KWWAU was limited to individual-based advocacy and legal measures for worker redress. Although grassroots counseling and advocacy were crucial for addressing the immediate needs of women workers, these strategies had done little to mitigate the wide-reaching and structural consequences of downgraded women's employment, especially in manufacturing-based regions. The Incheon Women Workers Association (IWWA), which had a more radical orientation due to its experience with massive job loss, raised the need to create alternative structures and strategies to address the current realities of women. During a forum celebrating the tenth anniversary of the KWWAU, Choi Sang-rim, the chairwoman of the IWWA who would become the first KWTU president, asked, "How can we organize women workers who lost their jobs, who now work as irregular workers, and who work now but don't know when they may lose their jobs?"[23]

Building on its commitment to international solidarity and exchange, the KWWAU began seeking new ideas by outreaching to international solidarity networks. Organizational exchanges with the Self-Employed Women's Association (SEWA) in India and the Women's Trade Union in Denmark led to new projects such as a garment workers' cooperative run by the IWWA and further research on the establishment of an autonomous women-only trade union. Internal conflict regarding the potential divisiveness of such actions on the broader labor movement stalled these plans in the preparation phase; however, the onset of the Asian debt crisis in late 1997–1998 decisively changed this debate's outcome.

National Terrains of Labor Movement Revitalization

Movement actors and organizations laid the groundwork for subsequent transformations to crisis-ridden labor movements by prioritizing the need to "organize the marginalized." In the United States this process took the form of a gradual and internal transformation within several of the AFL-CIO's major affiliates, most notably the SEIU. Rather than allow union membership to steadily dwindle in the face of industrial restructuring and a climate of heightened anti-unionism, SEIU union leaders adopted the corporate campaign and recruited staff organizers with prior social movement experience. In South

Korea, the 1997–1998 Asian debt crisis exposed the vulnerability of women and irregularly employed workers to a climate of intensified cost-cutting and anti-unionism. Although KCTU- and FKTU-affiliated unions did little initially to challenge such employer practices, women worker and left activists actively stepped in to create new organizations and strategies to revive the democratic labor movement's commitment to its historic base—the *minjung* (common people)—the most exploited segments of society.

The Union Corporate Campaign and the SEIU

While other major unions were struggling to stay afloat, the SEIU set out to integrate the ideological principles, tactics, and even individual activists from the vibrant social movements of the 1960s. Then SEIU President John Sweeney was an early advocate of reform in the 1980s. Under his leadership, the SEIU adapted the corporate campaign to its organizing efforts in health care and building services. The union corporate campaign consisted of "a combination of actions such as work site actions; jeopardizing the employer's relations with customers, investors, politicians or other source of funds, legal or regulatory challenges to the way the employer conducts its operations; [and] media campaigns and community pressure based on the common interests of workers and the general public" (Manheim 2000, 120 [quoted from SEIU Contract Campaign Manual, 1988]).

SEIU's earliest adaptation of the corporate campaign can be traced to January 1973. Like other employers, SEIU found that health care employers were also intent on expanding their nonunion business operations. To counter these efforts, the SEIU waged a joint corporate campaign in collaboration with the United Food and Commercial Workers (UFCW) against Beverly Enterprises (one of the nation's largest chains of nursing homes). At the time, Beverly Enterprises was waging an aggressive national anti-union campaign, training their management in "union avoidance techniques" and stalled contract negotiations with unions (Manheim 2000, 69). The SEIU, which represented workers at twenty-one Beverly Enterprises facilities, and the UFCW, which represented workers at ten facilities, responded by launching a nationwide organizing effort against the company's approximately nine hundred facilities. By equating the corporate approach to health care with deterioration in quality, the SEIU not only generated public support for its campaigns but also targeted public funders that supported the growth of anti-union health care organizations.

Although the union corporate campaign against Beverly Enterprises was one of the SEIU's longest and most resource-intensive campaigns to date, its strategic organizing model has become a model for union revitalization across the country. Many labor scholars use the term *union revitalization* to distinguish social movement–inspired forms of unionism from the industrial unionism of the past. This revitalization entails (1) acknowledging the limitations of the dominant servicing model of unionism, which has hampered the participation and empowerment of rank-and-file members, and (2) engaging in a process of organizational transformation, which can overcome internal resistance to change within highly, bureaucratized local unions. Union revitalization is also used interchangeably with the term *social movement unionism* to account for the broader set of actors and politics associated with revitalized unions. Rick Fantasia and Kim Voss (2004) astutely explain, "the vision of labor evoked by social movement unionism is entirely different than the one conjured up by business unionism: unions are seen as dealing with questions of social justice that extend well beyond the unionized work force, rather than advocating only for a narrow interest group" (Fantasia and Voss 2004; also see Lopez 2004, 11).

SEIU's social movement–inspired forms of unionism has generated the most public visibility under the Justice for Janitors campaign (JforJ), especially in California. Although JforJ also included a crucial bottom-up mobilization of rank-and-file workers, John Sweeney's commitment to reunionizing janitors, SEIU's historic base, manifested in a "top-down" initiative by established union leaders "to put pressure on the decision-makers in the industry" (Milkman 2006, 53–54; also see Milkman and Wong 2000). The corporate campaign provided a vehicle to identify these decision makers as the building owners, not the outsourced cleaning contractors. One SEIU union organizer explained:

> We do corporate campaigns. We do this whole strategy chart where we map out all the different relationships … politicians, development projects, media, public, field partners, tenants. … We would go to the tenants who would say, "If you don't stop this, we're going to move out." We would put massive media attention [on the tenants]. We would get people to write letters to the owners. If they were going to do a development project, we would get politicians to say, you've got to deal with this thing, this is the right thing to do. We would create this major compression around the owner so they throw up their hands at some point … and say, "Oh God, I don't want this to happen to us."[24]

The corporate campaign has also allowed the SEIU to circumvent traditional NLRB union elections, a disempowering process for many workers, and rebuild union density in an entire regional labor market through a process of "card check neutrality." By collecting signed union cards from over 50 percent of workers stating their desire to form a union, unions sought direct union recognition from employers. To convince smaller subcontracted firms to agree to the formation of a union at their worksite, unions promised not to wage "hostile union campaigns" against them. Rather, SEIU chose to target one high-profile employer in the area (Milkman 2006).

SEIU's Recruitment of Social Movement Organizers

Most accounts of SEIU's revitalization, both formal and informal, also highlight its recruitment of "talented" and inspired social movement organizers. In a study of 130 California labor leaders in 1984, Marshall Ganz et al. (2004) confirmed that over half of labor leaders interviewed viewed their work in unions as part of a larger agenda of "social reform." Many of these individuals were involved in student activism in the civil rights and antiwar movements of the 1960s and 1970s, and they viewed union work as a vehicle to continue political activism. "Motivated by their commitment to social justice, they generally believed political work was the best way to make the world a better place" (Ganz et al. 2004, 157). In their study of fourteen California locals, Voss and Sherman (2000) found that organizers with prior movement experience who were hired as staff organizers were present in all the locals they classified as "fully revitalized" with an organizational commitment and infrastructure that supported aggressive, strategic organizing efforts within the union. "Many leaders over 40 had had experience in community or welfare rights organizing or the United Farm Workers (UFW). Younger informants (in their twenties and early thirties) had also participated in community organizing or in student activism, particularly in Central American solidarity groups and anti-apartheid struggles on college campuses" (Voss and Sherman 2000, 328).

The UFW, and other organizations such as the Citizens Action League, served as important "bridging organizations" between the world of social movements and organized labor (Ganz et al. 2004, 191). The UFW, in particular, was an effective bridge because it represented a progressive model of unionism at a time when unions were quickly losing their political legitimacy. As the UFW escalated its civil rights–inspired struggles in California, it became a magnet for New Left and community activists from the 1960s seeking institutional outlets for their political ideals. Former UFW organizers could apply their knowledge and insight from previous campaigns in the fields to future campaigns in workplaces, although the path from organizations such as the UFW to the SEIU often reflected an organic and unexpected one.

The reflections of an SEIU union leader in one of its biggest California locals illuminates the important experiences that former farmworkers and UFW organizers bring to SEIU. When I asked about his beginnings at SEIU, this SEIU leader brought up his "life-changing" experience with the UFW:

> Part of the decision when I was in jail [for participating in a UFW strike] wasn't so much, what am I going to do, but what I needed to do…whether I wanted to become a leader with my union, or move out and become an organizer. And that's what I chose, to become an organizer, because I realized the need for more people who are aware of their reality, in terms of the social context in which we live and operate. There aren't very many organizers out there who take on the responsibility of going around, touching other people, helping them realize their potential, and put them in contact with their own power.[25]

After leaving the UFW, this union leader went on to work for various local community and service organizations before a former coworker from the UFW contacted him and offered him a job, first as part of an SEIU-led organizing campaign in 1985, and then as a staff organizer with a California local in 1988.

His experience "crossing-over" from a rank-and-file union leader to an SEIU staff organizer also brought perspective to SEIU's top-down and long-term organizing strategies:

> While I was part of [an eleven-month strike with] the United Farm Workers, there was an incident with the leadership of the union, in the fifth or sixth month of the strike…this is just an assumption that I'm making, [but] I think the leadership of the union—this includes everyone [including] Cesar [Chavez] and Dolores [Huerta]—thought they had lost control of what was going on in the fields with the strike…to a point where they decided…to call off the strike and pass a resolution to put all the resources of the union into the boycott. They had a meeting with…the rank-and-file leadership to announce the decision. Of course, we were by then already five to six months into the strike. For us, it was a war. We said no, we're not calling off the strike.…There was conflict. The leadership passed its own resolution and we passed our own, and the strike did not end. Back then I had a lot of resentment with those decisions. For years, I carried that resentment with me. I had to be in the kind of situation I'm in now, to finally understand, maybe not justify, but at least understand that maybe for the leadership of the union back then, the concern was to maintain the viability of the organization.[26]

Organizers, particularly those with on-the-ground experience with unions such as the UFW, played a major role in balancing the top-down approach of campaigns such as JforJ. Initially, this leader recalls that he had "a difficult time getting used to JforJ" because his experience of organizing was one that started with workers. In a relatively short time, however, he was able to see the difference it could make for unions:

> When I came to work for the local, the local was, and this is not an exaggeration, completely in shambles. The local had spent many, many years without doing any organizing....Nonunion companies were the dominant force, therefore the standards that they used in terms of pay and benefits were the prevailing standards. Union contractors were losing jobs left and right..., [but] in a period of three years...we went from 30 percent to almost 70 percent in terms of market domination of the local industry. And that obviously makes a difference in your ability to negotiate a contract and get better benefits for your members. Also, in terms of really helping the organization become a force, not just with the contractors, but with the industry, the respect we gained from the client companies was very noticeable. Toward the end of 1994, all we had to do was threaten a campaign.[27]

The unanticipated success of its California JforJ campaigns not only helped SEIU regain its dominance in commercial real estate sectors but also catapulted Sweeney into the presidency of the AFL-CIO.

SEIU's Road to Revitalizing the U.S. Labor Movement

The SEIU's dynamic approach to organizing corresponded with its stunning organizational expansion. At a time when most other major unions were declining en masse, the SEIU, under Sweeney's leadership, expanded from 650,000 members in 1980 to 1,321,790 in 1999 (see table 5). Today, according to SEIU's website (www.seiu.org), it has almost two million members in the United States, Canada, and Puerto Rico. Though a large part of this organizational growth can be attributed to union mergers and the growth of public-sector unions,[28] Sweeney pointed to the SEIU's organizing successes as the vehicle for overcoming union stagnation, and he criticized the AFL-CIO for refusing to do the same. As George Meany's successor, AFL-CIO President Lane Kirkland viewed corporate campaigns as costly and resisted channeling resources into nontraditional organizing efforts. In the early 1990s, unions spent only 5 percent of their

Table 5. Union Membership by Organization, 1980 and 1999, United States

UNION	1980	1999	CHANGE (%)
Service Employees International Union	**650,000**	**1321790**	**103.35**
National Education Association	*1,684,000*	*2,495,826*	*48.21*
Laborers' International Union of North America	*608,000*	*774,696*	*27.42*
American Federation of Teachers	*551,000*	*686,518*	*24.59*
American Federation of State, County and Municipal Employees	*1,098,000*	*1,300,000*	*18.40*
International Association of Machinists and Aerospace Workers	*650,000*	*737,510*	*13.46*
United Food and Commercial Workers	*1,321,500*	*1,391,399*	*5.29*
Communication Workers of America	551,000	490,621	−10.96
United Farm Workers	35,000	26,000	−25.71
International Brotherhood of Teamsters	1,891,000	1,400,700	−25.93
International Brotherhood of Electrical Workers	1,041,000	718,742	−30.96
International Brotherhood of Boiler-makers, Iron Ship Builders, Blacksmiths, Forgers and Helpers (Ironworkers)	184,000	126,004	−31.52
United Brotherhood of Carpenters and Joiners of America	784,035	515,986	−34.19
International Longshore and Warehouse Union	64,000	40,515	−36.70
Hotel Employees and Restaurant Employees	400,000	245,327	−38.67
United Auto Workers	1,357,000	762,439	−43.81
United Steelworkers	1,238,000	636,297	−48.60
United Mine Workers of America	245,000	124,803	−49.06
Union of Needletrades, Industrial and Textile Employees (UNITE)[a]	778,000	216,261	−72.20
United Electrical Workers	162,000	40,000	−75.31

Source: Court Gifford, ed., Directory of U.S. Labor Organizations, 1982 and 2000 ed. (Washington, DC: The Bureau of National Affairs).

Note: Data for the fastest-growing union are in boldface; data for the unions with positive growth are in italics.

[a] UNITE, established in 1995, was formed from the International Ladies' Garment Workers' Union (ILGWU) and the Amalgamated Clothing and Textile Workers Union (ACTWU).

total budget on organizing new members, which meant that 95 percent of all resources were being spent on the small percentage (15%) of workers that were already organized. According to one senior official at an international union, "They're [the AFL-CIO leadership] convinced we can't organize and they've devoted no resources to figuring out what we can do" (Meyerson 1998, 8). The inability of unions to reach the vast majority of the nonunion workforce was perhaps the final nail in the coffin. In a survey commissioned by the AFL-CIO, most nonunion workers answered that unions "were not an important part of how they see the world[, and] it literally did not occur to them to look to unions as a solution."[29]

As the existing AFL-CIO leadership continued to waffle and organized labor continued to lose its organizational and political base of power, Sweeney and his New Voice Coalition, which included Richard Trumka, president of the United Mine Workers, and Linda Chavez-Thompson, vice president of the American Federation of State, County, and Municipal Employees (AFSCME), promoted a new vision for organized labor's future, cultivated under the aegis of a revitalized SEIU. This model infused crisis-ridden unions with the dynamism of new social movements by prioritizing the importance of "organizing the unorganized." Recruiting and training a new cadre of organizers was an essential component of this strategy, and the new AFL-CIO sought to increase its base of committed, energetic, and inexhaustible organizers through programs such as the Organizing Institute and Union Summer. These initiatives drew inspired young people into the labor movement, although high rates of attrition among those trained by the Organizing Institute and Union Summer have also brought much criticism to the AFL-CIO's practice of training external organizers to promote union revitalization (Rooks 2004).

While much has been written—in both the popular media and academic circles—about the unprecedented change of guard in the AFL-CIO and the potential for union revitalization under Sweeney and his New Voice Coalition, the dominant consensus a decade after Sweeney's inauguration has been that the push for change has been uneven and insufficient. The realignment of alliances by Sweeney's successor at the SEIU, Andrew Stern, emphasized the continued crisis of leadership within the AFL-CIO. Despite the internal difficulties plaguing the unity of the U.S. labor movement, it is important to highlight that SEIU's shift to the center of the U.S. labor movement was the product of a dynamic process of change and institutional innovation with origins tracing back to emergent forms of community-based unionism and the corporate campaign. The infusion of resources and activists into social movement–inspired forms of unionism such as the JforJ campaign has also been pivotal in crafting the identity of the largest and most rapidly growing union of the past decades.

Overcoming Male-Dominated Unionism: Women's Trade Unions in South Korea

In South Korea, the 1998 national economic crisis exposed a major weakness of the KCTU and its 600,000-plus strong membership: It no longer represented the workforce at large, numerically or politically. The majority of its members were regularly employed, male workers in large, white-collar, and heavy manufacturing enterprises—an elite and shrinking segment of the total workforce. When mass layoffs and unemployment reached unprecedented levels during this time, the KCTU's proposals to mitigate the effects of job loss, such as the five-day work week and other forms of work sharing, were largely inapplicable to the majority of the workforce employed as nonstandard workers. The needs of women workers, who made up a small fraction of KCTU's membership and an even smaller fraction of its leadership, were consistently neglected and even actively sidelined by the KCTU. Requests that unions challenge discriminatory hiring and firing practices or address gender-specific grievances were often considered divisive and harmful to the labor movement's larger battle against neoliberal employers and the state.

KCTU's refusal to intervene against the blatant gender discrimination of their own member unions was highlighted in cases such as the Hyundai Motors Union. As I discussed in chapter 2, the Hyundai Motors Union's struggle against economic restructuring in the midst of the Asian debt crisis was one of the first and most militantly waged union struggles after the passage of 1998 labor law revisions. The state tried to intervene in the union's occupation of company grounds in Ulsan by dispatching 12,000 riot police. After two weeks, the union ended their strike by accepting an employer proposal in which 10,000 workers "voluntarily resigned" and 277 workers were formally dismissed. Of those dismissed, 144 were elderly women union members who worked in the company cafeteria. According to Kyoung-hee Moon (2006, 4), "The union's agreement to the proposal was a great shock to the female workers who were actively participating in the general strike, not only attending the collective actions but also providing all the unionists in the strike with three meals everyday." This case is particularly telling because women workers constituted only 0.04 percent of the company's workforce, yet they were willingly scapegoated to protect the interests of its primarily male union membership.[30]

To add insult to injury, the male-dominated union intervened in the women cafeteria workers' ongoing strike against the company by agreeing to rehire the 144 women union members as subcontracted workers employed by the union. The women workers launched a hunger strike against the union's decision and battled for three years against the union before they finally resecured direct employment from Hyundai Motors Company. Male unionists bitterly condemned women workers for being "selfish" during such difficult times and even used violent means such as physically blocking people from attending a documentary film viewing about the struggle to prevent women from telling their story. According to union leader Choi Jong-Hee, "the most difficult part of their struggle was the confrontation with male unionists who used to be their friends yesterday but turned out to be their enemies today" (quoted in Moon 2006, 5). This antagonism was true even among women union leaders. While conducting participant observation at a KCTU labor federation with a predominantly female union membership during the perceived height of the "IMF crisis," a staff member in the women's department explained to me that the union leadership viewed gender-related worker issues as subordinate and even detrimental to the more urgent struggle against structural adjustment. She recalled that she was even scolded by the General Secretary (who was also a woman) for raising gender issues at such a crisis-ridden time.

Women workers' movement activists grew increasingly weary of the male-dominated climate—from state welfare policies to the media to unions themselves. Regardless of the nuanced factors that contributed to differential gendered outcomes, from their perspective, the uneven economic impact of the crisis clearly pointed to a "women fired first" principle of restructuring. Choi Sang Rim, a former student activist who worked underground in the labor movement since the mid-1980s and later became the first KWTU president, explained:

> The IMF regime provided momentum for the change of Korean society as a whole. Without any social safety nets, the changes fell heavily on the society's margins, women. The trends on the informalization of women's work were also found in other countries' cases. However, when introduced, it was gradual or with social safety nets to reduce the total shocks. In the case of Korea, however, the coercive situation called the IMF [crisis] made the margins totally absorb the situation. Currently, the rate of non-standard women workers is over 73%. This is nonsense. (quoted in Seo 2004, 87)

In the absence of union support for vulnerable groups of women workers, KWWAU activists followed through with plans to create independent union structures capable of supporting the changing realities of the workforce. In 1999, the national Korean Women's Trade Union (KWTU) was officially inaugurated as well as two other women's unions, the Seoul Women's Trade Union

(SWTU) and the National Federation of Women's Trade Unions (affiliated with the KCTU).[31] All three unions were formed as a "definite and immediate reaction to the economic crisis and the neo-liberal restructuring which [had] thrown women workers out onto the streets and impoverished them."[32] All three unions also believed that existing unions—the vast majority of which were male-dominated in leadership and priorities—were ill-equipped to protect the needs and concerns of the vast majority of women workers employed as nonstandard workers, especially older women with limited job options in the larger labor market. Organizing women workers required paying attention to gendered forms of workplace discrimination and oppression, such as the gender wage gap, sexual harassment, and violence. It also called for alternative trade union models that considered the multiple responsibilities and concerns of women workers including maternity protection, juggling work and family, child care, relationship-oriented interaction at work, and skills training.

Although the predominantly male leadership of the KCTU largely resisted the formation of independent women's trade unions, women's trade unions have demonstrated the success of their approach. According to one KWWAU staff worker:

> When they heard that KWWAU was forming a women's trade union, they criticized and scoffed, "maybe we should also make a men's trade union." They did not acknowledge how much women are excluded within the labor movement and how much women are victims from restructuring policies that prioritize men. And actually, from what I remember, all the male unionists I knew opposed the creation of a separate women's trade union. They had absolutely no awareness around this issue. So, there was a lot of conflict and tension. Of course, now, they can't really say anything.[33]

Given the KWWAU's long historical experience organizing women workers and its organizational infrastructure, the KWTU has been the most effective of the three women's unions. Branch union offices were set up adjacent to KWWAU regional offices, sharing space, resources, and staff. Within the first year, KWTU recruited one thousand members and organized four local divisions: (1) for golf game assistants at the 88 Country Club, (2) for cooks at Kyeongsang University, (3) for script writers who work at broadcasting companies, and (4) for part-time workers at Daewoo Heavy Industries. During its first year, 80 percent of the members were nonstandard workers; 70 percent were married and in their thirties and forties. Since then, KWTU has grown to over six thousand members in over seventy industrial units (KWWAU 2007). "By actually expanding the labor movement and securing the constitutional right of workers to unite, the Korean Women's Trade Union is making significant strides in building a model of trade union organization for unorganized workers, which is a major task of the Korean labor movement" (S. Choi 2000, 11).

The KWTU's membership structure and organizing strategies accommodate its nontraditional workforce. While it aims to organize women workers who are not covered by existing unions and often are not covered by existing labor legislation, its bylaws allow any woman worker regardless of occupation or regional location to join as a member. Building the self-esteem and leadership of devalued groups through women- and family-friendly organizing strategies has strengthened the "overall good health" of its organizing, according to the second KWTU president, Namhee Park. The KWTU's return to "back to the basics" organizing strategies, Park adds, has also reminded other unions that "you just can't organize irregular workers without actually getting in there....Organizing is only possible by injecting money, time, and manpower.[34]

National Organizing and Policy Advocacy Campaigns for the Poor

In addition to its three-pronged strategy, emphasizing the principles of gender-specific, grassroots, and open membership–based approaches, the KWTU has focused on cultivating a nationally coordinated model of union organizing in which a specific group of workers by occupation and employment status is targeted as a strategic organizing priority in all regional union branches. Unlike in the United States, most union organizing in South Korea up until that point reflected two forms: (1) spontaneous workplace disputes that resulted in a struggle to create an independent union and (2) clandestine students who went underground as "disguised workers" and supported the creation of independent unions. In the latter case, while student movement organizations supported the flow of "disguised workers" into factories, the decision of where to go and who to organize was uncoordinated and often unbeknownst to other students. In contrast to the spontaneity of prior union organizing cases, KWTU noticed that a ripple effect from one university to the next was occurring among university janitors' unions in Incheon. After internal discussion, the KWTU decided to use this example as a model to promote the formation of unions among workers in similar jobs in other locations. First, a strategic organizing target was selected, such as university janitors or elementary and middle school cafeteria workers. To outreach to other women workers in similar occupations and workplaces, KWWAU and KWTU sent staff and union members to conduct research at various worksites. Next, if workers expressed interest in forming a union, they could seek approval from the executive committee of the regional branch union to form a local representing workers in a specific workplace or by occupation. KWTU's branch-union structure allowed workers to avoid the bureaucratic process of applying for union certification and instead, engage in an internal process for union recognition.[35] After a branch union was created, KWTU conducted trainings about the situation of other irregularly employed women workers, the labor laws, and the political climate of unionism. If employers resisted the formation of the union and the negotiation of a collective bargaining agreement, the union conducted a collective action campaign. Although not all the organizers in KWTU's branch offices support this top-down organizing approach, the KWTU has pursued this model since 2001.

Given its joint history with the KWWAU, the KWTU has also expanded its organizing to the realms of public education and policy advocacy. The KWTU Inha University branch union's struggle (detailed in chapter 5) sparked the first national campaign to raise Korea's minimum wage in 2001, which was jointly organized by the KWTU and its sister organization, the KWWAU. Although a minimum wage system was legally created under Articles 34 and 35 of the 1953 Labor Standards Act, it was not enforced until January 1, 1988 (Jeong 2008). In late 2001, minimum wage protections covered 100 percent of the workforce, which was a significant increase since 1988 when only 17.9 percent of workers were covered. However, few people, including union leaders, knew about the existence of a legal minimum wage, let alone the actual wage amount.[36] Through its organizing struggle with Inha University janitors, KWTU learned that, rather than protecting low-wage earners, the minimum wage rate actually functioned to depress existing wage standards by providing a bare legal minimum that employers could get away with paying.

To assess the pervasiveness of poverty wages among women workers, the KWWAU conducted a research survey based on 528 women workers in 107 service industries, which demonstrated the widespread existence of poverty wages for women workers. The research findings were publicized on June 8, 2001, during a public forum entitled, "Reform Measures of the Minimum Wage Standard from the Perspective of Irregular Workers." Marie Chol Soon Rhie, the executive director of KWWAU, and then KWTU President Sang Rim Choi began the forum with a joint statement that read, "paying workers enough wages to guarantee a minimum livelihood is a marker of societal human rights. However, the wage standards of non-standard women workers is not only extremely low…poverty is becoming much worse.…[Thus], the legal system must be advanced to protect the human rights and basic labor rights of workers located at the very bottom tiers [of society]."[37] The KWWAU and KWTU also invited representatives from the Minimum Wage Commission, KCTU, FKTU, the Grand National political party, the Ministry of Labor, the Ministry of Women, and a university research institute to discuss the implications of the study, all of whom acknowledged the societal need to raise the minimum wage.

To translate their policy goals into change, the Action Center to Secure the Rights of Non-Standard Women, led by the KWWAU and the KWTU, launched the first national campaign to raise the minimum wage standard. The major goals of the campaign were twofold: (1) to increase public awareness of the need to raise the minimum wage and (2) to pressure the Minimum Wage Commission to raise wage levels in their next annual meeting. To facilitate both goals, the KWWAU and KWTU launched a national petition campaign, and on June 25, 2001, they presented a petition with 10,488 signatures from ten different regions around the country to the Minimum Wage Commission. The petition drive and a mass media campaign eventually forced the Minimum Wage Commission to pass a new minimum wage, which raised the minimum wage standard to 2,100 Won an hour or 474,600 Won a month ($402 U.S.), which reflected a 12.6 percent increase. While this increase was significantly more than the 2 to 3 percent expected increase, it was still far short of what many considered an acceptable standard of living.[38]

"Awakening" the Labor Movement to the Struggle of Irregular Workers

By 2002 the KCTU, FKTU, and other labor organizations had made the "abolition of irregular employment" one of its main organizational priorities. However, it was not until the explosion of male-led, nonstandard workers' struggles in 2000 and the refusal of many KCTU-affiliated unionists to support irregular worker–led union fights that radical labor activists and students associated with the Left began recognizing the importance of the issue. Although some Left activists became increasingly aware of the dilemmas of irregularly employed workers throughout the 1990s, almost all the activists that I spoke with explained that "the discontent of workers on the shop floor far outpassed the consciousness of activists at the time."[39]

Immediately following the IMF crisis, many workers resigned and resumed employment as irregular workers under the assumption that their downgraded employment arrangements were short-term, crisis-alleviating measures. However, as the national economy started to recover and the government announced the formal end of the "crisis," many jobs remained "irregular" and some employers even continued wage and benefit reductions under the rationale that they were still embroiled in a "crisis." As more time passed, irregular workers began demanding some type of relief or action to mitigate wage cost-cutting and work intensification from KCTU affiliate unions. When their pleas were either ignored or rejected, many began organizing direct actions themselves. In 1999, union struggles erupted among golf game assistants, national insurance salespersons, cafeteria workers, home-based study tutors, and subcontracted manufacturing workers. The struggle of home-based tutors at Jaenung Educational Corporation was particularly important because, like the struggles of golf game assistants, it raised awareness about the vulnerability of workers in "special employment" and the need to redefine independently contracted workers into legally recognized workers.

Because many existing unions refused to allow irregular workers to join their ranks, many irregular workers' unions affiliated with regionally based union organizations such as the KCTU Seoul Regional Center (*sŏulponpu*). In the late 1980s, regional workers' centers represented the center of radical organizing efforts by newly formed democratic unions attempting to overcome the constraints of enterprise unionism. As more local unions affiliated with industry-based national federations and more radical regional centers were suppressed by the state, regional centers mainly focused on the grievances of nonunion workers and other workers that "slipped through the cracks" of existing unions' membership structures.[40] However, as the number of irregular workers demanding unions grew, regional centers began functioning as regionally based general unions that offered irregular workers open union membership without regard to occupation. The Seoul Regional Center was particularly important because it was one of the earliest hubs of irregular worker organizing within the KCTU. One staff organizer, Bak Sang-Yoon, played an instrumental role in raising awareness of irregular employment within the broader KCTU-led labor movement by conducting trainings on union formation and the labor laws, actively supporting public protests by various irregular workers' unions, and facilitating the networks of various irregular workers' unions' leaders across the country.

While these struggles raised voice and visibility to the issue of irregular employment, they primarily represented nontraditional and atypical women workers who were perceived by more militant labor activists as motivated narrowly by employment security and welfare issues. In 2000, however, the eruption of dozens more union fights, led by male workers, including the Korea Telecom (Fixed) Contract Workers struggle, the Remicon (ready-mix concrete) truck drivers, and the subcontracted workers at Carrier Corporation (air conditioning) thrust the urgency of the issue to the forefront of radical students and labor activists' agendas. Given the neglect and invisibility of their struggles, many irregular workers' campaigns have used extreme and desperate tactics aimed at raising public awareness about the severity of irregular employment. Chu Bong-hee, one of the most committed and passionate union leaders of the KBS Broadcasting Non-standard Workers Union, who was later elected a KCTU vice-president, shaved his head and had the words, "Eliminate Dispatch Employment" dyed into his hair every month during his almost one-year-long struggle to raise awareness about the hidden conditions of exploitation that pervade temporary agency employment. In 2003 alone, seven unionists committed suicide to protest the oppressive conditions associated with irregular employment and labor repression.[41]

Many radical activists, however, are most distressed by the ongoing "solidarity crisis" between regular and irregular male workers. The case of the Korea Telecom (KT) Contract Workers' Union was one of the first and most high-profile examples of this cleavage. From June to November 2000, 7,000 contract workers at KT were issued dismissal notices under a state-initiated effort to privatize public utilities and make its workforce more "flexible." KT had already shed 10,000 workers in 1998 through "voluntary resignations," and the public sector shed 131,000 workers between 1998 and 2000, 11 percent of the total public sector workforce.[42] Although contract workers were hired on an annual one-year basis, many had worked for the company for as long as ten years and stated that they endured low wages (less than half the average monthly wage of regular, full-time employees), sixteen-hour work days, and the lack of benefits such as paid overtime and paid sick and vacation leave in hopes of securing regular, full-time employment at one of the country's most well-known public companies.[43] According to one worker at the Daegu office, "For six years, I worked harder than the regular employees, hoping to become one. So, the dismissal felt like a betrayal. Formal employment had been my hope, what I'd given my youth to achieve."[44] This sense of "betrayal" was intensified by the actions of the existing KT union. Not only did the existing union forbid irregularly employed contract workers from joining as members, but they refused to act in solidarity with the KT Contract Workers' Union, which had formed a separate union from the existing KT union, during a December 2000 strike action. Once the KT management agreed to suspend the mass dismissals of regularly employed workers, the KT union returned to work, leaving the dismissed contract workers to continue their fight alone.

For the next nine months, the KT Contract Workers' Union engaged in many tactics to escalate their struggle against the nonresponsive company management, which union leaders described as a "fight for their livelihoods."[45] To draw attention to the desperation and seriousness of their plight, protesting workers shaved their heads; stormed and occupied the central KT headquarters building; climbed to the top of a major city bridge on a cold winter day; and camped out in front of the company headquarters in the middle of downtown Seoul. While the extreme militancy of their actions was pivotal in attracting the attention of the broader democratic labor movement to the plight of irregular workers, it also elicited increasing intervention by the state. The militant occupation of KT company headquarters by two hundred unionists ended with a violent crackdown by six hundred riot police, and arrest warrants and prison sentences were subsequently issued for union leaders who had engaged in the "illegal strike." The KT Contract Workers' Union struggle also had become increasingly isolated from other unionists, particularly other KT workers and the majority of rank-and-file regular workers affiliated with the KCTU. Faced with increasing police repression, little to no solidarity from other unionists, and no legal basis for their claims against the KT management, after 512 continuous days, the KT Contract Workers' Union ended their struggle with no resolution and dissolved their union.

Despite its "tragic end," the KT Contract Workers' Union struggle was significant because it "awakened" the broader movement to the severity of irregular employment. Within KCTU's leadership structure, KT Contract Workers' Union President Hong Joon-pyo was the first irregular worker elected as the KCTU vice-president. Within broader labor activist circles, one KSPW activist explained, "The KT Contract Workers' Union was significant politically. It was a fight against restructuring; it was the longest and most brutal of union struggles. Despite these difficulties, the union members stayed devoted. Through the sheer suffering their bodies endured, they awakened the rest of the labor movement to the severity of the issues facing nonstandard workers.[46]

The KSPW was established in 2000 to actively support the struggles of irregular workers. Its founding activists were members of both Old Left and New Left organizations and were key supporters of early struggles by irregular workers. As a solidarity organization, the KSPW focuses on worker education and training, research on irregular workers, policy advocacy and legal reform, and direct organizational support of union struggles by irregular workers. The KSPW prioritizes the self-organization of irregular workers' unions, although its strategies still emphasize the militant "fight to the death" (*kyŏlsa t'uchaeng*) approach to irregular workers' unionism.

Organizations such as the KSPW have become outspoken advocates of the irregular workers' movement and of the necessity to prioritize their issues with the broader KCTU-led labor movement. According to one KSPW activist:

> Trade unions cannot become the kind of organization that just seeks to benefit their own members. Even if they are not members of their trade unions, in our society they have to fight for the issues that affect

the entire working class. Concretely, if you think of it this way, what is an issue that affects the entire working class? It is the issue of irregular workers. Even though they do not work at my workplace, they have no rights, they face much discrimination. We must work together to secure their rights. So, in my opinion, unions have to be the kind of organizations that can understand working class issues broadly.[47]

Left activists, as well as the explosive struggles of irregular workers, have helped redefine the priorities of the broader labor movement. A 2003 Report acknowledged, "If the KCTU does not transform itself [in regards to irregular workers' issues] then there can be no future for the Korean workers movement" (T. Kim 2003). In February 2004, a dozen KCTU leaders occupied the offices of ruling party leaders, waged a hunger strike, and organized mass rallies and marches to condemn the proposed "Act for the Protection of Irregular Workers," which they described as an "evil law" (*akpŏp*) reminiscent of the repressive labor laws under authoritarian rule.[48] Progressive members of the Korean Democratic Labor Party, along with human rights activists and women's activists, are among the most ardent supporters of recent irregular workers' struggles. Examples include the five-hundred-day struggle for regular employment by KTX "bullet" female train attendants (similar to flight attendants) against KORAIL (Korea Railroad Corporation), which ended in July 2007 and a struggle that began the same month by hundreds of women cashiers and salespersons dismissed at Homever and New Core Outlet Stores, owned by the *chaebol* the E-land Group (discussed in greater detail in chapter 7). Thus, despite the KCTU's initial neglect and hesitation in supporting irregular workers, the plight of irregular workers is now recognized as one of the most urgent issues facing the future of the organized labor movement in South Korea.

Conclusion: New Cultural and Organizational Repertoires for Marginalized Workers

In both South Korea and the United States, the dynamic relationship between social movements and labor movements facilitated the creation of new organizations and strategies to overcome exclusionary forms of unionism. This relationship laid the basis for the development of a new arsenal of tactics and resources with which to organize the growing ranks of traditionally disadvantaged workers in downgraded forms of employment. The reconfiguration of national terrains of unionism along historically sedimented lines of inequality and difference highlights the importance of social movement legacies in challenging the reproduction of social and economic marginalization for workers situated on the bottom of labor market hierarchies. In the United States, activists and organizations influenced by the civil rights movement applied community-based organizing and corporate campaigns to help unions overcome embattled union frameworks, such as the NLRB election process, as well as the limits of business-oriented and service-oriented unionism. In South Korea, the scale and scope of the 1997–1998 Asian debt crisis revealed to Left and women workers' activists how far the KCTU had strayed from its democratic principles. These activists have worked outside but in solidarity with the organized labor movement throughout the 1990s, and they have provided crucial sources of organizational and political resources for the burgeoning struggles of irregularly employed workers.

In chapters 5 and 6, I discuss how prior social movement legacies have influenced how unions organize the marginalized in each country. In addition to cultivating a new set of tools with which to organize workers subject to multiple forms of discrimination and disadvantage, social movement legacies also provided the moral and organizational repertoires to transform the marginality of certain groups of workers into a recognized and potent form of symbolic leverage.

5

WHAT IS AN "EMPLOYER"?

Organizing Subcontracted University Janitors

As chapter 4 demonstrates, marginalized workers in both South Korea and the United States have been actively contesting the downward wages and employment pressures associated with social and economic marginalization. Social movement legacies play an important role in efforts to organize traditionally disadvantaged workers such as women, immigrants, and racial-ethnic minorities. By providing subordinated groups with protest tactics and moral vocabularies utilized in previous struggles, social movement legacies create organizational and cultural repertoires that can be reused and adapted during subsequent struggles. It is important to note, however, that social movement legacies do not simply reproduce themselves; they must be applied to new situations and settings to renew their power to persuade and mobilize. To investigate how the meanings and practices associated with social movements of the past are being reinvested in future struggles, this chapter examines the organizing efforts of a specific group: subcontracted university janitors.

By mobilizing support against corporations and universities that profit off the working poor, janitors in the United States have used colorful and dramatic protests to call attention to the inequality and poverty associated with unjust employment, especially for the predominantly immigrant and racialized workforce. Although the influence of janitors' unions is much less pronounced in South Korea, union struggles waged by janitors (*hwankyŏng mihwawŏn*) there have also invoked public outrage over the extremely low wages of the predominantly female and elderly custodial workforce. Janitors' struggles reflect divergent national properties in terms of scale and organization, yet in both places, workers and their collective organizations are using social movement–inspired forms of unionism to cultivate leverage against recalcitrant employers during the course of a labor dispute. As I discussed in the introduction, symbolic leverage derives its power from the contested arena of culture and public debates about values. By redefining exploitative employment practices as broader violations in a society's conception of justice and fairness, janitors' unions are attempting to convert the socially and economically vulnerable status of disadvantaged workers such as women, immigrants, and racial-ethnic minorities into potent forms of symbolic leverage. Specifically, janitors' unions are waging highly dramatic and mobilized struggles in the public arena to rebuild the nature of employer-employee relationships associated with triangulated arrangements such as outsourcing and subcontracting.

A team of UCLA researchers published one of the first studies documenting the innovative organizing strategies of Justice for Janitors (JforJ) in the commercial building services sector of downtown Los Angeles (Waldinger et al. 1998). Subsequent studies have expanded the geographic scope and scale of janitors' organizing campaigns, highlighting the importance of local politics and gender as well as the spatialization of urban labor struggles (Milkman 2006; Rudy 2004; Erickson et al. 2002; Wilton and Cranford 2002; Milkman and Wong 2000; Savage 1998; Cranford 2007). In this chapter, I build on the insights of these case studies by extending the analysis to a cross-national comparison. Selecting janitors at universities controls for occupation and workplace. In the United States, I examine janitors' struggles that took place at the University of Southern California (USC) in Los Angeles between 1996 and 1998 and at Harvard University in the metropolitan Boston region between 1999 and 2001. In South Korea, I focus on janitors' struggles that took place at Seoul National University (SNU) in Seoul between 1999 and 2000 and Inha University in Incheon between 1999 and 2001. I look at two sets of cases in each national context to address the anomalies that Harvard University and Seoul National University (SNU) may present as unique icons in the national imagination. For each case, I draw on union archives and primary documents as well as in-depth interviews and site visits conducted between July 2001 and May 2004 with workers, union organizers, labor and community activists, and students.

In the following sections, I first discuss how the system of subcontracting obscures the employment relationship between janitors and those entities that use and benefit from their labor, which not only facilitates downward wage and employment pressures but also create barriers to unionization. Next, I present detailed case narratives of janitors' struggles, outlining how their ambiguous and contradictory employment conditions lead to heated classification struggles over who is considered the moral as well as economic "employer." The use of high-profile, shaming tactics that can redefine narrow workplace disputes into broader struggles over justice and fairness are key characteristics of public dramas waged by subcontracted janitors aimed at shifting the balance of power between workers and their opponents during the course of a heated classification struggle (Chun 2005).

The Legal Liminality of Subcontracting

Subcontracting, a business practice in which labor needs are outsourced to a secondary or intermediary firm, is one of the oldest and most enduring forms of labor exploitation. By externalizing labor costs and legal employment responsibilities to a separate entity, companies can more easily treat labor as an abstract (rather than human) cost of production. Although subcontracting is conventionally associated with "sweatshops," the drive for flexibility in organizational and industrial structures has diversified this managerial practice into a wide array of service sectors. More companies are outsourcing "noncore" business functions such as building maintenance, human resources, and other service-related sectors. The proliferation of subcontracting networks is not only transforming entire industry structures but also influencing labor market dynamics. By contracting out custodial services, firms can impose arbitrary wage cuts without having to physically move to another location. Subcontracting also allows firms to exert rationalized and masked forms of anti-unionism. For example, unless regulatory restrictions are in place, when building owners change the cleaning companies with whom they contract, the latter can choose to terminate the employment of existing workers, masking any unlawful employer practices that take place in the turnover process.

A defining feature of subcontracting employment is a state of "legal liminality." By creating a legal distinction between the entity that pays for and benefits from a particular form of labor and the entity that establishes and manages the terms of compensation, the system of subcontracting locates subcontracted workers in the "interstices" of formal employment relations: "betwixt and between the positions assigned and arrayed by law, custom, convention, and ceremonial" "(Turner 1977, 95; quoted in Rothenbuhler 1988, 70). In the case of building maintenance, the money that is disbursed to janitors technically originates from the building owner; however, their wages are legally dispensed through an intermediary agency—the cleaning contractor—which serves as the official employer-of-record.

This triangulated employment relationship complicates the legal and fiscal obligations of a single employer to a single worker. Because the terms of the contract have already been agreed on, cleaning contractors can shirk union demands for increased pay or improved working conditions during collective bargaining negotiations by arguing that they have not been allocated additional funds to raise wages and benefits. Building owners can claim that they are not the official employer-of-record, which releases them from any formal accountability or liability to workers, especially during labor disputes and grievance procedures. Consequently, janitors become subject to a multitiered employment system that severely weakens their capacity to negotiate collectively over wages, working conditions, and workplace benefits.[1]

Subcontracting trends are apparent when analyzing the shifts in the building services industry in the United States. Restructuring in the janitorial industry in the 1980s resulted in a major shift from unionized, in-house custodial workers to those employed by nonunion subcontracting companies. Initially, janitorial work was outsourced to small cleaning subcontractors; however, today, multinational cleaning contractors dominate the market share. While this shift occurred mainly in the commercial real estate sector before the 1990s, colleges and universities have not been exceptions to aggressive restructuring (Harvard Workers Center 2001, 1.) Figures published in *American School and University* in 1999 show that 22.7 percent of custodial work in colleges and universities is contracted out, but industry experts comment that this number will continue to grow as colleges continue to "explore every opportunity to outsource any activities that are not at the core of teaching and research" (Van der Werf 2001, 1).

In major cities such as Los Angeles and Boston, the real estate construction boom in the 1980s contributed to the massive expansion of the nonunion, subcontracted janitorial workforce. Wages deteriorated as the industry became dominated by nonunion subcontractors. Nationally, the average wage of janitors dropped significantly, with nonunion janitors earning approximately $4.00 per hour and union janitors $7.00 per hour. In 2000 the U.S. Bureau of Labor Statistics (BLS) reported that janitors who work in the building services industry earn less than $18,490 per year, the lowest occupational income bracket in the labor market. Falling wages also coincided with the intensification of work tasks, more competitive payment schemes, and unpaid wages. According to Cynthia Cranford (2000, 11):

> Workers were pressured to prepare their supplies before they clocked in, they often worked split shifts clocking in under different names at

each shift, and they were encouraged to bring family members, often children, to "help" with the work without being paid. Many janitors worked for weeks without pay, to "practice" in order to get a recommendation. Janitors worked by the piece, rather than by the hour. They would be given 3 floors to clean and they would have to stay until they were finished. Often this meant working 10 or 11 hours but only being paid for 8.

The growth of subcontracting also coincides with a demographic shift in the racialized and, increasingly, gendered composition of the janitorial workforce. During the 1960s and 1970s, the majority of janitors in U.S. urban labor markets consisted of working-class white and black workers. Since the mid-1970s, the shift to nonunion contract companies was followed by the increased recruitment of immigrants, with the racial-ethnic concentration of people from Central and Latin America and the Caribbean in major urban centers (see Milkman 2006). National data on employment trends among Latinos in this sector support these trends, with the proportion of Latinos increasing from 13 percent in 1970 to 68 percent in 1990. The proportion of women among Latino janitors has also increased significantly from 28 percent in 1980 to 40 percent in 1990 (Cranford 2000).

Unlike the recent trends in outsourcing among U.S. colleges and universities, the outsourcing of the janitorial sector at universities represents one of the oldest areas of subcontracting in South Korea. During the 1960s, President Park Chung Hee made cleaning and security work at universities "exceptions" to existing labor laws that prohibited intermediary employment agencies in sectors where work could not be completed within a finite period such as construction or research for a book. Since Park Chung Hee knew that revising the labor law would lead to confrontations with labor unions, he decided to arbitrarily place cleaning and security sectors under the auspices of the Sanitation Law. First Park created a contract firm in a public enterprise such as a university, and then appointed a retired military officer as the president of the company. According to Lee Kwang-taek (2000), this allowed the Park regime to create a source of managerial employment for retired military officers, who at the time functioned as crucial sources of support for his military dictatorship.

From early on, janitors were employed under atypical employment arrangements. Unlike other workers who were not employed under a fixed contract, some janitors were hired under one-year contracts, with the option to renew. Contract renewal was considered a formality, however. Although the official name of the subcontracting company would change periodically, the workers, wages, and the employment conditions remained relatively the same. It was not until the 1990s, however, when employers began aggressively promoting labor flexibility, that workers' contractual employment status became a viable route to downgrading wages and working conditions. Slowly, universities with directly employed janitors began outsourcing custodial jobs to intermediary cleaning contractors. When employers began using the so-called IMF crisis as an excuse to arbitrarily reduce labor costs, outsourcing janitorial work became more pervasive. Employers began cutting welfare protections that workers previously received such as vacation and sick pay, menstruation leave pay, retirement compensation, and meal and housing stipends. However, under the rationale that all employers were suffering from the "IMF crisis," employers began arbitrarily cutting workers' wages and denying them these so-called fringe benefits.

Elderly, women workers in their fifties and sixties were directly impacted by labor cost-cutting in the late 1990s. As discussed in chapter 2, older women have extremely limited job opportunities in a gender- and age-segregated labor market, and they composed the majority of the low-paid, low-skilled, and socially devalued janitorial workforce. According to an independent study on contract firm employers conducted by Park Jin Young (2001) of the Korean Women Workers Association, among the janitors surveyed (who composed 84.5% of the sample), 42.1 percent of contracted janitors were between fifty and fifty-nine years old, 26.3 percent between forty and forty-nine, and 25.1 percent were over sixty. The overwhelming majority (89.7%) also received less than 600,000 Won per month, with the average wage being 496,234 Won, which was just slightly above the legal minimum wage at the time (421,900 Won a month). The working conditions of contracted janitors were also worse than other nonstandard workers. For example, the average workweek of contracted janitors amounted to 52.8 hours versus 47.5 hours for other nonstandard workers (Park 2001, 13, 15). Since janitors' wages were already so low, the further reduction of their wages threatened the basic survival of many workers, many of whom are heads of households with the responsibility of taking care of dependent family members.

The Symbolic Leverage of Janitors

Outsourcing can be described in Pierre Bourdieu's words as the creation of a new classificatory scheme. Such schemes usually occur without notice because "there is nothing of the conscious, deliberate commitment or the voluntary contract about it" (Bourdieu 2000, 11). Although most individuals gradually accommodate to the expectations and rules of new classificatory schemes, there is always a possibility of contestation—especially when the imposition of a new classificatory scheme grossly violates the subjective expectations of affected individuals and forces them to accept harsher conditions. In the case of janitors, the system of subcontracting is rife with such moments, including the transition from direct to indirect employment via an outsourced cleaning contractor (as in the Harvard and USC cases) and arbitrary changes in the work allocation and compensation (as in the SNU and Inha cases).

To understand how and under what conditions such violations lead to contestation, the following section examines the temporal dynamics of labor's symbolic struggles at four different universities—two in each national context. While the particulars of each case vary in terms of the timing and the nature of involvement by social actors, the mechanics of cultivating symbolic leverage involve two interrelated processes: (1) oppositional classification struggles between campus janitors and universities and (2) the escalation of classification struggles into public dramas aimed at generating widespread moral crises in a given community's conception of "justice" and "fairness."[2]

Oppositional Classification Struggles

Struggles over classification initially erupted when a violation occurred between janitors' expectations and new employment practices associated with subcontracted arrangements. To reestablish existing wage and benefit standards and working conditions, janitors joined trade unions and organized collective protests at their worksites. When cleaning contractors refused to recognize the legitimacy of their claims, janitors quickly redirected their demands to university administrators (see figure 4). As external parties to labor disputes between campus janitors and their direct employer, the cleaning company, university administrators argued they were under no obligation to negotiate with janitors' unions. Despite the contradictions inherent in triangulated employment arrangements, janitors opposed such interpretations, highlighting the existence of a clear, hierarchical employment relationship between janitors and the universities that use and benefit from their labor. Given their opposing viewpoints, the first stage of classification struggles usually reflected a prolonged stalemate in which janitors and their advocates prepared to escalate their demands for recognition as "legitimate interlocutors, equal in honor" to university administrators at the bargaining table (Bourdieu 1999, 236).

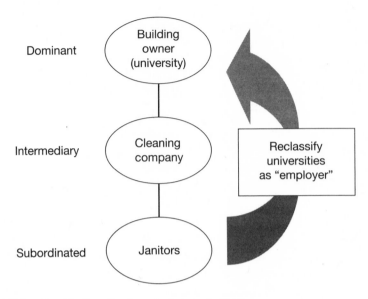

FIGURE 4. Classification struggles of subcontracted janitors.

University of Southern California

The classification struggle between campus janitors and the university administration began soon after the university decided to terminate employment contracts with 160 janitors at the University Park Campus. On February 1, 1996, USC issued a memo stating that affected janitors would be laid off in one month and offered comparable employment with ServiceMaster, an external contractor that was already providing custodial services to twenty-two other buildings on the University Park Campus. While this was a small fraction of USC's total janitorial workforce, it was part of a general trend at the university to streamline operating costs through outsourcing. From the perspective of the administration, outsourcing custodial services, which were considered secondary to its primary role as an academic institution, was a simple cost-benefit issue. Thomas Moran, the vice-president of Business Affairs, explained, "The university now pays $5,310,000 per year for custodial services on 3,100,000 square feet with its own employees. The per square foot cost is $1.71. With ServiceMaster, the university will pay 99 cents per square foot."[3] Moran emphasized that the decision to hire ServiceMaster was "consistent with the Division of Business Affairs' commitment to providing high quality service while reducing the financial burden on academic units."[4]

For many janitors who were longtime employees at the university, some of whom had worked at USC for as long as thirty years, news of USC's decision to outsource their jobs generated feelings of shock, skepticism, and opposition. According to Manuel Lizarraga, one USC janitor, "For the past four months, they've been telling us, 'You're doing a good job, you're doing a great job.' And then they turn around and say, 'Your work is not good enough.' If we were so bad, what happened to a warning?"[5] For years the administration had emphasized the motto that everyone on the USC campus—from students to faculty to employees—were part of one valued family, the "Trojan family." The university's decision to sever legal employment ties and eliminate USC-related benefits such as tuition remissions for students of employees at USC sent a clear message of the "second-class" status of campus janitors in the social order of the university.[6] Although university officials issued public statements that janitors' pay rates and benefits would not change, the majority of employees "predicted a bad outcome of their employment with ServiceMaster," expressing fears that their wages would drop from eight or nine dollars per hour to as low as five dollars per hour.[7] For janitors, USC administration's claims about the "benign" practice of subcontracting looked quite different when viewed through the experiences of janitors whose jobs had already been outsourced across campus. Twenty-five percent of campus janitors were already employed by ServiceMaster, and many were well aware of the deteriorating pay rates, benefits, and working conditions that corresponded with subcontracted employment on campus.

To challenge the university's claims and assert their views about the "dark side of subcontracting," USC janitors quickly organized several public actions including a campus rally on February 8 with the support of Local 11 of the Hotel Employees and Restaurant Employees (HERE) union and a "sick out" on February 21 involving approximately ninety janitors who called in sick for work. Engaging in public acts of protest was crucial for making the janitors' opposition to outsourcing explicit. Public protests not only portrayed the act of subcontracting as an assault on their rights, job security, and livelihoods, but they also rendered visible janitors' subordinated location in the social order of the university. From the perspective of the administration, janitors performed a necessary yet fundamentally peripheral function to its core mission as an academic institution. However, from the subordinated perspective of janitors, subcontracting represented an arbitrary method of cutting wages as well as obscuring the basis of their social ties to the university as campus workers.

Janitors also took immediate steps to establish a trade union and assert their collective opposition against the university.[8] They placed a call to SEIU Local 399 (which would later merge with Local 1877 at the end of the campaign), which had gained widespread recognition as a major hub of the "Justice for Janitors" campaign (JforJ) and a powerful force for improving the living and working conditions of low-paid janitors in the city of Los Angeles. Up until that point, the Local's success in securing gains for unionized janitors had come from strategically selected, comprehensive campaigns in the commercial real estate sector that combined card-check unionization, corporate targeting, and colorful direct actions to win wage and benefit contracts for low-paid janitors. One organizer remarked in retrospect, "Had we any sense of the time, we would have said no [to the USC janitors' request to form a union]. USC [was] like an island…[and it wasn't] clear that [winning a contract for USC workers] would win higher wages for anyone else." However, the timing of the campaign and, more important, the presence of a highly mobilized and committed group of rank-and-file janitors that had already defined the labor dispute as a justice issue, highlighted "[the Local's] moral obligation…as a janitors' union."[9] Within three days, workers successfully collected enough cards from the majority of workers (out of 230 workers total) to seek union recognition and lead a union delegation to voice janitors' concerns to the university administration.[10]

Although the union did not have previous experience organizing janitors at universities in Los Angeles, local union organizers assumed that USC would not be a hostile employer since it was a university, not a commercial real estate company. USC janitors were also extraordinarily committed, indignant, and self-organized, which led local union organizers to believe that the campaign would be an "easy win." However, when the local union approached USC administrators for union recognition, the university refused to recognize the janitors' union. According to the university, the issue of subcontracting was an operational matter, not a labor dispute, and the university proceeded to dissolve its legal employment relationship with janitors exactly one-month after giving formal notice. The university's unilateral actions proved to the union that it would most likely need to escalate its tactics into a full-scale public drama to pressure the university administration to recognize the union as a "legitimate interlocutor." Legally, union organizers were well aware that they could not target the university due to secondary boycott laws that made it illegal to target any party except the direct employer. However, the Local's experience in previous JforJ fights taught them that building owners, which represented the highest link in the chain of power in custodial contracts, could be pressured into resolving labor disputes when their images and reputations were in jeopardy, especially with key stakeholders. Rather than allow the university to "wash their hands of the responsibility to deal with the issues [related to subcontracting] before these workers," explained Lety Salcedo, the lead organizer on the campaign, "the union's main strategy relied on making USC take accountability for the 'unjust' working conditions of campus janitors, whether or not they were legally liable under the law."[11] Thus, from the very beginning, Local union leaders told the janitors that they would not be following the conventional protocol of National Labor Relations Board (NLRB) elections. Instead, through extensive outreach and education, union organizers told janitors to prepare for a heated, confrontational, moral battle through which they could attempt to subvert the "power equation" that undergirded the triangulated system of subcontracting.[12]

Harvard University

At Harvard University, the classification struggle waged by the union displayed many similar characteristics to the USC case. Rather than accept the legitimacy of subcontracting arrangements that dissolved the university administration's ties to campus janitors, the union, also represented by an SEIU Local, aimed to reclassify subcontracting from a rational managerial practice to increase efficiency to an exploitative labor practice that had deleterious consequences on vulnerable groups of workers. However, several features distinguished the classification struggle at Harvard from USC. First, it was the SEIU International union, not a group of indignant janitors, that initiated a union campaign to challenge the university's decision to outsource custodial jobs and secure a better collective bargaining contract for campus janitors. Second, it was a group of students, not the union, that would establish the contested positions of the classification struggle between the university and the janitors that cleaned campus buildings and grounds.

In February 2001 SEIU International placed Local 254 in trusteeship. The International leadership had been long frustrated by the "old guard" at Local 254, which represented approximately 700 janitors at Harvard University as well as 10,000 janitors in the larger Boston metropolitan area. While janitors' wages were steeply declining at Harvard and in the broader metropolitan area of Boston, SEIU Local 254 was "content with business as usual." When a videotape had exposed Edward J. Sullivan, the Local's business manager, driving a union car under a suspended drivers' license due to drunk driving, SEIU quickly used it as an opportunity to dismantle the existing union leadership and give the Local a signature JforJ makeover. The International later installed Rocio Saenz, one of the leaders of the JforJ struggle in Los Angeles and (perhaps not so) coincidentally, the lead organizer during the USC campaign, to step in as the deputy trustee. It also sent several other staffers from the International to help run the union and prepare it to wage a contract campaign against the city's commercial real estate owners the following fall 2002 when the city's master contract was set to expire.[13]

When Saenz arrived, an active and mobilized student presence at Harvard University directed the Local's attention to the negative impact of outsourcing on campus janitors.[14] She recalls, "When I got here, it [the labor struggle against Harvard] was already in motion. The Local had union members, so it was already organized, but the contract was no good—50 percent in-house, 50 percent contract, eight different contractors...Harvard workers had lost almost everything in terms of benefits."[15] Before 1988, Harvard University did not outsource any of its janitorial work. Janitors directly hired by Harvard with four years of service earned about $14 per hour. However, in 1992 and 1996, when the university began giving contracts to external cleaning contract firms, Harvard's in-house janitorial department shrunk from 980 workers in 1980 to 260 workers in 1996. The onset of outsourcing had a direct effect in depressing the wages of janitors. According to a report conducted on wages in Harvard's service sectors, the median wages of directly hired janitors dropped from $10.96 in 1994 to $9.55 in 2001, which does not capture the reduced costs to the university in the form of eliminated health insurance provisions, paid vacation, and seniority benefits for some of its longest serving janitors.[16] Thus, the first order of business was to secure a better contract for union members, which meant directly challenging the university's decision to outsource janitors to an external cleaning company.

The university selected a company named Trammell Crow, which in turn selected American Cleaning Company to take over custodial work in July 2001, upon recommendation by a special university committee. During the first meeting between union representatives and university officials, the union stated that it "did not care what deals may have been made between Harvard and the union in the past; the union now wanted Harvard to reverse the decision to outsource janitorial work in the medical school."[17] From the union's perspective, outsourcing was synonymous with eroding wages, benefits, and job security. Although David Jones, a representative from the university, first informed the union that "the ship has sailed" concerning the issue of outsourcing, he later qualified this statement by explaining that the university would consider placing a moratorium on the decision to outsource until further research was conducted.

The union recognized the university's response as a familiar "delay" tactic, which reproduced previous patterns of neglect and disregard concerning the well-being of low-paid janitors on campus. However, the union's decision to initiate a JforJ–style campaign at Harvard and the effects of the ensuing public drama cannot be understood outside the context of the escalated actions of an organized student group, the Harvard Progressive Labor Movement (HPLM), which pitted the university administration against student activists on the issue of subcontracting. Unlike other JforJ campaigns, in which SEIU International dispatched energetic union organizers to propel a crisis around a high-profile corporate target in an identified labor market, a highly contested classification struggle against the university administration had already been launched by students two and a half years prior. Inspired by a city living wage ordinance in which public-sector workers in Boston won a living wage of $8.43 an hour and preparations by the Cambridge City Council to pass its own living wage or-dinance at $10.25 an hour, several Harvard students contacted the Cambridge Living Wage campaign and began attending meetings to learn how to bring the issue to the Harvard campus. In the fall of 1998, the HPLM initiated a living wage movement on campus. "Cambridge public officials had set the commu-nity standard," explained one student activist, "and Harvard as a community citizen had to [abide] by it."[18] The HPLM had already established a United Stu-dents Against Sweatshops (USAS) chapter, but "there was a real concern about focusing on issues in our immediate environment…[which included] concern about outsourcing, contingent labor, and the way janitors are being treated."[19]

Students took issue with Harvard for instituting profit-driven business prac-tices that deprived workers of decent wages for themselves and their families, especially at a time when other local businesses had begun paying living wages to low-wage workers in the community. Aaron Bartley, a Harvard law school student who had helped initiate the campaign and went on to become a union organizer with Local 254/615, emphasized, "We're not just consumers here at the University, we're students and we have a role to play in shaping the attitude of the University."[20] Student activists urged then President Neil Rudenstine and pro-vost Harvey Fineberg to pay workers $10 an hour, the living wage rate passed by the city of Cambridge and emphasized the importance of "the entire Harvard University community ris[ing] together, especially out of the depths of poverty which claim too many of Harvard's own employees."

The university administration acknowledged the potential importance of further research on the effects of subcontracting; however, it repeatedly refused to engage in discussions with a student group, especially an increasingly mili-tant one, over operational and human resource matters. Although the students occupied a more privileged position than janitors in the social order of the uni-versity, students did not possess a "seat at the bargaining table" when it came to the issue of campus labor policies. Students did not ordinarily have input into the business operations of the university nor were they members of a legal organization such as a trade union, however attenuated the associational power of the latter was in the case of subcontracted service workers. As such, the administration ignored student requests to negotiate on behalf of campus service workers regarding a living wage. It was not until the entry of a more "legitimate" representative of campus janitors, the trade union—in the context of a highly escalated public drama spearheaded by student activists—that the university would begin taking concrete steps toward resolving the ongoing classification struggle over the relationship between the university and campus janitors.

Inha University

Like the beginnings of the USC campaign, the janitors' struggle at Inha University reflected a classic example of a "hot shop" campaign, a union struggle that erupts spontaneously after a workplace dispute. The early stages of union formation reflected one that was common to workers across South Korea, especially those in small- to medium-sized enterprises. First, disgruntled workers took steps to form a union that could collectively represent their interests, usually due to an employer violation in wages or working conditions. Second, workers engaged in a recognized set of actions to establish their identity as a union, including formally establishing a union and then physically marking themselves as union members in the workplace to get the union "noticed...and [to] win a place in the social order" (Bourdieu 1984, 480–481). Third, the union's struggle to negotiate a collective agreement was fraught with a barrage of anti-union practices by employers that resulted in a heated workplace battle by unions to secure their basic collective labor rights. However, unlike other unionized workers, the struggle waged by campus janitors at Inha University included an additional dimension: a classification struggle aimed at exposing the ambiguous and exploitative relations that underpinned triangulated employment arrangements. And similar to the classification struggles waged at USC and Harvard, the janitors' union at Inha University waged their classification struggle by emphasizing the university's moral obligation to janitors as "employers" and their responsibility as such in intervening in and resolving union disputes, regardless of their formal status under official employment contracts.

For years, Inha University outsourced janitorial services to external cleaning contractors, which employed workers under a one-year contract, subject to annual renewal. This practice was consistent with the system established under

Park Chung Hee in the 1960s and 1970s, which allowed universities to legally subcontract cleaning and security work to intermediary companies. Although the formal name of the intermediary cleaning company would periodically change, denoting an official change in the employer, the actual workers as well as their wages and working conditions often did not. The same workers, the majority of whom were women over the age of thirty-five, cleaned the same campus buildings and grounds year after year, and their average monthly pay hovered around 400,000 to 500,000 Won (approximately $360–$500 U.S.) a month, representing some of the lowest wages in the labor market. Although workers were required to renew their employment contracts every year, most considered this a formality. Even if there was an official change in company ownership, workers' annual contracts were renewed without fail and the terms of their employment remained the same.

For most unions, the formal conditions under which subcontracted university janitors labored remained unknown. To both unions and the general public this was a highly "invisible" workforce. The majority of janitors consisted of older women workers, with extremely limited job opportunities in a highly age- and gender-segregated labor market. As in the United States and elsewhere, janitorial work was considered menial service and "dirty" work that merited low pay and substandard working conditions. It was not until the so-called IMF crisis, however, that the downward pressures on wages and working conditions associated with "long-term temporary work" for women janitors would catalyze a series of highly contested and mobilized struggles over the class relationship between janitors and universities, the first of which occurred at Inha University in the city of Incheon.

In February 1999, JH cleaning company—one of three companies with cleaning contracts at Inha University—informed workers that they were going to change the wage payment system for all workers upon renewal of a new one-year employment contract. Previously, workers' wages were dispensed according to a monthly wage payment system, which included a basic rate of 400,000 Won a month, plus a 200 percent bonus. The wage allocation system was in accordance with the national Labor Standards Act (LSA), which required employers to pay workers a base wage on a specified day of each month as well as a minimum welfare compensation package such as paid sick and vacation leave and retirement compensation.[21] Even though workers did not technically "retire," the termination of the previous one-year contract and the renewal of another obligated the employer to pay severance, which corresponded to the average amount of a thirty-day period for each year of service. Under the new annual salary payment system, however, the company stated that workers would not receive severance pay nor would they receive bonuses such as paid leave, thereby allowing the company to reduce the total amount paid to workers to 470,000 Won a month. JH company also required workers to take an additional shift at another worksite with which JH had a cleaning contract at a much lower pay rate. While "other people [who were not already working at Inha University] received 45,000 Won, we [cleaners at Inha University] only received 15,000 to 20,000 Won."

Sun-ho, a janitor at Inha who noticed these unfair employer practices, did not understand why the company was arbitrarily changing its wage and employment policies. "After IMF, the company converted our contracts into annual salaries [and] they stopped giving us our bonuses.... [However], we were not high-skilled workers, we did grueling work [so it didn't make sense that our wage payment system would be arbitrarily changed].... Then, I found out that even in an annual salary payment system, companies must give workers their legally entitled retirement compensation."[22] Upon learning that the company was manipulating the wage allocation system to unilaterally cut their monthly wages, Sun-ho voiced her discontent to management and filed an official complaint to the local labor board office. In response, the company promptly switched back to a monthly wage system. However, it carried on with plans to reduce labor costs by eliminating "fringe" benefits that they were not obligated to pay under the LSA. When it was time to sign the new annual contracts, the company demanded that workers agree to a 30,000 Won a month deduction, which eliminated their monthly lunch stipend, in order to continue their employment with the company. It also stated that workers could no longer leave the premises for lunch. Since many workers ate lunch at home, this policy change seemed like a punitive one. In response to the company's arbitrary policies, Sun-ho refused to sign the new contract. In retaliation, the company sent her a transfer assignment to a remote location to clean apartment buildings.

For Sun-ho, getting transferred was tantamount to getting fired. Since Sun-ho knew that she would eventually be forced to quit due to the exhausting two-hour commute after a hard day of manual labor, she refused her transfer assignment and continued to work in her current position, despite her transfer notice, which was a common practice for workers that felt wronged by their employer. By refusing to accept the new terms of her employment, Sun-ho was directly challenging the legitimacy of the action. The pervasive insecurity characterizing her daily work and the realization that she could be fired at any moment, however, led Sun-ho to begin taking more proactive steps to protect herself. "I knew we needed to form a union, but I did not know who we could make an appeal to," explained Sun-ho, until she remembered the students. Every day she cleaned the student union, which housed the student cafeteria and many different student organizations, including the progressive student association (*hak-saenghoe*). "I collected myself, climbed up three flights of stairs to the student association office, and told them about the situation facing the *ahjummas* [older women]." The student leaders immediately referred her to the Korean Women's Trade Union (KWTU) Incheon branch. The KWTU was one of the few unions in the region, and the country, that was organizing women in irregular or nonstandard employment. The KWTU was created to address the inability of Korea's existing unions to sufficiently protect the rights and eliminate the discrimination of women nonstandard workers, many of whom were unfairly targeted by so-called economic recovery efforts. With the help of the KWTU union organizer, Sun-ho eventually convinced her coworkers to join the union, and the janitors' branch union of Inha University was officially established on October 24, 2000. Although older women workers never dreamed that they would be a "union member," which they associated with young militant male unionists, many recognized the injustice of their situation. One worker explained: "Because we are employed under contract [with an external cleaning company], when we are finished with our work at the school, we are taken to work at other places by the company president. But, we don't get paid more money. We can no longer endure being dragged from place to place."[23]

The first action the union took was to demand negotiations with both the cleaning contractor and the university administration over wages and working conditions. Both, however, refused. The university explained that as a secondary party, it was not legally involved in a union dispute between campus janitors and the cleaning company, regardless of the fact that the janitors physically worked on university grounds. The cleaning contractor also shirked its responsibility to resolve the union dispute. Because the unit price for labor costs was already fixed in their contracts with the university, the cleaning company explained that workers' wages were non-negotiable. To clarify the ambiguity and negligence of both the cleaning company and the university administration, the KWTU Incheon branch union decided to make their presence and their demands public. After the fifth failed round of negotiations, the union planned a collective action on campus. Union members showed up to work in bright union vests with the name of their branch union and the slogan, "Eliminate the discrimination of nonstandard workers." Within five minutes, "the school was turned upside down," explained the KWTU field organizer. The sight of older women workers in militant union vests "shocked the university." While images of striking male unionists could frequently be seen on the downtown streets of Seoul or on the evening news, the image of mothers and grandmothers in militant union garb was unprecedented. In addition, the university did not want the union vest-clad janitors to gain the attention of students, who had a history of supporting militant union struggles. Although the university administration had clearly told the union that it would not intervene in union disputes, university officials immediately called the cleaning company and told them to resolve the issue swiftly. Instead of getting immediately fired, as many suspected, the union won a small wage and benefit increase. Their initial victory, however, set the stage for retaliation by the cleaning company and a more escalated public drama directed against the university by the janitors' union.

Seoul National University

Like janitors at Inha University, janitors at Seoul National University were already employed under an external contractor when they decided to form a union. In May 1996, SNU began contracting out custodial work. At first, the shift toward outsourcing happened gradually. Instead of replacing workers who vacated their positions due to mandatory retirement (*chŏngnyŏn t'oejik*) one by one with another directly hired worker, the university would eliminate these positions and reclassify them as slots to be filled by a janitorial contractor. In the aftermath of the "IMF crisis," however, SNU officials decided to eliminate most directly employed janitors from the university payroll and contract out all custodial work to external cleaning companies. To convince workers to voluntarily switch their employment to another employer, university officials assured workers that nothing would change. They would retain their jobs, they were told, and their wages and benefits would remain the same, including their retirement compensation. University officials even convinced workers that it might be in their interest to switch to an external cleaning company: Since SNU's official retirement policy required all directly hired employees of the university to resign at age sixty-five, they hinted that the policies of the janitorial company might allow workers to work past the official retirement age." Since many janitors were older and nearing the age of sixty-five, switching to an external contractor thus seemed like a potential benefit in the long run. One of the organizers who supported the janitors' later struggle explained, "For them [the university], the rationale was that they needed to start reducing their operating costs. If they switched to a contractor, they could reduce the cost allotted to wages in half. So, they started with the weakest workers."[24] By the year 2000, the university outsourced all custodial work, except in the main University Administration building.

At the time, there was no real social understanding of the downward pressures on wages and working conditions associated with long-term irregular employment for janitors and other low-paid service workers. Although janitorial work was on the bottom rungs of university employment and the larger urban labor market, janitors who were directly employed by SNU received the standard compensation package with benefits allotted to all workers under the LSA such as retirement and paid sick leave and vacation. According to one of the main labor activists who supported the SNU janitors' struggle, "[M]ost workers were all directly employed by the university and had been working at the university for many, many years. Even though there was no union, most workers could expect that the university would raise their wages every year until they retired, at which time they would receive relatively hefty retirement compensation."[25] Thus, when university officials told janitors to sign contracts with a different employer and assured them that nothing would change, most workers accepted that the university was telling them the truth, especially because SNU was the most prestigious university in the country.

During the first year of the contract, little had changed to alarm workers that they had agreed to reemployment under a less secure and more exploitative employment system. However, with each successive contract, and sometimes during the middle of their contract period, the janitorial company arbitrarily reduced workers' wages. In December 1999, the janitorial company announced that for the 2000 contract, janitors' wages would be cut by another 100,000 Won (approximately $90–$100 U.S.), along with the elimination of their retirement bonuses. One worker, who later became a branch union officer, explained "Workers were very angry. Over the years, their anger had been brewing and intensifying. They [realized that the university] essentially deceived workers. Workers were able to continue working, but at half the wages they used to receive."[26] Over the prior three years, SNU janitors who were indirectly employed watched their wages drop by almost half: The wages of male workers dropped to 650,000 Won and women workers to 420,000 Won. At first, workers accepted that wage reductions were a necessary fact of life facing all workers during the national economic crisis in 1997 and 1998. Hundreds of thousands of workers were laid off during this period, and wage reductions were perceived as a daily fact of life for all workers. However, when the janitorial company announced that workers were facing another set of wage cuts in their 2000 contracts, workers were no longer convinced that the company was suffering from the economic crisis. The national government had also released reports that the economic crisis was officially over, highlighting a contradiction between the company's justifications for continued wage reductions and the national narrative. Although there was a time lag, the imposition of the new employment classificatory scheme and the harsh realities that it generated provoked outrage and indignation among workers.

Although most of the workers were elderly and had never thought they could form a union, as was the case at Inha University, a few janitors went directly to the progressive student association to request assistance. These janitors also knew who the student leaders were because they cleaned their offices every day and watched them stay late for meetings and events. The students contacted two organizations—the Korean Confederation of Trade Unions (KCTU) Seoul Regional Center and the People's Solidarity for Social Progress, a progressive social movement organization that had been conducting workshops on the issue of nonstandard workers. Representatives from both organizations met with the janitors and explained that janitors needed to form a union if they wanted to secure their rights. "When we first started talking about the union, the older workers did not know what the union was and just thought it was something for younger workers. But, when the organizers from KCTU Seoul Regional Center began explaining that we needed to form a union to secure our rights, regardless of our age, this really resonated with all of us, since it matched what people felt they had experienced their whole lives," explained one worker who would become an elected officer of the SNU janitors' branch union.[27] After convincing 80 percent of the workers to join, one month later, the Seoul National University Building Services union was established on January 25, 2000.[28] On the same day, the union confronted the subcontracting company and told them that workers would not sign the 2000 contracts under the stated conditions. The company threatened that if workers refused to sign, they would not recognize their reemployment.

Although the union did not have much legal leverage against the cleaning contractor, labor activists immediately recognized their potential symbolic leverage against the university. "It seemed like the right situation to start a struggle," according to a labor activist who supported the janitors. She goes on to explain, "It was Seoul National University. It is a national university and it is the very best university in the country. Socially, it is very symbolic in the national imagination. It's the place where all the most elite intellectuals are gathered and the place where those who lead the nation are educated."[29] The idea that the best university in the country would subject workers to cost-cutting labor practices seemed like an issue that would have shock value and widespread resonance. The union approached university officials to resolve the issue. As in the other three janitors' struggles, SNU insisted that they had no connection with a labor dispute between the union and the independent cleaning company as a secondary party and told the union that it should direct its grievances to the latter. Thus, to carry their struggle forward, the SNU janitors' branch union would have to escalate their classification struggle to a more public arena.

Public Dramas

In all four cases discussed in the section above, the perspectives of janitors and universities conflicted over the issue of "who is the employer." To overcome this stalemate, janitors attempted to strengthen their position by escalating their classification struggle into a full-scale public drama. The main objective of the unfolding public drama was control over the "moral high ground" regarding which party would be deemed the "distinguished possessors" as opposed to the "pretentious challengers," as Pierre Bourdieu (1984, 252) puts it. Differences in symbolic recognition between opposing parties structured the ensuing public drama in distinctly different ways. As the "more authorized party," each university was saved from waging a "symbolic struggle of all against all" (Bourdieu 1990, 239–240). The university's capacity to make itself heard and believed was embodied in the formal authority of recognized social actors. Thus, the classifications struggles waged by universities usually entailed a continuous pattern of nonresponsiveness. They would simply refuse to negotiate with unions and, therefore, to recognize the legitimacy of their demands.

As the "less authorized party," however, janitors' waged an all-out symbolic struggle in the public arena for the "belief, credit, perception and appreciation, knowledge and recognition" to be recognized as a legitimate authority "in the eyes of all" (Bourdieu 1984, 251–252; 2000, 184–185). Discrediting the moral authority of the university entailed dramatizing the unequal power relationships that facilitated "unfair" subcontracted employment arrangements between universities and janitors. Janitors' public dramas consisted of collective actions and public shaming rituals that generated the sense of an ongoing crisis for the community. The support of a broader constellation of social actors, especially students, was a crucial dimension to escalating the crisis, although the characteristics of this support varied on a case-by-case basis. Appealing to culturally and historically contested notions of "justice" and "fairness" that acquired meaning during previous symbolic struggles was also a crucial dimension for strengthening the moral legitimacy of janitors' public dramas in each case. Once university administrations accepted the terms of janitors' classification struggles, each crisis subsided and collective bargaining agreements were negotiated accordingly.

University of Southern California

At USC, the ensuing struggle waged by the local union reflected classic elements of a public drama. As the "less authorized party," the union engaged in a barrage of colorful, public shaming–oriented tactics to capture the "moral high ground." Union members distributed leaflets to students and passersby, organized campus marches and rallies at the entrance gates and in central spaces of the university, and delivered "fax bombs" (i.e., mass fax-outs) to two hundred administrators, faculty, staff, and student organizations to alert the campus community to the "dirty tactics of both USC and ServiceMaster."[30] The union also targeted key symbolic events such as commencement and university recruitment events to alert the families, alumni, and broader public of USC's actions as a "bad employer." Although USC had previously dealt with the union by ignoring their demands, the union's public escalation, especially at high-profile university events, elicited a more active response. Spokespersons for the university administration issued formal letters to students, parents, and alumni emphasizing the value of outsourcing secondary functions such as custodial services to the university's primary mission.[31] Once USC handed over the janitorial contract to ServiceMaster, the university placed ads in the school newspaper justifying its position, stating that it was "illegal" for the university as a "secondary party" to intervene in the labor dispute between SEIU Local 399 and ServiceMaster.[32] Although the university administration did not wage colorful, public protests like the union, it utilized strategies that had become standard fare in anti-union campaigns by aggressive employers, such as the use of university police to "harass and shadow workers as they tried to leaflet and disseminate information to students and faculty" (Wilton and Cranford 2002, 382). The university also filed a court injunction against the union to prevent union members from freely protesting on campus grounds.[33]

Despite the injunction (or perhaps because of it), the union took further steps to tilt the balance of power toward the janitors' side by exposing contradictions in the university's own public relations image. The university administration repeatedly made references to the "Trojan family" to emphasize the cohesiveness of the entire USC community, including students, alumni, trustees, staff, and faculty (see Wilton and Cranford 2002, 380). This message was part of the university's public relations effort to improve its negative image as a hostile, wealthy, private employer in a predominantly low-income

African American and Latino community, but it was also a message that many long-term employees, including janitors, took to heart, equating tuition remissions as a chance for their children to achieve the "American dream." A Local 399/1877 organizer explained,

> Janitors worked there year after year after year and that was really for one reason—to be able to send their kids to the university....People want to move up...the whole American dream thing of having your kids go to college, right? That message really resonates with people. People felt really angry that that opportunity was taken away from them....It's about opportunity, it was just ripped out of people's hands.[34]

Other members of the USC family, especially students and faculty, strengthened the symbolic leverage of the "Trojan family" reference by repeating sentiments about the university's obligation to treat all members, including low-paid service workers, as important members of the "Trojan family."[35]

The union also exposed the "two-faced and hypocritical" nature of USC in the community by "unmasking" USC's "Good Neighbor" facade and highlighted this with the slogan "USC=Poverty in South Central Los Angeles." Because of the university's history of antagonism with their mostly African American, poor urban neighbors and the violence and destruction that occurred in many parts of South Central Los Angeles after the civil uprisings that erupted after the Rodney King verdict in 1992, USC began trying to improve its image in the community.[36] The university donated money to neighboring schools, created tutoring programs, and supported cross-training programs that helped local students become accustomed to university life through its "Good Neighbors" program. The president of the university gave speeches about the "integral role [it has] to play in forging a promising future for this city, particularly the central city" (Roseman and Wassmansdorf 1994). One of the union's core symbolic messages, thus, contrasted the wealth of USC as the largest private employer in the city of Los Angeles and the South Los Angeles community against the poverty and devastation of the surrounding community. "USC tries to always project that they are a responsible partner with the community and blah blah blah and they have bullshit community programs, well some of them are good...[but], they are not a good corporate partner to the community—in fact, they are contributing to the hunger and the poverty and the despair that has plagued south LA."[37] In public events the union invited senators and city councilors to listen to the "Tale of Two Universities": There was the USC that received over a hundred million dollars in donations as well as tax subsidies from the government to stimulate economic development in low-income communities and the other USC that denied the American dream to its primarily Latino and African American campus workforce. Julia Lopez, a USC employee for seventeen years who later became a paid staff organizer for Local 1877, voiced workers' indignation against the USC administration: "The university is a billionaire, but they pay [low] wages. We're fighting for our overall dignity. We will not allow them to step on us."[38]

Securing the support of other campus unions and students also helped redefine the labor dispute into a moral crisis that engulfed the campus community. To show the university administration that they would be fighting a "much bigger group" than just campus janitors, HERE Local 11 organized a "symbolic referendum" with posters and fliers reading "Shall We Escalate Our Actions?"[39] Maria Elena Durazo, HERE Local 11 president, explained that while the university's subcontracting plans did not directly involve the housing and dining workers that were members of her union, it was an issue that affected all "poor, working people."[40] A small group of undergraduate and graduate students also became active supporters in the union campaign.[41] The goal of the student support committee and the formal organization that it spawned, the Student Coalition Against Labor Exploitation (SCALE), was to make sure that students understood what was going on in their own university and take an active interest in what happens in the lives of the janitors who "clean the areas they use on a daily basis."[42] In a petition delivered to USC President Steven B. Sample, signed by over seven hundred students, student activist Steve Sidawai, a student support committee member, stated

> I think that it's important for students to recognize that this is not just about the workers, but that this struggle affects the community because, first of all, the local economy of South Central is at stake.... If USC is really committed to being a "good neighbor," it should start by paying its workers decent living wages, making sure they have adequate benefits like health coverage, and making sure they have some minimum level of dignity and respect on the job.[43]

Union organizers also reached out to local community organizations that worked with residents in South Los Angeles such as the Esperanza Community Housing Corporation, AGENDA (Action for Grassroots Empowerment and Neighborhood Alternatives), and Strategic Action for a Just Economy (SAJE) to strengthen its normative claims about the "community."[44] At a "community hearing" event at St. Vincent's Church on October 12, 1996, over 120 supporters gathered to hear testimony from "workers, community leaders, politicians, and others to uncover the truth about USC's 'Good Neighbor and fair Employer' façade."[45] As the union's public dramas became more dramatic and colorful, their base of supporters grew to include the mobilized urban public that had become active supporters of the many fights that the JforJ campaign waged across the city. During a particularly colorful, public shaming action against the university, over two hundred university janitors and their families marched from Figueroa Street at Exposition Boulevard to the corner of Jefferson and Hoover dressed in "mop wigs, prison uniforms and witches costumes" "trick or treating" for union contracts. The USC newspaper *Daily Trojan* reported that the action was widely supported by USC students as well as a diverse range of community constituents including representatives of SCALE, College Democrats, Movimiento Estudiantil Chicano de Aztlán (MECha), and the Gay, Lesbian, and Bi Assembly that all pledged, "Every time you walk out, we'll walk out, until you have a fair and equitable contract in your hands."[46]

The union's public shaming tactics projected the labor dispute involving USC janitors onto the public consciousness of the city; however, USC remained steadfast in its refusal to submit to the union without an NLRB election. The university had defeated unionization efforts by janitors twice in the past and was confident that an NLRB election would morally discredit the union and end the campaign. One of the union organizers explained, "I believe that the university saw it in their interest to show the students as part of their education how to fight a union. I don't have any proof, but it was a very ideological fight on their end." From the perspective of the university, its insistence on holding an NLRB union election reflected its desire to control "the definition of the legitimate means and stakes of the struggle," which, according to Bourdieu (2000, 183), "is in fact, one of the stakes of the struggle." To demonstrate that the union possessed the collective will and the community backing to chance a full-out strike, something that had become increasingly risky for low-paid service workers, the union called a one-day strike in December 1996 and another week-long strike in February 1997. "The week long strike culminated in the arrest of 14 demonstrators, who stopped traffic by linking arms at the corner of Figueroa Street and Jefferson Boulevard. The strike and subsequent protest were held the same week as the AFL-CIO held its executive council meeting downtown."[47] Despite these intense, crisis-escalating tactics, it was clear that its ideological stalemate with the university administration would be resolved only with an election. To survey how much worker support they could count on during an election, the local organized a community-coordinated election in March 1997 in which janitors voted overwhelmingly in favor of unionization

(132 for, 5 against, 2 invalid votes). After their attempts to gain recognition by the community election had failed, the union was confident, to some extent, that "a year of organizing and taking actions that had built solid trust between the workers and the union [would] enable the workers to withstand the company's anti-union campaign." On May 23, 1997, the union held an NLRB election in which janitors voted 107 to 79 to unionize, demonstrating that, even in the face of employer intimidation during the period preceding the date of the NRLB election, the union could express their clear right to collectively represent workers' interests.[48]

After the NLRB election, the university finally conceded its loss, both on ideological and legal grounds, which then left ServiceMaster with little choice but to begin negotiations for a collective bargaining contract with the union. "Until the last vote was counted, they [USC] really thought they had this [the election] in the bag. [When we won] it was proof that they just had to shut up."[49] The union recognition victory pressured the university administration, as the dominant party, to recognize the union as a "legitimate party" and to agree to negotiations as "equal parties," a victory that is the basis of symbolic power for dominated social actors and evidence of a shift in the preexisting balance of power (Bourdieu 2000, 199). Due to the high level of worker participation and ownership in the campaign, the union bargaining committee was able to win a solid first contract, which secured job protection against arbitrary dismissal, restored seniority in pay scales, and provided full family health care benefits.[50] In the second round of contract renegotiations, the union won key provisions such as a tuition remission for workers who had worked at USC before the shift in university policy. More important, the janitors' struggle developed a highly mobilized constituency of active students and community members that continued to advocate for the interests of low-paid workers against the university.

Harvard University

Highlighting the link between the Harvard administration's market-driven outsourcing policies and the degraded living and working conditions of campus service workers was the first step toward escalating a moral crisis on campus; the second step was to undermine the symbolic authority of one of the most elite and prestigious institutions. The HPLM decided to strike the university where it seemed to matter most—Harvard's public image. Two major themes became the driving force of the students' public drama. First, students condemned the "unacceptable" conditions under which vulnerable groups of workers labored: poverty wages, eighty-hour work weeks, multiple jobs to make ends meet, and lack of health and medical benefits. Second, students exposed the "shocking" inequality between the richest and poorest members of the Harvard community. Amy Offner, a key leader of the HPLM, highlighted these inequalities in the student newspaper *Harvard Crimson* by juxtaposing the "immigrants and people of color…whom Harvard administrators consider not quite important enough to dip into [Harvard's] $14 billion endowment" and the "Harvard fund managers that take home up to $80 million a year… 800 times as much as [what the former take home]." Offner explained, "Poverty at this university might not be so shameful if it were not so needless. We attend the richest university on the planet."[51]

With the support of other members of the university community, including faculty, parents, and alumni as well as famous guest speakers such as Hollywood celebrities, politicians, and progressive activists, HPLM organized dozens of public shaming rituals to define the issue of a living wage as a central moral issue facing the campus community. Students disrupted speeches by university officials during Parents Weekends (March 1999), chartered airplane messages during periods of high public traffic on campus such as commencement weekend (May 1999), sang Christmas carols to university administrators in their offices about the poverty they create for workers on campus (December 1999), held mock teach-ins in administrators' offices to educate them about the need for a living wage (March 2000), organized arts festivals and musical concerts with celebrity guest appearances to put "Workers First" (May 2000), and delivered Valentines cards to the home of President Neil Rudenstine to "love his workers" (February 2001). Public shaming rituals worked to reframe the values of the university community, from one that valued profit to one that valued responsible community employer practices. During October 1999 when SEIU Local 254, in its unreconstructed form, was in the midst of renegotiating contracts for 200–300 directly employed janitors, HPLM supported their efforts to raise workers' wages by staging colorful campus rallies in which they "threw bags of garbage at the base of John Harvard's bronze likeness, then draped a T-shirt with the words, 'Janitors for Living Wage' above the statue's feet."[52]

Since the student living wage movement had an uneasy relationship with the janitors' union, some students began directly organizing workers. Harvard students, mainly from the law school, had started a Worker Center on campus that began outreaching to campus janitors. Because Local 254 at the time was notoriously corrupt, it was "difficult for us to ask workers to mobilize for the union."[53] However, more and more students began realizing the need to organize workers on the ground. One student who attended the meeting recalls, "I sensed that worker outreach was the type of thing we should be doing.…It's not enough to say that rich universities should pay a living wage....We need to be organizing a reform movement within the union."[54]

When SEIU International installed a former rank-and-file leader to run the Boston local, student activists decided the time was right to escalate the campaign into a crisis point. Although Harvard did not wage the kind of ideological campaign that the janitors' union accused USC of, the university administration repeatedly refused to move forward on any discussions regarding the wages and working conditions of campus janitors. To break the ideological stalemate, HPLM decided to wage an "occupation" of Massachusetts Hall, the administration building that houses the president's and the provost's office. Crucial to its execution was the consolidation of support from students and the broader campus community on the moral necessity of a living wage. Offner (2004) explains,

> By the time of the sit-in, the campaign had already built a consensus among students, workers, and faculty in favor of a living wage policy, had involved hundreds of people in a campaign of escalating direct action, and had convinced most people that the university would never implement a living wage policy without a major escalation of pressure. The sit-in would have been a disaster if the community had not been prepared and supportive.

In effect, the students' ongoing public drama on campus had effectively reconfigured social hierarchies on campus in support of campus janitors.

On April 18, 2001, fifty student members of the Harvard Living Wage Movement entered Massachusetts Hall carrying sleeping bags, food, and laptop computers and began what would be the longest sit-in in Harvard history. Although students knew that there could be repercussions to their act of civil disobedience, they challenged the notion that protesting for a living wage of $10.25 was a "criminal act." In an official statement, they stated, "Harvard is falling short of basic standards of economic fairness and human dignity, and in acting to make it meet those standards, we are acting to make our community what it ought to be. We are acting to make it the kind of place that thousands of students, workers, faculty members, unions, alumni/ae, and community members have said it should be. We are acting to make it a better university. This is not a criminal act."[55]

As the "occupation" continued inside Massachusetts Hall, students began holding solidarity demonstrations and protests outside the building in Harvard Yard, including setting up tents that "dramatized the private struggle inside to the outside world." Unions representing campus housing and dining workers and the Harvard Clerical Workers Union also began supporting the student sit-in, and, for the first time, SEIU Local 254 organized public rallies and speak-outs in conjunction with the progressive agenda of the Harvard Living Wage Movement.[56] The email distribution list included over 1,200 names and the rallies were among the largest that the campus had seen so far, with the biggest rally numbering 2,000 participants. The faculty also publicly supported the sit-in, including signing an open letter supporting the students' efforts to secure a living wage on campus. The Boston chapter of Jobs with Justice also played a critical role in supporting the sit-in, providing students with speakers' lists and circulating information about the sit-in to the broader Boston community.

These major public actions were largely successful because they "direct[ed] local attention to the national low-wage problem at places where local decision-makers [could] address it" (Freeman 2001).[57] Images of Harvard Yard draped in tacky colored tents and plagued by noisy protesters drew the national media's attention as well as the attention of famous public icons. Offner (2004) explains,

> The most important part of tent city was that it changed the feel of the campus: it killed huge patches of the university's perfectly manicured grass and made the place look like it belonged to the community. At the same time that tent city was growing, the inside team was producing beautiful signs and sticking them all over the outside of Mass Hall. We also made signs for students to hang in their windows, and invited supporters to make their own. Quickly, the campus became covered with homemade art, and Harvard Yard became an amazing, unrecognizable eyesore.

National media attention helped push the stand-off to a resolution, and on May 8, 2001, Harvard University decided to end campus protests by reaching a mutual agreement with the students. Harvard President Neil Rudenstine explained in an official statement, "As a socially responsible institution, Harvard is committed to employment practices that reflect a human and principled concern for the well-being of all individuals who work here…"[58] Although the students failed to win a commitment from the university to pay all workers a living wage, the University agreed to freeze all new subcontract hires and made a commitment to collectively bargaining with SEIU Local 254 before its existing contract expired in November 2002.[59] It also agreed to create a university committee with student representation to reassess the "economic welfare and opportunities of lower-paid workers at Harvard, both those directly employed by the University and those employed by companies that contract to provide on-campus services to the University."[60]

Once the university acknowledged the students' demands as legitimate, students effectively won the symbolic struggle. At this point, the public escalation took a back seat to the report that was to be issued by the Harvard Committee of Employment and Contracting Procedures (HCECP)—the bureaucratic committee created to resolve the dispute. The findings of the university committee helped finally push the drama to a point of resolution. The Katz Committee, headed by Lawrence Katz, a friend of then Harvard president Lawrence Summers and the former chief economist of the Department of Labor under Robert Reich during the first Clinton administration, had largely legitimated what the students and the union had been saying all along. Subcontracting by the university had contributed to a 13 percent decline in workers' wages during a time when Harvard's endowment had earned record surpluses. The committee also recommended that a "parity wage" be created that requires companies under contract with Harvard to pay the same wages as unionized employees at Harvard doing comparable work. Legitimation of these issues with an academic report exposed the university's role in contributing to the larger national problem of economic disparity in their very own community. According to Robert Kuttner, "If Harvard were a conventional corporation, it would cite competitive pressures and pay low-wage workers as little as it could get away with. But Harvard, by definition, is a different sort of creature. In an era of cutthroat capitalism, institutions like Harvard need to stand for different values."

After the report legitimated the students' and unions' moral claims, the next round of contract negotiations commenced with minimal escalation. After several public rallies and a brief civil disobedience action, the union quickly accepted a proposal by the university based entirely on the HCECP guidelines. The resulting contract gave workers an immediate pay raise to $11.35 and increases over the next three years to $13.50, with those employed for three years guaranteed $14.00 per hour. The contract also eliminated distinctions between directly hired workers and indirectly hired workers and stipulated that 60 percent of Harvard janitors would receive full-time employment by the end of the contract. For the union, the Harvard contract signified a major victory and a building block for a major strike planned for the following fall, when master contracts for the city's 10,000 janitors were set to expire. For students, however, the union's quick acceptance of Harvard's proposal was bittersweet, with many students still believing that the union could have won far greater wage increases and benefits for workers (DiMaggio 2004).

Inha University

Publicly declaring the janitor's union presence at Inha University helped resolve the union's first dispute with both the cleaning contractor and the university administration. However, it also set the stage for a typical offensive attack by the cleaning contractor against the union. On June 28, 2001, JH company mailed dismissal notices to two long-time employees who cleaned the dormitory buildings. The notices cited "negligence on the job" as the reason for the dismissals, but according to union members, "To fire them for 'work neglect' was clearly an excuse to threaten us [the union.]" The union feared that all thirty-four other union members would soon be the target of similar "contract terminations." Within days, the company sent notifications via certified mail to each individual union member and the KWTU Inha University janitors' branch union that their employment contracts would be officially terminated on August 31, 2001, when a new cleaning company would take over the contract. When the KWTU Incheon union field organizer confronted JH company management about the wholesale "sacking" of union members, the company president disclosed that the "new" contract company was under the official ownership of his wife and brother. According to the KWTU Incheon branch field organizer, "In the new contract, there was a change in name only. It was clear they fired the women to drive the union out."[61]

Although the company insisted it was acting in accordance with formal procedures, exercising its legal rights violated workers' subjective expectations about the terms of their employment. A branch union leader explained,

> At first, I thought this was a usual occurrence. I had started working at JH company [relatively recently] in 1998. But, the most senior union member who had worked at the university for 18 years explained, "Up until now, the entire time I have worked [at Inha University] I have been continuously employed, even though the company's [official name] continuously changed. There was never a case when someone was laid off because their contract was up. As long as you worked hard, it was enough. Termination? It was unheard of."

Unlike at USC, where the university and the cleaning contractor also engaged in illegal dismissals of workers, going so far as to falsify legal documents, the JH company's misuse of legal policy and its attempts to mask repressive actions with legal loopholes evoked a strong sense of indignation among union members. "At first people did not know what to do. But, soon people started thinking that we needed to fight. Even though the school did not directly employ us, and we weren't even [technically] laid off, no one was daunted. We could not sit still and do nothing."[62] Although JH company management justified their policy change by invoking legal language, workers refused to recognize its authority, highlighting a breach in customary practices.

Due to the triangulated nature of subcontracting relations, the union demanded to meet with all relevant parties under the new contract. However, its efforts to arrange a meeting with the president of JH company failed. JH company representatives informed the union that "there's no need to meet" since they were technically acting in accordance with the law and refused to engage in any negotiations with the union. The union also directly confronted university officials about the company's attack against union members, including the administrative director of the dormitory. However, university officials informed the union that the dispute with JH company was out of its "jurisdiction." On July 31, JH company went ahead as planned and formally dismissed the two workers who cleaned the dormitories. The company's refusal to rescind its decision sent a clear message to the union. "Contract termination" was a legal loophole that masked illegal anti-union actions by employers. The KWTU Incheon union field organizer, who had a long history fighting repressive employers during the authoritarian period, immediately condemned JH company for violating the spirit of the law—a spirit that the democratic labor movement in South Korea had shed blood, sweat, and tears to uphold. The union released an official statement saying, "These women have been continuously employed as the companies changed [every year] for as long as 13 or 14 years. Their dismissal is a clear case of unjust dismissals. Women in the union are the only workers out of three different contract companies with the university who were not renewed. Their dismissal is a clear indication of illegal efforts to break the union."

To strengthen their positional advantage, the union initiated the first stage of the public drama: asserting the existence of an alternate set of meanings and practices that shape social understandings of the social exchange of labor for a wage. Despite their formal termination, the two dismissed workers showed up to the campus dormitory at 8:00 a.m. ready to work a full day's shift. Their physical actions corresponded to their subjective understanding of how the social world should operate, rather than an act of "propaganda" or strategic, "purposive action."[63] Even when workers were hired under an annually renewed contract by a subcontracting company, customarily workers could expect to continue their employment without a lapse in time or pay over multiple contracts. "Terminating contracts" was simply a guise for "firing" workers, and workers, thus, refused to accept its authority. In response,

JH company representatives immediately instructed the workers to vacate the premises, which resulted in a physical altercation between union and company officials and the arrival of the police on the scene. After a JH company worker informally agreed to arrange a face-to-face meeting with the branch union, the police left the site of conflict and both "fired" workers finished their full day's shift at the dormitory.[64]

The next day (August 1) the union held its first public rally between noon and one o'clock at the front gate of Inha University and Inha Professional School. For the union, it was important to win their demand for reinstatement, but it was also important to publicly condemn the university. While Inha University benefited day in and day out from the hard work of low-paid janitors, university officials refused to take any responsibility for the harsh and discriminatory conditions of employment under which the older women janitors labored. In the subsequent petition the union stated:

> Over half of the women workers are heads of households and they are responsible for the livelihoods of their families. On one morning women who have worked for 10 years suddenly found themselves out on the streets after news that their contracts were terminated. Women who are in the lower economic group have no where to go and no way to provide for the livelihoods of their families.... Both the contract company and the school are responsible for unjust employer practices and they are named as the parties who are clearly responsible to bring justice to the situation. Schools must stop avoiding responsibility and actually resolve the right to livelihood for workers.[65]

Over the course of the next thirty-five days, the union intensified its public drama by transforming the campus into a symbolic battleground. Many of the older women union members who initially felt uncomfortable and embarrassed about publicly chanting their grievances and demands became more confident as the public struggle ensued. The repeated refusal of the cleaning contractors and the university administration to abide by the moral spirit of the law fueled their indignation and strengthened their confidence. The KWTU Incheon union field organizer recalled that, "as each day past, ajummas [women in their 30s, 40s, and 50s] turned into union workers who vigilantly raised their voices and fists to demand 'continuous employment.'" Emboldened union members also berated the university for throwing out "like garbage" the women who "loyally" and "faithfully" cleaned the campus buildings and grounds day after day. Despite the sweltering summer heat (average temperatures of 30 degrees Celsius—almost 100 degrees Fahrenheit), union members never took off their union vests even once before resolving their dispute, which to the KWTU Incheon union field organizer demonstrated their place in the larger struggle of the democratic labor movement. The broader significance of the branch union rallies was strengthened by the solidarity and active participation of local activists from the Incheon Women Workers Association, the regional branch of the KWWAU, KCTU-affiliated unions in Incheon, and local members of the Democratic Labor Party. Although university officials could scoff at the threat of older women workers waging a strike, it could not so easily dismiss the support of unionists and activists associated with the militant social movement struggles of the past and present.

The Inha University Janitor's Branch Union also solicited the solidarity and active support of the Inha University Student Union as well as the Inha Professional University Science Student Association to help escalate and resolve the public drama. This was particularly crucial in the union's efforts to emphasize the university's accountability in resolving the public drama. From the very beginning of the public campaign, student leaders were persistent in their efforts to meet with university officials on behalf of the union. While student leaders received the same responses as the union—"go to the company and resolve it legally"—they wanted the university administration to know that they would not allow the university to abandon their responsibility in the matter. In addition to participating in the union's public daily rallies and passing out printed material on the janitors' union's struggle to other students, student activists also voiced their opposition to the university by hanging huge banners in front of the student union building reading, "Secure total job security for the women janitors" and "School must apologize for skirting responsibility for the unfair firing" (KWTU 2001). Students also organized a spontaneous "occupation" of the president's office to force the university to acknowledge their responsibility in securing reinstatement for union janitors between August 10 and 17. Although the vitality of the student movement had dwindled over the past decade, the university administration knew what students were capable of when they organized. The very rebirth of Inha University as a public city university was linked to the immense pressure of student organizing during the early 1990s when students demanded an end to the corrupt management of the school by a private corporation.

Steps toward resolving the public drama began to move forward in the final days of August. Although previous rounds of contract negotiations broke down, mainly due to the refusal of the new cleaning contractor, JH company, to formally participate, the university began sending a formal delegate to attend union negotiations. Although university officials continued to emphasize their "neutrality," the refusal of JH company to engage in "good faith" bargaining became increasingly apparent. After the next round of revisions to the agreement were presented, a temporary agreement was finally reached, which stipulated that Inha University and the dormitory administration would not use the existing subcontracted company and instead contract out custodial services to another company, which would guarantee continuous reemployment for all union members. Thus, on the thirty-fifth day of their struggle, the public drama came to a close.

On September 3, the union's demands for official participation by members of the student association and the university administration in the collective bargaining agreement were met, and on September 4, 2001, the KWTU Incheon branch signed its first collective agreement. The official collective agreement guaranteed the following: (1) that the new cleaning company would reemploy the entire janitorial workforce that was employed in the dormitory and the university as of September 1, 2001, (2) that the new cleaning company would reinstate two dismissed workers (on July 31) and pay them August wages, and (3) that JH company would dispense retirement compensation for all employees with contracts over one-year and that the new cleaning company would pay those workers who were officially employed under one-year 50 percent of their retirement compensation, based on calculations in accordance with the national Labor Standards Act. Despite the complexity of the case, the escalation of the union's classification struggle into a full-scale public drama, with the participation of key social movement actors such as democratic labor activists and militant students, helped shift the power equation in favor of some of the newest and most unlikely union actors.

Seoul National University

As in the other three cases, the ensuing public drama at SNU escalated its classification struggle over the terms of employment for subcontracted campus janitors. Between April 19 and May 20, 2000, the KCTU-affiliated Seoul National University Janitors' Union set up tents for three hundred striking janitors in front of the university's main administration building. While its public drama most closely resembled a typical strike in the South Korean context, it is important to note its symbolic dimensions. Historically, democratic trade unions set up strike camps in a specific workplace to render the repressive anti-unionism of employers and the state visible in the public eye. Today, while the purpose of strikes in Korea vary—from an isolated grievance over employer abuses to annual strikes over wage increases in collective bargaining agreements—strikes still contain a very public and symbolic dimension. Strike camps prominently display flags bearing the union name and wide banners stating the specific grievances of the union throughout the duration of the struggle. The number of days a strike camp is erected commonly depicts the degree of employer repression as well as the moral resolve of striking unionists. Striking unionists usually spend day and night at the strike site to demonstrate that their everyday lives cannot go on due to their conflict with employers. In addition, since Korean unions do not have strike funds, most workers go without their wages during the strike period. The duration of the strike, thus, is often highlighted by labor activists to "show how long workers [are] willing to endure and sacrifice because of the larger cause."[66]

Several major features, however, clearly distinguished the characteristics of the SNU Janitors' Union strike from other typical strikes on the streets of Seoul. First, although strike camps were fairly common to passersby in front of the office buildings of major corporations such as Korea Telecom and Hyundai Motors as well as public buildings such as hospitals and schools, the participants of the strike usually represented male unionists and often younger workers engaged in military-like protests. As at Inha University, the sight of older women workers and even grandmothers engaging in a militant union strike was an extremely rare and unconventional public sight. Second, although the strike camp was set up in front of SNU's main administrative building, SNU was not the official employer-of-record for striking janitors. The university had contracted out most custodial services to external cleaning contractors by the time of the strike. However, like the other three cases, the union publicly identified the university administration as the materially and morally responsible "employer." Third, the major organizers of the janitors' strike were not primarily rank-and-file workers. Rather, militant student activists as well as labor activists affiliated to external unions and worker organizations were the main agents planning and escalating the public drama. Every morning, several SNU janitors' union leaders would meet with key organizers from the KCTU Seoul Regional Center and the People's Solidarity for Social Progress to discuss the plans for the day, explain which university administrators they would be meeting that day, and strategize how negotiations should take place. After the eight o'clock morning meeting, the rest of the workers would then be updated on how the day's events would unfold.[67]

For workers, students, and external support activists, the moral issue was clear. The fact that SNU—the only national public university and the nation's most prestigious educational institution—would engage in the same abusive, cost-cutting labor practices as other employers in the aftermath of the so-called IMF crisis highlighted a gross contradiction between its role as a public entity and their actions as profit-seeking, exploitative employers. When the wages of workers dropped below the national minimum wage, organizers immediately exposed this violation to garner public attention, emphasizing "Workers at the best national university suffer from minimum wage violations." One organizer explained, "It is very difficult to organize unions at private companies. They will do anything to break a union. If we can expose that the government is abusing laws and exploiting workers to this extent, it gives us symbolic capital. We can expose that the government is violating its own laws. The responsibility of the government to uphold the laws has more resonance, especially since they are the ones that make the laws."[68] The university's increased vulnerability to public opinion also made it a more strategic target than the unknown cleaning contractor, which the union already recognized was implicated in asymmetrical power relations as the intermediary employer.

"The internal conditions were also good" to engage in a public drama against the university, recalls a support organizer. As the social fabric of the university community, faculty and students play a major role in defining its values. Many professors and university officials had daily physical contact with the campus janitors, greeting each other daily in the halls and their offices; however, they had "no idea how little they were getting paid." "Many of the professors did not know that the women over 60 who clean their offices and classrooms do not even receive 500,000 Won a month, and they work so hard....They all agreed this was terrible, so they were friendly to the struggle of janitors."[69] Although students did not doubt that campus janitors received low pay, many students also recalled their "shock" at how extremely low the wages really were. In the city of Seoul, living on 400,000 Won a month seemed an impossible feat, and both students and faculty recognized the cruelty of cutting janitors' already low wages.

As in the previous three cases, especially in the Harvard and Inha cases, students played a central role in supporting and escalating the public drama. In addition to referring disgruntled janitors to a local union, student leaders quickly formed a Student Support Resolution Committee to work in solidarity with the union struggle. According to one student activist,

> Even though they [students from the support committee] were not union members, they participated exactly like they were union members. From the beginning, they helped workers create a union and elect union leaders. They were this active mainly because many of the

workers were elderly and did not know how to form a union. Students are usually not supposed to do all this, but essentially, they did all the work that rank-and-file leaders do and participated in the same way. I was the representative of a social organization on campus that worked in solidarity with the struggle.[70]

For student activists who were closely connected to the "participatory democracy" wing of the movement, where class struggle was deemed the pathway to national liberation, supporting the struggles of janitors at their own union seemed like a "natural" alliance.

As the struggle continued to escalate, however, it became clearer that SNU, like all the other universities, would not be easily shamed into "doing the right thing." Appealing to the symbolic authority of official contractual relations allowed the university administration to repeatedly deflect and ignore the union's demands to intervene in the conflict. The university administration continued to insist that they had no connection with the independent (sub) contractor and that the union should focus its pressure on the latter. As in all the other cases, the pattern of nonresponsiveness by the university sparked a more intense escalation in the public drama. Unlike in typical union struggles, where the union could highlight the anti-union practices of the employer to imbue their struggle with deeper moral significance, the SNU janitors' struggle had to engage in other tactics to escalate the public significance of their struggle. To push the struggle to a crisis point for the administration, union organizers decided to elicit key support from student activists. Like at Harvard and Inha, students "occupied" the central administration building and hung a huge banner on the face of the building that read, "Participate in Union Negotiations, University Administration!" This very visible and desperate act was pivotal in pressuring the university administration to finally meet the union's demands. Since it was clear that the public drama would not simple go away, the university began taking steps toward its resolution. University officials told the union that they were willing to meet, but only if that meant ending the turmoil on campus.

After forty-four consecutive days of the public drama, the cleaning company agreed to pay workers the wages that they had not received while on strike and restore the wage rates to the amount set in their 1999 employment contracts. An official collective agreement was signed between the SNU Janitors' union and the cleaning company on May 30, 2000. One of the organizers explained, "While SNU was never an official part of the collective bargaining, we forged what we call an *imyŏn* [behind the scenes] agreement...even though in the official agreement it says the contractor will raise wages, unofficially and off the record, we knew that [SNU renegotiated] their contract with the janitorial company and gave more money to the contractor to cover the wage increases. But, there is no record of this officially."[71] Despite the invisibility of the university administration from the actual bargaining process, their role was an essential component of the resolution process. The continued centrality of its role was clear in the months following the collective agreement. Although SNU only contracted custodial services to one company between 1996 and 2000, in 2001, it began giving out contracts to three or four different cleaning companies. "If there's just one contractor, it is easier for the union to be united across all three campuses, since they bargain together. But, if they start using three or four different contractors, the union has to negotiate with all the different companies separately…with workers at one company getting paid slightly more than at another. Of course, SNU did this purposely to essentially break the union."[72]

Conclusion: Redefining What Is an "Employer" through Symbolic Leverage

In all four cases, a triangulated employment relationship among janitors, universities, and the cleaning companies with whom they contract resulted in the cultivation of a distinct form of symbolic leverage. To overcome resistance to their collective demands to change employment conditions, janitors and their advocates waged full-scale public dramas aimed at reclassifying the moral and economic responsibilities of all employers, regardless of their formal obligations under the law. A key aspect of each public drama was the "power of recognition," or what Bourdieu (1989, 23) calls the "power to consecrate or reveal things that are already there." In each case, public dramas highlighted that janitors worked hard every day to service the needs of students, faculty, and the entire campus community and, thus, deserved to be valued as important members of the university community.

Since janitors possessed limited leverage in the workplace, due to their ambiguous employment arrangements and devalued social locations, the support of a specific constellation of social actors and institutions was crucial to strengthening the legitimacy of their collective claims. SEIU's "JforJ" campaign provided significant organizational and cultural repertoires for janitors' struggles at both USC and Harvard. Because Los Angeles, and SEIU Local 399/1877, was the moral epicenter of the JforJ campaign, the USC janitors' struggle was organized by local union activists that already had experience mounting "in your face" public shaming campaigns. They could also count on the support of a highly mobilized urban public, which had grown throughout the 1990s, to support USC janitors at key events during the campaign.

At Harvard, despite the lack of a revitalized SEIU local, the janitors' struggle was initiated and actively supported by the campus living wage movement, which drew support from progressive student groups and the campus-based chapter of the United Students Against Sweatshops movement. Other organizational networks such as the Cambridge Living Wage campaign, the campus HERE Local, and the Boston chapter of Jobs for Justice also served as important components of escalating the public drama of Harvard janitors.

At Inha and SNU, union, student, and women worker activists with experience organizing militant democratic unions against authoritarian developmental regimes during the 1970s and 1980s also played a crucial role in supporting janitors' struggles. At Inha, janitors benefited from the support of the KWTU Incheon branch union, which was run by staff from the Incheon branch of the Korean Women Workers Associations (KWWA). As a historical site for democratic union struggles in textile and auto factories in the 1980s, Incheon city also provided the Inha janitors' union with active public support from student movement groups and other KCTU-affiliated unions. At SNU, the KCTU Seoul Regional Center was the primary KCTU-affiliated organization that supported nonstandard workers' organizing. Movement organizers with the People's Solidarity for Social Progress (PSSP), who went on to establish a national workers' center focused on organizing nonstandard workers, Korean Solidarity Against Precarious Work (KSPW), also played a crucial role in supporting the janitors' unionization efforts during the course of the campaign. At both Inha and SNU, the participation of radical student activists in supporting campus janitors was crucial to adding political weight to their demands. Although the power of the student movement has waned throughout the 1990s, students are still perceived as the moral conscience of society (N. Lee 2007). Movement activists who supported the push for independent democratic unions also emphasized the role of unions as democratizing forces, even after the formal democratization of the state.

Specific constellations of social justice actors and organizations influenced the forms of symbolic capital that each struggle drew on. At the heart of janitors' struggles in the United States was a mobilizing narrative about corporate and community accountability. Janitors' struggles criticized the hypocrisy of wealthy universities that purport to be pillars of the community yet contribute to the poverty of workers "in their own backyards." Community outrage was directed at Harvard University for refusing to act as a responsible community member and comply with local living wage ordinances that had already been passed in the cities of Cambridge and Boston. At USC, unions criticized the university for refusing to help alleviate the kinds of racial and economic tensions in South Los Angeles that contributed to widespread riots just a few years earlier. For both U.S. cases, the crux of janitors' associational power rested in their ability to strengthen the union's image as a representative of the community interest. This entailed securing a broad range of support—from local politicians to community organizations to student advocates. Public support from different elements of the "community" allowed the union to contradict employers' claims about the legally suspect nature of the union's demands and instead, affirm the validity of the union's claims.

At the heart of janitors' struggles in South Korea were oppositional struggles against the welfare-depriving tactics of oppressive employers during authoritarian industrialization. Janitors' struggles condemned the unjust practices of employers as labor law violations and drew on the support of movement actors that had historically led oppositional movements against the state for national democracy. Janitors' struggles not only exposed the shockingly low wages that forced older, women janitors to work in a state of chronic poverty, but they also exposed the responsibility of public institutions that blatantly disregarded the legal letter of the law, specifically in regard to the provision of basic minimum wages. At SNU, the union increased the moral weight of its demands by criticizing the nation's premier national university—a university where many of the nation's lawmakers were educated—in violating basic laws for workers. By appealing to the morality of legality, unions strengthened the institutional weight of their demands against "negligent" employers.

Each of the case narratives demonstrates the similar and different ways in which janitors cultivated symbolic leverage to strengthen the basis of their associational power. A key component of this process was the ability to use highly escalated classification struggles to redefine the expectations between janitors and those entities that used and benefited from their labor, thereby showing that changes to contractual relations are possible only in so far as they elicit the consent of affected parties. They also reveal that struggles take place on distinct culturally and historically contested terrains. From the organizational actors that supported janitors' struggles to the cultural repertoires of justice, the cases highlight the significance of local and national factors in shaping the dynamics of labor's symbolic struggles. Chapter 6 turns our attention to another group of marginalized workers and their struggles to redefine ambiguous, contradictory and exploitative employment relationships.

6

WHAT IS A "WORKER"?

Organizing Independently Contracted Home Care Workers and Golf Caddies

After repeatedly being denied their collective labor rights as "independent contractors," 74,000 home care workers in Los Angeles voted to unionize on a single day in 1999, snowballing into successful union campaigns in almost every major county in California and in several states across the country including Washington, Oregon, New York, Michigan, and Illinois.[1] Under the motto, "invisible no more," SEIU locals, in coalition with disability rights advocates, consumer groups, and community organizations, provided voice, visibility, and political representation to hundreds of thousands of home care workers—the majority of whom represent an "invisible" population of women and immigrants. Likewise, in South Korea, despite the contractual obstacles to unionizing as "specially employed" (*t'ŭksu koyong*) workers, a status equivalent to independent contracting, golf caddies at the 88 Country Club (88CC) established one of the first branch unions of the Korean Women's Trade Union (KWTU). Under the motto, "Stand Firm as a Worker," the 88CC golf game assistants' (*kyŏngki pojowŏn*) branch union negotiated a historical collective bargaining contract for workers in ambiguous and contradictory employment arrangements, sparking a wave of labor unrest by golf game assistants across the country. Unionists renamed their occupation from golf "caddies" (k'aedi) to golf "game assistants" to eliminate the derogatory connotations associated with the Korean use of the word "caddies"—images of highly sexualized women serving a primarily male clientele in places such as bars, singing rooms, and country clubs. Newly formed golf game assistants' unions not only pressured management to recognize their collective organizations as legitimate political actors, but they also projected the issue of "special employment" and the gender discrimination associated with the disproportionate number of women working in specially employed jobs onto the consciousness of the broader labor movement.[2]

What made two groups of women workers in highly atypical and socially devalued forms of personal service work across the world choose unionization as the vehicle to improve their everyday working and living conditions? How and under what conditions can traditionally disadvantaged workers classified as "independent contractors" overcome the seemingly insurmountable obstacles to forging unions and securing collective bargaining agreements? What do these struggles reveal about the creativity and resourcefulness involved in organizing one of the most rapidly growing and diverse occupational categories in today's global economy: low-paid personal service work?

This chapter examines the dynamics of how and under what conditions independently contracted personal service workers, another group of workers in the lower tier, are cultivating symbolic leverage to reconfigure the relations of power and authority underpinning triangulated employment arrangements. I focus my cross-national comparison on two specific cases: (1) the home care workers' struggle in Los Angeles County between 1987 and 2000, affiliated with SEIU Local 434B and (2) the golf caddies' struggle at the 88 Country Club in Kyonggi-do County between 1990 and 2001, affiliated with the KWTU. Although I mentioned earlier that the Korean usage of the term "caddies" is associated with derogatory traits of the kinds of women engaged in this form of service work, I primarily use the occupational term *golf caddies,* which does not have the same gendered and sexualized connotations in countries outside South Korea and Japan where the workforce is not predominantly female. In the case of Los Angeles home care workers, due to the numerous published sources on SEIU Local 434B's campaign and the struggle in California to organize home care workers, I rely primarily on secondary sources and narrative accounts of the organizing campaign (Cobb 1999; Delp and Quan 2002; Heinritz-Canterbury 2002; Rivas 2005; Walsh 2002). I also rely on primary documents such as union-produced materials (including press releases and periodicals), as well as newspaper and magazine articles. In the case of golf caddies at 88CC, I rely on fieldwork conducted between June to September 2000 and July to December 2002. In addition to attending union meetings, events, rallies, and trainings, I interviewed key rank-and-file and union leaders at the local and national levels. Union-produced reports and newsletter articles by KWTU as well as independent labor research organizations such as the Korean Contingent Worker Center also serve as important data sources.

Despite the obvious differences between them, home care workers and golf caddies share several key features that make them a valuable, cross-national comparison. As a predominantly female workforce involved in low-paid and devalued personal service work, both cases involve highly "invisible" sectors of the labor market that have not historically been unionized. The overwhelming majority of home care workers in the United States are women, a high proportion of whom are immigrants and women of color, who take care of the elderly and disabled in their own homes. Most golf caddies in South Korea consist of disadvantaged women workers who assist wealthy golfers in geographically remote and exclusive country clubs.[3] The primarily female workforce of golf caddies in South Korea (as well as Japan) is in stark contrast with the primarily male workforce of gold caddies in North America and Western Europe. The ability of atypical groups of women workers to successfully form unions and win collective bargaining agreements ruptures conventional understandings about *who* can be organized and *how*. Rather than view each case as "exceptional," I argue that an in-depth comparison of each case reveals striking similarities about the mechanics and dynamics of organizing workers subject to new forms of employment exclusion.

This chapter proceeds as follows. First, I discuss how the system of "independent contracting" produces highly contested struggles over classification during the course of a labor dispute. Second, I provide narrative detail for each case, outlining how each group sought to redefine what it means to be a "worker" and an "employer" through highly escalated classification struggles. Unlike conventional union tactics such as the strike that generate leverage for workers solely by refusing to work, symbolic leverage relies on a broader repertoire of meanings and actions that shift the terrain of struggle from narrow contractual interpretations to public contestations over basic moral values in a given community.

The Legal Liminality of "Independent Contractors"

Personal services represent a rapidly increasing employment sector in today's new economy. Although certain types of personal services, such as domestic care, have existed for a long time, the growth of dual-income households in the latter decades of the twentieth century have increased the number and variety of commodified personal services available in the labor market. Home care workers and golf caddies are just a few of such diverse personal services jobs, which also include waitresses, nannies, housekeepers, nail salon workers, beauty stylists, fitness instructors, personal chefs, and career coaches. While the range of personal services varies in terms of skill and pay levels as well as employment types, working conditions, and workplace arrangements, a high proportion of personal service workers are women who can be found in atypical forms of employment, including "independent contracting."

Independent contractors are broadly defined as individuals who "work for themselves (or their own company), bearing the responsibility for obtaining clients, seeing what work assignments are executed, and otherwise running the business" (Cohany 1996, 2). For highly skilled and better-paid workers, being classified as an "independent contractor" can offer greater flexibility and choice. For less-skilled workers in lower-paid jobs, such a classification often results in lower wages, harsher working conditions, more job insecurity, and less institutional protection against employer abuses (Hudson 1999, Kalleberg, Reskin, and Hudson 2000). Independent contracting positions workers in ambiguous and contradictory ways with respect to conventional employer-employee relationships, which tends to exacerbate poor working conditions for individuals on the lower rungs of the personal service job ladder. If we subject both home care workers in the United States and golf game assistants in South Korea to an "economic realities test to determine who is an employee," according to Susan Houseman (1999), we find that neither group truly represents "independent entrepreneurs performing services for clients" because they are economically dependent on the entity for which they perform services.

As in the case of subcontracting or outsourcing, which I discussed in chapter 5, independent contracting represents a form of ambiguous or hybrid employment (also discussed in chapter 1). By locating workers in the "cracks" and "fissures" of formal employment, irregular employment arrangements such as independent contracting exacerbates a state of *legal liminality* for workers—that is, a state of institutional exception in which workers are neither fully protected by nor fully denied the rights of formal employment. As such, labor struggles increasingly take the form of classification struggles aimed at redefining the terms and conditions of the employment contract. At stake in the classification struggles of so-called independent contractors are contested public struggles over what it means to be a "worker" in the eyes of the public, as opposed to narrow legal interpretations over the nature of their employment status.

Home Care Workers: Between Public Employment and Public Assistance

Home care work is the single fastest growing occupational category in the U.S. economy. When specified as "personal and home care aides," the U.S. Bureau of

Labor Statistics (BLS) (2000a) estimates that there has been a 226 percent growth in the number of workers nationwide, from 127,000 in 1992 to 414,000 in 2000. Of the thirty fastest growing occupations over the next decade, personal and home care aides far outpaces other low-wage job categories, with a projected 62 percent increase between 2000 and 2010.[4] The California Employment Development Department (2000) reports that personal and home health workers also account for two of the fastest growing occupations in the state, although the exact numbers are difficult to determine through official statistics.[5] Popular accounts indicate that the California home care workforce has doubled since the late 1980s, from 100,000 to 200,000, and nearly tripled in Los Angeles County from 60,000 to nearly 160,000.[6]

Part of the difficulty in generating precise estimates of home care providers can be attributed to the occupational distinction between home health care aides and personal home care aides in official statistics. According to the BLS, home care work is classified as a service occupation that combines the duties of caregivers and social service workers. *Home care workers,* also referred to as personal attendants, caregivers, and home care aides, provide daily assistance to elderly and disabled adults who wish to continue living independent lives in their own homes. Their activities include routine personal care services such as cleaning, laundry, changing linens, as well as planning, shopping for, and preparing meals. *Home health aides,* a separate BLS occupational category, also provide in-home care, but their work consists mainly of higher-skilled forms of medical care. They check their clients' vital signs, administer oral medications, and assist with medical equipment in addition to the basic daily tasks of bathing, dressing, grooming, cooking, and cleaning.

The working conditions of home care are highly unregulated, and can vary from day to day and from client to client. Workers can be hired to work on an on-call hourly basis or as long-term care providers for one or several clients who set the fees and arrange work schedules on their own terms. Some home care workers find work through social service agencies, home health agencies, or residential care facilities, but in the state of California, 96 percent of home care providers are self-employed with no affiliation to an agency (Heinritz-Canterbury 2002, 18). Some home care workers find work through word of mouth; others find work by responding to employment advertisements in newspapers, on church bulletin boards, and in other community locations. Home care workers are also one of the most poorly paid occupations in the labor market. Before unionization, most home care workers earned the minimum wage and did not receive health insurance, pensions, vacation pay, overtime pay, or compensation for travel time between clients' homes (Delp and Quan 2002, 3–4).

Home care work is characterized by ambiguous and contradictory classifying practices by the state.[7] In some states, home care workers are direct employees of the county; in others, they are employed under contracts with private health care agencies. In the state of California, home care workers are neither. This is due to a "consumer-directed model" of care provision in which "consumers retain the right to hire, train, and terminate the direct-care worker who provides assistance and support in the consumer's home" (Heinritz-Canterbury 2002, 7). This model was the result of intense lobbying efforts by senior citizen and disability groups in California who advocated for the creation of home care programs that would allow elderly and disabled persons to live independently in their own homes in their own communities, instead of being dislocated into health facilities. In 1973, each county officially established an In-Home Supportive Service System (IHSS) under the Department of Social Services to administer public financing for home care services for elderly or disabled patients who meet specific income and disability criteria.

From the beginning, this model contributed to the creation of a three-tiered employment structure for home care workers. The funds to pay for home care services came from a public fund, which included a mixture of federal, state, and county funds. The state government also assigned county governments the administrative responsibility of managing home care programs and evaluating the eligibility of prospective recipients of home care services. The responsibility of finding a care worker, defining their work responsibilities, and hiring and firing them, however, were delegated to individual clients. In other words, the state issues home care workers' paychecks, the county decides whom they can work for, and the consumer hires and fires them (Cobb 1999). Because no single party is deemed to be the formal employer, no single party is legally responsible to ensure workers' basic labor rights. As in the case of previous public work programs (such as the Works Progress Administration in the 1930s), the state created a "hybrid" category between public employment and public assistance, which, however unintentionally, gave rise to contradictory claims over the legal employment status of home care workers (Goldberg 2005, 342–344).

State policies regarding the administration of home care programs have provided a growing client base of low-income elderly and disabled persons with a highly exploitable workforce. There is no formal training provided by the county's IHSS program or by the state government, and there is little opportunity for career mobility. The county also determined the maximum number of hours for which a home care worker can be paid (up to 283 hours per month), but it does not regulate how the time is dispersed. Thus, home care workers can work up to 65 or 70 hours a week at the fixed minimum wage without compensation for overtime or any restrictions on times of the day or days of the week actually "worked." In addition to highly unregulated working conditions, home care workers are vulnerable to injuries on the job such as overexertion when assisting patients. They also spend a significant portion of their workday traveling from home to home, which is also uncompensated. In the *Occupational Outlook Handbook for 2000,* the BLS describes their working conditions as follows: "Aides may go to the same house every day for months or even years. However, most aides work with a number of different clients, each job lasting a few hours, days, or weeks....Some homes are neat and pleasant, while others are untidy and depressing. Some clients are pleasant and cooperative; others are angry, abusive, depressed or otherwise difficult" (U.S. Bureau of Labor Statistics 2000b).

Part of the rationale for why home care workers can be paid so little, despite the life-sustaining care that they provide, is attributable to the devaluation of care work as gendered and racialized labor (Glenn 1992). Historically, home care was performed by either unpaid (usually female) family members or racial-ethnic minority women. "The nonwage labors of the wife or mother, performed out of love, obligation, and duty, morph into the low-wage tasks of the housekeeper, personal attendant, health aide, and child or elder minder" (Klein and Boris 2007, 178). These racialized and gendered patterns have remained consistent for today's home care workforce in California. Depending on regional location, family members compose a significant proportion of the home care workforce. In the state of California, 40 percent of all personal and home care aides are family members (Heinritz-Canterbury 2002, 18). The California Department of Social Services reported in 2001 that of 202,000 home care providers in the state, 77 percent are women and 50 percent are between forty-one and sixty years of age (Heinritz-Canterbury 2002, 18). A recent survey conducted by the University of Southern California (USC) supported these findings, stating that 83 percent of 1,230 home care workers in Los Angeles county were women. The USC study also found that the workforce was ethnically and racially stratified with 39 percent Latina, 25 percent African American, 14 percent Armenian or Russian, 7 percent Asian, and the remaining 15 percent white or other (Delp and Quan 2002, 3).

Golf Caddies: Between Cash Tips and Wage Labor

Golf caddies assist individual golfers during the course of an eighteen-hole game. As a luxury sport with a primarily male, wealthy, and socially exclusive clientele, almost all golf courses in South Korea require that players utilize a golf caddie and, as in Japan, almost all golf caddies are women. Despite the stereotype of young, flirty, single women whose presence on the golf course is mainly to entertain male golfers, golf caddies provide a variety of assistance on the course including carrying and delivering golf equipment; operating golf carts; scoring and recording the scores of individual golfers; providing technical information about game rules, golf club selection, the characteristics of the course, and wind patterns; and giving advice about golfers' form and swings. They work between five and six hours a day during the week (i.e., the equivalent of one thirty-six-round course) and as long as thirteen to fourteen hours a day during peak seasons (two thirty-six-round courses). They often work six days a week, and their schedules fluctuate depending on the weather conditions and the number of golfers for the day. The first shift usually starts at 5 a.m., and golf caddies are assigned a number that corresponds with the order in which they will be assigned individual clients. For workers whose number is early in the rotation, they might work two sets of thirty-six holes before the day is over. For workers whose number is later in the rotation, they might not get any work at all for the day. Golf caddies' livelihoods also fluctuate according to seasonal changes in the golfing season throughout the year. During the low season winter months, it is not unusual for golf caddies to go without any earned income.

The golf caddies' workforce in South Korea has grown significantly over the past two decades, as the number of golf courses has grown.[8] In 1984, when plans for the construction of the 88 Country Club began, there were only 27 country clubs in South Korea. However, by 2000, the number of golf clubs increased to 180, with 50 more under construction, and the number of golfers more than doubled from 116,521 golfers to 265,189 between 1989 and 1999 (Korean Contingent Workers Center 2002c, 72–73). The KWTU estimates that approximately 20,000 golf game assistants are employed as independent contractors. However, like home care workers, the actual size of the golf game assistants workforce is difficult to assess due to the fact that "specially employed" workers are not counted in official government statistics (Korean Contingent Workers Center 2001).

Golf caddies are officially classified as "specially employed" workers, which represents an ambiguously defined category of workers who are placed in it simply because they are hard to define under the traditional definition of a worker (see chapter 3). Although the employment conditions of golf caddies vary by country club, four major factors exclude them from unequivocal legal recognition as traditional workers: (1) the lack of a clear labor contract relationship, (2) flexibility in initiating and determining one's own work schedule,

(3) payment in the form of a service tip directly from consumers, and (4) exemption from paying income tax on their caddie fees (K. T. Lee 2000). As in the case of independently contracted home care workers, their employment conditions reflect a hybrid state.

The majority of golf caddies' earned income is based on cash tips from clients, which technically make golf caddies "self-employed," but similar to waiters and waitresses in the United States, most country clubs pay golf caddies a basic wage of 5,000 Won (approximately $4.50–$5.00 U.S.) per game. Most country clubs also directly hire and fire caddies, determine their work schedules, and regulate their working conditions, in the same way they would if golf caddies were directly hired employees. Golf caddies are also directly supervised by so-called caddie masters who are directly employed by the country club and work in the game department. Supervisors are infamous among many golf caddies for their harsh and arbitrary forms of punishment. For example, if golf caddies are late to work, caddie masters can decide to assign them to weeding the grounds all day long. Consequently, caddies are denied the ability to earn any wages for the day and are forced to perform free labor for the country club.

As in the case of California home care workers, the South Korean government is responsible for classifying golf caddies in ambiguous and contradictory ways. In the early 1970s, the state defined such workers as legitimate laborers under the rationale that caddies received wages from an identifiable employer and worked in the labor user's facilities. However, contradictory decisions by the court and under administrative interpretation since then have resulted in a highly inconsistent state of employment. On May 25, 1993, the Supreme Court ruled that golf caddies are considered workers under the National Trade Union Law. However, on July 30, 1996, the Supreme Court ruled that golf caddies could not be considered workers under the national Labor Standards Act (LSA), which defines workers according to a more narrow set of conditions (K. T. Lee 2000).[9] The Ministry of Labor also delivered contradictory decisions on the legal status of golf caddies. During four pending legal cases, the Ministry of Labor recognized golf caddies at two out of the four country clubs in question as legitimate workers. At 88 Country Club and BuGok Country Club, the management was held responsible for illegal firing practices and labor law violations because employers at these two establishments were directly involved in hiring, firing, internal operations, and wage setting. However, caddies at Hanhwa Country Club and Han Yang Country Club were denied recognition as legitimate workers because it was stated that an independent caddies organization, not the employers, determined caddie fees and working conditions (K. T. Lee 2000).

Due to their ambiguous employment status, golf caddies are also responsible for all injuries they incur in the workplace. Because golfing is a physical outdoor sport, golf caddies experience many different kinds of accidents ranging from golf carting accidents to injuries from wayward golf balls to pesticide poisoning from the lawns. When injuries happen, golf game assistants are responsible for covering all their medical costs. KWTU organizing director Choi Soon-im explains, "Even at the hospital, doctors wonder why [golf caddies] cannot receive industrial accident compensation."[10]

The hierarchical relationship between caddie masters and golf game assistants, as well as the marginalized status of golf game assistants in the labor market, must be understood in the context of gendered service. The KWTU explained that violence and sexual abuse from both male supervisors and clients is widespread: "When some clients experience unsatisfactory play, they sometimes vent their feelings on the caddies and even turn physically violent.... [Some country clubs] force caddies to accompany clients for drinks."[11] Golf game assistants, as well as other gendered (and often sexualized) labor such as retail salespersons, flight attendants, bank tellers, and clerical workers are subject to discriminatory physical requirements including age, weight, and height restrictions. There is also an assumption among employers and the general public that caddying is a temporary job, in which women can earn cash for a short period of time. Although some women do work as golf caddies on a temporary basis, many golf caddies have worked as such for long periods and characterize caddying as highly skilled work that requires accumulated experience.

Classification Struggles

For workers with atypical employment conditions, unionizing efforts often stall at the level of classification. Home care workers and golf caddies are not in typical employer-employee relationships; thus, their efforts to form legally recognized unions and secure collective bargaining agreements have often been contested. The first step in the struggle for union representation for both groups of workers entails asserting the class identity of each group as legally recognized "workers," rather than as independent entities engaged in mutually beneficial employment relationships. This involves clarifying the employment relationships between "workers" in subordinated and dependent positions with respect to clients and, more important, "employers" with control and authority over the terms of workers' employment. (See figure 5.)

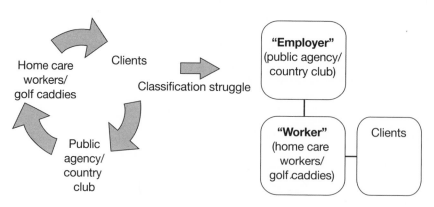

FIGURE 5. Classification struggles of independently contracted home care workers and golf caddies.

Because the symbolic authority of official classifications directly contradicts the veracity of workers' claims, winning the authority to determine the class status of "independent contractors" as "workers" depends on publicly escalating classification struggles. As discussed above and in chapter 6, classification struggles represent competing struggles over whose vision of the social world should be recognized as authoritative and capable of changing social relationships accordingly. Given the lack of recognized forms of symbolic capital as marginally employed and socially devalued women, home care workers and golf caddies have waged morally laden symbolic struggles aimed at winning recognition for the legitimacy of their claims in the face of opposition. In the following cases, I will explain how both groups of workers discredited the classificatory schemes associated with "independent contracting" by redirecting their struggles away from narrow contractual interpretations to more public understandings about care, social inequality, and injustice. Not only did union struggles draw on recognized signs, symbols, and slogans associated with oppositional unions, but they also drew on support from other social movement actors to illuminate the broader moral implications of workers' struggles for the community at large.

Home Care Workers: Confronting Obstacles to Winning Union Recognition

The Los Angeles campaign to organize home care workers began in 1987 as a strategic, resource-intensive organizing drive under SEIU's Home Care Division. SEIU had experienced success unionizing home care workers in other parts of the country and decided to expand its efforts to Los Angeles, where SEIU had already gained prominence in efforts to unionize the city's low-wage and predominantly immigrant workforce in the janitorial sector. According to Andrew Stern, former organizing director and current SEIU president, "A decade ago people thought we were crazy to try to organize California's 180,000 home-care workers once the courts said they were independent contractors. We said, 'if we can't organize the fastest growing occupation in America, then what does that say about the labor movement?'"[12]

Before the union's intense classification struggle began, organizers faced the daunting task of recruiting members. Verdia Daniels, one of the union's earliest rank-and-file leaders, who later become SEIU Local 434b president, recalls that when she was first contacted by a union organizer, "I thought I was the only home care worker in L.A. County" (Cobb 1999). Unlike traditional workers, home care providers did not share a common workplace; they were isolated in tens of thousands of individual homes and dispersed across 4,061 square miles. To locate potential members, the union sent out a mass mailing, which immediately generated responses. Claudia Johnson, who later became the Local's vice-president, explained, "It was phenomenal…once they saw a flyer or heard about the union, they would call in to the union for more information because we were only getting $3.72 an hour at that time" (Delp and Quan 2002, 6). Organizers also engaged in intensive grassroots organizing tactics such as outreaching face-to-face at markets, bus stops, community centers, and churches. Their outreach to churches was crucial to building community support and providing a centralized meeting space for potential union members to congregate. According to the union's first general manager, Ophelia McFadden, the home care workers campaign was "born in the black churches of Los Angeles.…Ministers provided space for meetings, reassured elderly parishioners about concerns about organizing."[13]

The union also encountered difficulties recruiting members because many home care providers did not see themselves as "workers" in a class-based sense. One organizer recalls, "When I started doing the visits for home care…they [potential union members] wouldn't admit they were home care workers. And I think that's the way we started a lot of our conversations with people, with them not admitting that they were home care workers. They would tell me, 'I'm the daughter, I'm supposed to take care of my mother. I'm the neighbor…'" (Nancy Romero, quoted in Walsh 2002, 12–13). To promote a sense of shared identity and purpose, the union identified the most pressing work-related issue for home care workers: low-wages. In 1987, home care workers received the minimum wage ($3.72 per hour) and no benefits, which was already over 50 percent less than the average wage of the bottom 20 percent of California's workforce at the time. SEIU initiated a statewide political action and grassroots education campaign to raise the California state minimum wage (Delp and Quan 2002, 6–7). For example, in December 1987, hundreds of home care workers participated in a union-organized public rally during a Los Angeles County Board of Supervisors meeting, demanding a raise in the minimum wage. While livelihood issues were an important concern, home care workers were also motivated by concerns about dignity and respect for their clients. According to researcher Rachel Cobb (1999, 2), "Homecare workers place a high value on their service to others, and share a deep concern for their clients. Consequently, in the drive to organize homecare workers, one of the most persuasive arguments for joining the union [was] to generate respect for their clients as well as themselves."

Through a combination of aggressive grassroots organizing strategies, a focused political action campaign, and mass worker mobilizations, SEIU organizers were able to sign up 15,000 workers and hold a founding convention with 1,500 workers by January 15, 1988, reaching their goal of "15/15/15" (Cobb 1999). When the union presented its NLRB petition to the County Board of Supervisors, the Board refused to acknowledge any responsibility as the "employer-of-record." Citing a previous court ruling, the Board stated that home care workers were technically classified as "independent contractors" not "workers"; therefore, neither the county nor any other government entity was obligated to recognize their union or engage in collective bargaining.

Reclassifying Home Care Workers

The SEIU's failure to gain formal recognition for Local 434B from Los Angeles County forced the union to rethink how to proceed. The first difficulty entailed operating a union in the absence of legal recognition. Rather than focus immediately on collective bargaining, SEIU turned the local union office into a centralized venue for advocacy and service-related concerns. The SEIU created a registry designed to help match potential clients with home care providers. The union also helped workers file lawsuits over late paychecks. These efforts were aimed at making the union a valuable resource for home care workers and creating a place for them to congregate and share experiences, which was especially valuable because many home care providers worked in isolation. One home care worker explains, "Sometimes in this job, you feel like you're all alone. You might be with your client 8 hours a day, even longer. You lift them out of bed, put them on the potty, put on their clothes. You pray with them, and you try to keep them from getting too depressed. I don't think most people understand what it's like. At least here in the union, you meet other people who are going through the same thing."[14]

The union also continued to mobilize members to win basic improvements in wages and working conditions. After winning a statewide minimum wage increase to $4.25 in 1988, the union turned its attention to wage violations. Union members held a series of demonstrations demanding the county's IHSS department improve the payroll system, especially the way in which it dispensed late paychecks to home care workers. Public pressure helped home care workers secure an initial set of concessions from Los Angeles County, including an agreement to establish a countywide home care provider registry, provide health insurance, and grant a small wage increase.[15] In late 1989, the union won another set of incremental gains, including the authority to collect dues from home care workers' paychecks, which provided a more stable foundation for the expansion of the local's membership base. According to Local 434B General Manager Ophelia McFadden, these early successes helped "ground the operation and galvanize the membership. People started realizing what could be done collectively" (Delp and Quan 2002, 7). The following year, SEIU signed up 5,000 additional members.

The second difficulty was reclassifying the employment status of home care workers. Although the consumers represented a possible employer whom the union could pressure for recognition, neither their dispersed nor vulnerable status made them a likely choice. "Consumers, who by definition need to be impoverished in order to qualify for IHSS, did not have any resources to improve wages and benefits. Furthermore, negotiating with each individual consumer was a legal and organizational impossibility" (Rivas 2005, 5). Instead, SEIU legal counsel filed suit against Los Angeles County. Richard McCracken, the San Francisco labor lawyer who prepared the suit, argued that the county should be deemed the official employer because it already set workers' wage rates, determined their hours, wrote their paychecks, maintained their employment records, and regulated working hours.[16] The union's legal battles in California courts, however, faced many dead ends. Their 1988 suit as well as their 1991 appeal failed. Despite existing precedents for deeming the county the official bargaining agent for home care workers, the "law was quite confused as to who was and who was not the employer for various purposes" (Cobb 1999, 3). Amanda Figueroa, a home care worker who testified in front of the Los Angeles County Board of Supervisors in 2002, explained that the legal confusion surrounding their employment status made home care workers feel like " 'ping-pong balls' tossed between the state and county, neither of which was willing to accept fiscal responsibility for wage increases or benefit coverage."[17]

Rather than pursue a narrow litigation strategy, the union changed course and focused its efforts on building an alliance with consumer groups (see Rivas 2005; Delp and Quan 2002, 11–14). Initially, disability rights and elder advocates worried that working with the union would threaten consumer autonomy and control over the quality of care. Hale Zukas, a disability rights movement leader, stated, "We were clear that unionization would be good for [personal attendants], we just weren't sure if it would be good for us" (quoted in Rivas 2005, 13). Home care workers justified the importance of their demands as both a livelihood and a quality-of-care issue. Theresa Edwards, who cared for two women in their nineties and a younger client who had been left partly paralyzed by a stroke, was paid for 291 hours a month, which did not include the bus commute between her clients, who lived in South-Central, Los Angeles, and Santa Monica. She explained, "I'm a nurse, a mother, a cook and more for these people. I do it because I like working with people, and they need someone to help them. But I have to live too."[18]

Threats to the independent consumer service model and to public funding for home care assistance strengthened the mutual interests of home care workers and consumers against the state. The National Home Health Care Corporation proposed to take over the cost and operation of the state's home care services as an external contractor. Consumers viewed the elimination of the independent provider model as a direct loss of consumer autonomy in the care of their bodies and lives. Disability rights activist, Lillibeth Navarro, explained, "We did not want to see IHSS become like an HMO [health maintenance organization], where companies come in and dictate the hours, what's to be done and for how long."[19] What is more, a 12 percent reduction in the state's IHSS budget in October 1991 heightened a state of crisis among consumer advocates, sparking the formation of a "spontaneous caucus between various representatives of disability rights, senior rights, and the union" (Rivas 2005, 6–7).

To preserve the independent service provider model of elderly and disability care, consumer advocates and the union formally collaborated on an innovative legislative strategy that laid the groundwork for an alternative route toward identifying Los Angeles County as the formal "employer-of-record" for home care workers.[20] After much research, they recommended creation of county-level public authorities who could ensure better quality and care for the state's 200,000 plus recipients of IHSS benefits.[21] Despite the legislature's initial orientation toward the contract mode of IHSS delivery, in 1992, the California Senate passed SB 485, the Public Authorities Act. This Act allowed the creation of a "new quasi-governmental entity—an unprecedented 'home care public authority'—with a sole focus on IHSS delivery issues" at the county level (Heinritz-Canterbury 2002, 4, 7). In addition to establishing a consumer-majority board to oversee the public authority, an official registry to match consumers with home care providers and to provide both consumers and workers access to training, SB 485 created a provision that allowed for the creation of public authorities as the official employer-of-record for home care workers.

Publicly Escalating the Home Care Workers' Classification Struggle

Despite this historic policy victory, SB 485 did not automatically result in the creation of a formal employer for home care workers. Under SB 485, every individual county had the option to create a public authority. Counties were not, however, mandated by law to do so. Los Angeles County was particularly unreceptive to the idea of creating a public authority and bearing the fiscal and administrative responsibility for its operation and maintenance. To escalate its classification struggle against the county, SEIU hired David Rolf as the local's general manager to lay the groundwork for an ensuing public drama. For Rolf, the Los Angeles County Board of Supervisors' refusal to create its own public authority was directly connected to the continued invisibility and marginality of home care workers in the urban polity; although SB 485 provided the legal framework for the Local to secure union recognition, home care workers had yet to be regarded as a community worthy of limited county resources.

To "sway" the Board of Supervisors' attitude toward creating its own public authority, the Local framed the union's struggle to create an employer-of-record as a broad-based public issue. To shift the site of struggle from the policy to the public arena, one of the first orders of union business was to repair its relationship with consumer groups. Although consumer advocates and union leaders worked together closely on policy measures, their relationship quickly disintegrated after the passage of SB 485. According to researcher Jess Walsh (2001, 227), "the coalition was challenged by the lack of fit between the structures and processes of the union with those of the disability community." The union found it difficult to work with the individualistic and loose network of disability rights advocates that lacked an entity to which it was accountable; disability rights advocates criticized the SEIU's bureaucracy and lack of transparency as well as its failure to view them as "equal partners."

To mend relations with consumer advocates, Local 434B began attending social functions in disability and senior advocacy circles. "From early 1996,

SEIU organizers and rank-and-file activists went to senior dances and bingo sessions, Alzheimer's groups, polio groups, and senior citizen housing complexes; it also organized community town hall meetings" (Walsh 2001, 228). The Local also recognized its previous failure to treat consumer advocates as "equal partners" in the coalition and sought to improve transparency and communication. During its public confrontations with County officials, the Local and consumer groups framed their political alliance as one that benefited all of Los Angeles, from elderly and disabled consumers in need of vital assisted living services to low-wage workers deserving of decent and fair working conditions. According to Kirk Adams, former AFL-CIO director of organizing and early architect of SEIU's home care organizing campaign, "Homecare organizing...is much broader than an organizing issue. It is also a policy issue—how will we care for the elderly in our society? Will we put the burden on families who must make do with limited resources? Do we expect women to provide their services as an act of faith which we will take advantage of? Or are we willing to commit the funding to reimburse providers adequately for the services they provide?" (quoted in Delp and Quan 2002, 5).

To make home care workers a more visible public force, the Local focused on improving their internal organizing capacity and on cultivating workers' leadership skills. Since the union's early years, the Local had focused on overcoming the invisibility and marginalization of home care workers. According to union shop steward Rosie Byers, "We're interested in taking home care workers from the back burner to the front burner. We are not only concerned about wages and benefits; we also want home care workers to be recognized for the work they do."[22] However, since 1993, the union had invested little energy into fostering active member participation. To address this problem, the Local began training members—whom they designated as "member political organizers" (MPOs)—to actively participate and take a leadership role in the union. According to Teresa Lingafelter (2003, 4–5), "MPOs take action at their worksite[s] in the neighborhoods, on the phone in the call center and through e-mail; to educate other members and their families, to get out the vote on Election Day, register members to vote, build community coalitions, recruit volunteers, and raise COPE (Committee on Political Education) funds."

The Local also reinitiated their statewide political action campaign to raise the California minimum wage, which had remained at $4.25 since 1988. In March 1996, the Local organized home care workers to support Proposition 210, which aimed to raise the statewide minimum wage to $5.15 per hour. Grassroots outreach was an important component of its political mobilization. Local 434B organized members to collect 80,000 signatures to put on the election ballot. The Local also educated members about candidates running for office, organized precinct walks to educate other voters, and "even ran an election campaign from the Local's office" (Walsh 2002, 228).

Redefining unionization into a broad-based community issue strengthened the union's position in its classification struggle against Los Angeles County. The support of religious and consumer groups, community-based organizations, and local politicians was pivotal in pressuring Los Angeles County to accept responsibility as home care workers' formal "employer-of-record" (Delp and Quan 2002, 8). Ten years after its organizing drive began, the County Board of Supervisors unanimously voted to establish a fifteen-member public authority (including eight clients)—the Personal Assistance Services Council (PASC)—to act as legal "employer-of-record" for the county's home care workforce. According to L.A. County Supervisor, Zev Yaroslavsky, who wrote the 1997 ordinance, unionization was a crucial element in protecting a highly vulnerable and marginalized workforce: "Without being organized, these workers are vulnerable. They work unorthodox hours. They certainly have unorthodox demands placed on them by their clients. In order to protect their quality of life and the quality of their workplace, given the incredibly difficult work involved, it makes sense for them to be represented by a union."[23]

After winning its classification struggle, the union took swift steps to formally unionize home care workers. Local 434B hired twenty-two full-time organizers, bringing seventy-five additional organizers from other locals. To locate workers to vote in a union election, Local 434B used a variety of tactics such as polling, focus groups, electoral maps, canvassing, phone banks, telemarketing, and direct mail. Local union meetings helped build the basis for new organizing committees and member-organizers who outreached door-to-door and talked to over 30,000 workers at home to spread the union message. The union also gathered workers together for neighborhood meetings in libraries, churches, and community centers. Through these efforts, the union collected 10,600 signatures and created forty local chapters. After securing enough cards to demonstrate a "showing of interest," the Local then petitioned the PASC to hold a union election.[24]

On February 25, 1999, Local 434b won the right to legally represent 74,000 home care workers in the county. The union then secured a collective bargaining agreement, which raised wages to $6.75 per hour and, for the first time, provided health and medical benefits to county home care workers. From the perspective of public officials, the results of the election were more than just about the union. According to the future Los Angeles mayor, Antonio Villaraigosa, "Part of this is about crafting a future where all the boats rise together."[25] For SEIU Local 434B General Manager David Rolf, "[The victory] has implications that are fascinating and wonderful for the life of the labor movement. We're talking about low-wage workers, women of color and immigrant workers—the largest segment of the labor pool in Southern California. It's the kind of workforce that has to be brought into the labor movement."[26]

Golf Caddies: Challenging Discrimination

Unlike home care workers, golf caddies were not considered a strategic organizing target by national unions in South Korea. In fact, their existence to the broader labor movement was largely unknown. Only when a group of golf caddies at 88 Country Club (88CC) mobilized against management, with the key support of seasoned women worker activists from the Korean Women Workers Association (KWWAU), did the union organizing campaign take off. Golf caddies who had worked for some of the wealthiest of Korea's elite experienced highly unregulated employment conditions for years. When an immediate grievance over gender and age discrimination unleashed these accumulated feelings of deprivation and injustice, golf caddies demonstrated that they could be just as militant as the 650,000 other union members who were the driving force of the Korean Confederation of Trade Unions (KCTU)-led democratic labor movement.

The golf caddies' struggle began in 1999, after the 88CC management ordered the dismissal of all caddies over the age of forty under the rationale that they were too "old" to avoid accidents and were thus unfit for the job. The management's actions followed an incident that occurred the previous year when a caddie over the age of forty broke her leg on the job. For the twelve women directly affected by the "forced early age retirement" policy, the management's action was viewed as an example of blatant discrimination. According to one of the dismissed golf caddies, Kwang Soon Lee, the managers did not investigate whether or not the accident was due to faulty machinery. Rather, they used it as an excuse to hire "young caddies with pretty faces."[27] Another worker explained, "Management told us that customers did not want old caddies. But, I could not understand. This is a specialist job, why does age matter? And in fact, older women who have worked as golf game assistants have more experience that make them better at their job. Service should not be defined by one's body."[28] Despite the fact that golf caddies were subject to insulting treatment from customers and society at large, "these women took pride in their job expertise."[29] Thus, when management treated them as "sexualized objects" rather than as professionals, the twelve dismissed workers began taking concrete steps to fight their dismissals.

The initial efforts of dismissed golf caddies to join the existing union at 88CC were rejected on the grounds that golf caddies were not direct employees of the company. The dismissed golf caddies then turned to the KWWAU's Action Center for Unemployment, which was formed in the aftermath of the "IMF crisis" when a disproportionate number of women, particularly socially marginalized women, were the targets of discriminatory job loss and abusive employer practices. With the help of a veteran KWWAU women worker activist, Choi Sang Rim, the dismissed caddies formed an organization called "Chang Po Hoi" (Iris Group) and began a fourteen-day collective struggle for reinstatement. They hung posters on 88CC company walls at dawn before everyone else arrived, and they wrote letters to the president, managers, and other caddies to publicize their unjust dismissals. Their actions were met with hostile resistance. Managers tore down the posters and hurled insults and threats at protesting golf caddies. Despite the 88CC's intimidation tactics, two weeks later, the 88CC management submitted to the protesting golf caddies' demands (but never apologized) and allowed all twelve women to resume their work.

Although this particular labor dispute was resolved, members of Chang Poi Hoi began discussing the need for a union. Initially, many workers were averse to the idea. Even when choosing a name for their group, golf caddies rejected names like Dandelion (*Mindŭle*), a common symbol of resistance and resilience in South Korea due to the flower's fast-growing and ever-present nature. The golf caddies did not initially want to be associated with such symbols of activism. However, when Chang Poi Hoi leaders learned that the Korean Women's Trade Union (KWTU) was being established in close association with KWWAU specifically to organize nonstandard women workers, they decided it was the right time to start a union and convinced other golf caddies to join.[30] Planning for the establishment of a women's trade union had been in place for years as a direct response to the widespread neglect of women workers, particularly those most vulnerable to exploitation, on the parts of male-dominated and large enterprise-based unions (see chapter 4). The KWTU encouraged women workers to join "regardless of their workplace, the type of work they do, and the region they work in," making the affiliation process a relatively smooth one. In October 1999, sixty golf game assistants pledged to join the union and 88CC registered an official branch union under the KWTU.

Like home care workers, the dispersed and isolated working conditions of golf game assistants required the union to cultivate a sense of collective solidarity both with other golf caddies and with the union. Although golf caddies did not work in separate locations, they worked in relative isolation from one another throughout the day, accompanying different golfers on the course during staggered tee times. In addition, while some golf caddies had worked at 88CC for many years, others viewed the opportunity to earn a fair amount of cash quickly as a temporary solution to a difficult period in their life. Thus, to cultivate a group consciousness as "workers" and "union members," the KWTU held meetings, trainings, and gatherings that emphasized the importance of relationship building, women's leadership, and self-empowerment. KWTU leaders held discussions and trainings about the meaning of one's status as a "worker," the role of labor unions in securing basic labor rights for caddies, and labor law more broadly. They also discussed the many problems related to working at 88CC, including verbal, physical, and sexual harassment by supervisors and clients, poor working conditions, and unnecessary health hazards such as exposure to pesticides sprayed on the greens.

In her internal report on the 88CC branch union, KWWAU researcher Jin Young Park describes the effectiveness of strategies such as "team meetings" in which union representatives met with members in informal settings: "These small meetings were [held] at dinner tables in a comfortable atmosphere [to overcome] women's reluctance to speak in a formal meeting. [Union leaders] tried to encourage the members to express everything they wanted to say." The union activities were a crucial component in cultivating a sense of ownership and collectivity in the union. One union leader explained, "To be informed fully and do everything together is really important. When you follow the union without knowing the reason, you will regret it and be discontent" (Park et al. 2001). Thus, as in the case of home care workers, forging a "class" identity required a deeper understanding of (1) the factors contributing to the subordinated and unequal position of golf game assistants as "workers" and (2) the importance of challenging "unjust power relationships" through collective organizing and solidarity.

Reclassifying Golf Caddies as "Workers"

Unlike the home care workers' unionizing drive, however, the golf game assistants' classification struggle was not aimed at defining a formal employer-of-record. Rather, its goal was to force the 88CC management to recognize their union as a "legitimate and equal party" with which it was legally required to engage in good faith bargaining. In this sense, the classification struggle of golf caddies more closely resembled that of a more typical union organizing drive in South Korea, especially one waged by workers in more vulnerable occupations and workplaces. Although union leaders were careful to maintain a low profile, especially during the low season for golfing, news about the formation of the 88CC golf game assistants branch union reached management.

Like the Los Angeles County Board of Supervisors, the 88CC management refused to recognize the golf caddies' union on contractual grounds. During their first meeting with union representatives, management representatives refused to negotiate with golf caddies under the rationale that they are not "real workers." Management considered golf caddies to be "independent contractors" providing services to clients, who compensated them directly with "tips." They were not, management argued, legally recognized "workers" with the right to form unions and demand collective bargaining rights.

While the union prepared to bring legal suit against 88 Tourism Development, Inc., (88CC's parent company), management began actively and aggressively trying to "break the union" through personal intimidation and direct threats to union members. In a typical anti-union fashion, the 88CC management also suspended eleven union leaders for periods ranging from three months to indefinitely on April 25, 2000. Management argued that union members "illegally" organized meetings during work hours and that they had physically assaulted company managers.

Up until this point, many other golf caddies still "had nothing to do with the union." However, the management's "outrageous" accusations and outright dismissal of eleven union leaders led to widespread feelings of indignation and anger.[31] In May, the 88CC branch union almost unanimously voted (92.7 percent) in favor of a strike. Although most union members did not expect to win, they explained that the strike was for "justice and dignity" (Park et al. 2001). Union members organized pickets on company grounds, collected signatures petitioning for reinstatement for the eleven dismissed workers, raised strike funds, and prepared meals for striking workers.

As they had before, management responded to union militancy with intense employer repression. On May 13, 2000, eleven union leaders were assaulted on company grounds by fifteen male employees. "Company-hired thugs" barged into the lobby, destroyed all the union's literature, and kicked and stepped on protesting workers. One manager justified the violence, stating "caddies are not like other women who will just take a beating."[32] This aggressive and inflammatory anti-unionism was not unlike many other cases of unionism in South Korea, particularly in smaller workplaces where there was a clear power imbalance between workers and management. The gendered aspects of the company's anti-union stance was also familiar to many female-led union struggles since the 1970s. The union strengthened its claims by repeatedly calling attention to the harassment and violence directed against it. In this way, unlike home care workers' struggle to define an employer-of-record, the classification struggle of golf caddies was deeply rooted in a historical sensibility about how gender and class warfare is waged in South Korea.

Escalating Golf Caddies' Classification Struggle

To strengthen their positional advantage against the 88CC management, the union escalated their struggle to more public venues, including the busy shopping district in Myongdong where union activists wore protest banners and passed out flyers about their ongoing labor dispute with the 88CC to the general public. 88CC branch union members also held public protests in front of downtown government buildings such as Ministry of Labor, demanding that golf caddies be recognized by the law as legitimate workers. Advocates from KWWAU and KWTU not only supported their public protests in solidarity but also brought signed petitions that had been collected since January 2000 by the "Committee Advocating Labor Rights for Women in Irregular Employment." This committee demanded that the LSA be applied to golf caddies as well as other "specially employed" workers. Kim Kyung Sook, the 88CC branch union general secretary, emphasized, "Could those at the Ministry of Labor or the Labor Committee work for just three months as a golf game assistant and then not make a decision based on the actual reality [that golf caddies are workers]?"[33]

Although the Ministry of Labor avoided making a decision for nearly five months, it finally released a statement on May 17, 2000, reading that "The caddies of 88CC are workers in accordance with the Labor Standards Act." The Ministry of Labor then ordered 88 Tourism Development, Inc., to "withdraw unfair disciplinary measures" and ordered 88CC management to "provide lunch for the caddies, an office for the union, guarantee the union's activities and maternity leave, prepare measures against sexual harassment, reconstruct the working conditions which had worsened since the strike[,] and withdraw complaints it had made to the Labor Department."[34]

Despite the clarity of the Ministry of Labor's decision, this ruling did not immediately pressure the 88CC management to submit to the union's demands. However, the Ministry of Labor's decision did intensify the resolve and perseverance of union members as the conflict continued to escalate.[35] Shin Yoon-Ja, president of the 88CC trade union explained, "I always viewed my employer as a special hero to be afraid of who inhabited a different world. But not anymore. They are just the same as us. Now I can speak up for myself and get angry at their unjust treatment of us. My colleagues and I are now recognized as workers."[36] After forty-three days of intense conflict, management shut down the entire facility and finally agreed to participate in collective negotiations. On July 12, 2002, the 88CC golf caddies branch union signed its first collective bargaining agreement with 88 Tourism Development, Inc. The bargaining agreement included the following provisions: (1) recognition of the 88CC branch of the KWTU as the only representative body for collective bargaining, (2) agreement to discuss matters related to golf caddies with the union, (3) guarantee of the right of the union to conduct its activities, (4) measures for the prevention of sexual harassment by employers and clients, (5) permission for golf caddies to wear glasses, (6) commitment to better treatment for golf bag carriers, (7) permission for union members to have access to golf courses for their own recreational use.[37] While the resolution of this struggle reflects a familiar example of militant unionism, it was nonetheless critical to validating the class status of golf game assistants as "workers."

By 2002, over two-thirds of golf game assistants at 88 Country Club had joined the union, providing it with substantial leverage in that year's round of contract negotiations, when management proposed to invest in equipment that would seriously undermine working conditions and job security. They proposed to introduce golf carts that would reduce the number of workers from 180 to approximately 130, and to install lights around the golf course that would significantly increase working hours. With strength in numbers, the union was prepared to engage in collective action once again. General Secretary Kim Kyung Sook describes their position: "If golf game assistants work [double shifts] the intensity of work would be too severe and golf game assistants would not last more than two or three years....In order to halt the deterioration of working conditions, we have no choice but to fight."[38]

The members of 88CC branch union voted once more to mount a collective struggle against the club. Comfortable in the knowledge that they had the law on their side, 88CC branch union leaders felt confident in their ability to challenge their management's abusive and unfair tactics. Having discovered in the previous struggle that 88 Country Club was actually a public corporation called 88 Tourism Development, Inc., and was managed by the National Social and Welfare Ministry for Veterans, the KWTU held public protests in front of the Ministry of Veterans building in downtown Seoul to exert additional pressure on the 88CC management to recognize and negotiate with the union. After twenty days of picketing and marching across the country club grounds, the union signed a collective agreement on August 31, 2002. In this agreement, the company agreed to enroll golf game assistants for accident insurance and to assume responsibility for the entire cost. They also agreed to stop favoring non-union members on the basis that doing so was indeed a form of discrimination against union members.

The Symbolic Leverage of Labor's Classification Struggles

Both home care workers and golf caddies continued their struggle despite initial legal failures to be recognized as unions. A key component of each case was an escalated classification struggle that challenged narrow contractual arguments that denied both groups union recognition. After failing to make Los Angeles County the formal employer for home care workers, SEIU Local 434B created broad-based political alliances with consumer advocates to pressure the state of California to allow individual counties to create their own "public authorities" to act as official "employers-of-record" for home care workers. While its top-down, policy-driven approach was critical in securing collective labor rights for home care workers, it is important to note that it took the home care workers' union almost five years to cultivate enough pressure to force Los Angeles County to accept this responsibility. A key part of this effort was to publicly mobilize home care workers *and* consumer advocates into a visible community force capable of holding public officials accountable to the needs and interests of constituent groups; namely, consumers and caregivers.

The KWTU 88CC golf caddies branch union also escalated public pressure against the 88CC management and various national government offices to secure recognition and a collective agreement for its union members. With the help of veteran activists in KWTU and KWWAU, golf caddies waged militant and public struggles to expose their discriminatory employment status and to condemn belligerent managers and the state for depriving workers of their basic labor rights. Their militant struggles reflected the oppositional tactics and political spirit of the democratic unions of the 1970s and 1970s, which forced repressive employers and state regimes to recognize independent unions.

The specific ways in which workers in each national context strengthened the legitimacy of their oppositional claims are clarified by examining the trajectories of union struggles once initial victories were secured. In the case of home care workers, although unionization signified a historic victory, SEIU Local 434B faced many challenges in its future efforts to secure wage and benefit gains for the county's highly underpaid home care workforce. As part of the SEIU's statewide lobbying efforts, in 1999, SEIU convinced Governor Gray

Davis to allocate $100 million to raise the wages of home care workers, which provided for an increase of $7.50 plus $0.60 in benefits an hour. However, the state's offer of $1 per hour wage increases over the next four years was contingent on a matching commitment from Los Angeles County. County officials, however, refused to allocate any additional moneys for home care workers wages: "We are not the deep pocket, the state's the deep pocket," said Supervisor Zev Yaroslavsky, comparing the state's $12.3 billion surplus to the county's $48 million.[39]

To escalate pressure against the county, the union took its campaign to the streets of Los Angeles. As in the case of janitors, the union launched an intense public campaign that exposed the city's unwillingness to ensure quality care and dignified living standards to important members of the Los Angeles community. The home care workers' union also argued that home care workers saved the county valuable dollars because they allowed clients to live in their homes rather than in costly state-run facilities. During the spring of 2000, the union spent twelve weeks marching, rallying, writing letters, and holding vigils. It even set up a tent city in downtown Los Angeles. During public demonstrations, home care workers marched with their clients, some of whom were in wheelchairs, and demanded respectable living conditions for themselves and those they cared for. The following fall (September 2000), the union won a $0.50 wage increase for all home care workers; however, $6.75 per hour was below the union's demand of $7.50 per hour and still far below the level of a living wage. Tyrone Freeman, the general manager of Local 434B, told the county's supervisors, "You have taken a step....However...our struggle and our quest for a respectable wage has not been respected."[40]

SEIU officials continued their policy battles at the state level and secured the passage of AB 1682, landmark legislation requiring all California counties to establish a public authority that could serve as an employer-of-record for IHSS home care workers. Meanwhile, SEIU Local 434B escalated its efforts to secure a living wage for its low-wage, immigrant members.[41] In the summer of 2001, SEIU Local 434B members were active participants in the AFL-CIO–endorsed Immigrant Freedom Ride, a nationally coordinated event that sought to resurrect the spirit of the 1960s civil rights movement freedom rider, who rode racially integrated buses across state lines to protest racial segregation laws. During the Immigrant Freedom Ride, approximately 900 immigrant workers and their allies boarded buses in major U.S. cities and rode across 20,000 miles of U.S. highways to protest anti-immigrant attacks and demand decent wages and benefits for immigrant workers. According to Amanda Figueroa, former home care worker and the secretary treasurer of Local 434B, "Just as the Freedom Rides of the 1960s revived the cultural consciousness of the nation, we hope to create a climate that rewards the contributions of immigrant workers who make up this great nation."[42] In the fall of 2003, SEIU Local 434B also launched the "Poor People's Campaign" in Los Angeles—a coalition made up of labor, civil rights, community, elected officials, clergy, and business leaders—to "revive Dr. Martin Luther King Jr.'s historic effort to address and resolve poverty and the injustices workers and communities suffer."[43] The Poor People's Campaign was more than just a response to Governor Arnold Schwarzenegger's proposals to eliminate the IHSS program and to decrease wages to $6.75 per hour. According to General Manager Tyrone Freeman, it was a call to "all Angelinos… to act" to eradicate all the injustices of poverty in Los Angeles.[44]

Sustained pressure against public agencies also influenced the trajectory of unionism after the 88CC golf caddies' struggle. After the 88CC branch union was formed, golf caddies at country clubs around South Korea also initiated unionization efforts. However, despite the 88CC branch union's success in gaining recognition from the Ministry of Labor as legitimate workers, these would-be unions faced greater difficulties. Court interpretations in Pusan and other regions rendered contradictory rulings about the status of golf caddies as legally recognized workers. A ruling by the Seoul Regional Court on August 21, 2001, also overturned a previous ruling by the Kyonggi Regional Courts that recognized the right of golf caddies as workers to hold employers responsible for unfair labor practices (Kwon 2001).

Such contradictory rulings at the regional level highlighted the need for a uniform, national standard applicable to all workers, regardless of regional location. The KWTU tried to make this happen by pursuing a larger, more ambitious national strategy to organize a broader range of nonstandard workers. This campaign strived to include not only golf game assistants but also other "specially employed" workers such as home-based tutors and insurance salespersons in the protections mandated by the LSA. In March 2000, during the women workers' assembly, the Committee Advocating Labor Rights for Women in Irregular Employment was launched. The committee began a petition campaign calling for the LSA to be applied to women workers under "special employment conditions." It argued that because women workers are not protected by the LSA, they are denied even the most basic labor rights, such as the right to get paid on time, to be protected from unreasonable dismissals, gender discrimination, employer abuse, and to enjoy the right to maternity protection. Other women's organizations such as the KWWAU and WomenLink Korea also joined together to create the Committee on the Promotion of Basic Labor Rights and the Prevention of Discrimination against Nonstandard Workers.

In 2001, the KWTU, KWWAU, and other women's organizations joined together with major trade union organizations and hosted solidarity events calling for national attention to be paid to the issue of gender discrimination and non-standard employment. On March 3, 2001, the KWWAU and KWTU embarked on a ten-day nationwide bus tour to commemorate International Women's Day. They held rallies and cultural festivals in nine major cities, calling for "the abolishment of part-time work and the application of labor laws to contract workers—the end to the devastating consequences of IMF restructuring that struck Korean women workers."[45] The KCTU also hosted a National Women Workers' Rally on March 10, 2001, which gathered 1,000 workers under their union flags: "The speeches were filled with horrifying stories of the oppression and exploitation of women under the IMF prescription and the Kim Dae Jung government. Lay-offs, transfers to part-time work, the attempt to abolish or de-crease maternity and menstruation leave were the main targets of the rally."[46]

Conclusion: Redefining Who a "Worker" Is through Symbolic Leverage

The "particular" nature of these cases frequently raises concerns about their "exceptional" character in relation to other union struggles in each respective national context. For example, some would argue that because home care workers were not confronted by a hostile, private-sector employer applying direct intimidation during the course of the campaign, the union was able to pursue creative and diverse strategies to escalate political pressure against its targeted employer. Others might argue that the union's successful collaboration with consumer advocates in creating public authorities that could act as formal bargaining agents for independently contracted home care workers highlighted the importance of cultivating formal political leverage in support of union struggles. Likewise, some would argue that because the 88 Country Club operated under the jurisdiction of a national governmental office, the National Social and Welfare Ministry for Veterans, the union's demands for state intervention were imbued with more political weight than would have been the case for golf game assistants at private country clubs.

While these particularities are useful and necessary for understanding the complexities of each organizing campaign, they do not discount the importance of the union's classification struggles in strengthening the associational power of so-called independent contractors. By applying the symbols, slogans, and strategies associated with oppositional unionism, both the SEIU and the

KWTU were able to reconstruct the class identity of home care workers and golf game assistants, respectively, into recognized social groups who possessed the right to form trade unions and secure concessions from a targeted employer. In the United States, home care workers circumvented legal barriers to unionization by bringing voice and visibility to the "invisible" workforce of immigrant women in low-paid home care work. In South Korea golf caddies drew on the moral discourses and historical experiences of past democratic union struggles—as well as the women worker activists that were directly involved in them—to expose the continued discrimination against women workers in "hidden" forms of nonstandard employment.

In both cases, redefining the status of "independent contractors" into workers through the process of unionization and collective bargaining also entailed eliciting the intervention of broader sectors of society. The struggle of home care workers was about more than pay increases and job security; it was about the quality of public health care, the dignity of work, and the everyday living conditions of poor and disadvantaged workers, many of whom were women of color. Likewise, the struggle of golf caddies was about the pervasiveness of gender discrimination against vulnerable groups of women workers and the need to expose the continued links between employment discrimination and gender discrimination. By recasting the seemingly negative state of marginality for both groups of workers into recognized forms of social injustice, unions in each case were able to begin securing improvements in the material conditions of workers' lives.

In the final chapter, I discuss the significance of marginality for the future of both the Korean and U.S. labor movements.

7

DILEMMAS OF ORGANIZING WORKERS AT THE MARGINS

This book has sought to compare the seemingly incomparable: labor movements in South Korea and the United States. For most of the twentieth century, the U.S. labor movement has stood as a stark exception to other parts of the world. Whether characterized by a relative absence of class consciousness or exceptional employer hostility toward labor radicalism, its trajectory—up until the 1970s—reflected a steady path toward bureaucratic, service-oriented unionism in which unions traded better wages and benefits for industrial peace. Since then, however, organized labor's compromises with capital and the state have resulted in a continued deluge of job losses as well as wage and benefit concessions. Today, any mention of the U.S. labor movement includes at least a passing remark about its dismal state of decline over the past fifty years—from roughly one in three unionized workers to barely one in twelve in the private sector.

By contrast, the South Korean labor movement is commonly viewed as one of the most militant and mobilized in the world. As in other late industrializing countries such as South Africa and Brazil, Korean workers capitalized on their growing leverage at the point of production to help topple authoritarian regimes. Since the late 1987 transition to an electoral democracy, Korean unionists have wielded the strike to routinely bring Korean capital to its knees. Today, references to the Korean labor movement, especially by pro-business interests, usually mention the billions of dollars of production losses incurred when unionized workers at the ports, factories, hotels, and retail stores walk off the job.

Despite these clear and important distinctions, stopping our analysis here overlooks striking convergences taking place in this unlikely pair of countries in the twilight decades of the twentieth century. In both South Korea and the United States, unionized workers have witnessed renewed employer offensives amid intensified global competition, transnational capital mobility, and financial liberalization. Both groups have also experienced declining wage and employment standards under state regimes that increasingly favor the interests of organized capital over organized labor. Perhaps most surprisingly, the shifting character of employment growth has dramatically redefined the priorities of crisis-ridden labor movements in each country. Whereas the interests of manufacturing-based workers in traditional union strongholds largely determined the direction of the broader labor movement, the ability to organize less powerful workers, especially the growing ranks employed in vastly nonunion service-producing sectors, now serves as a crucial barometer of change. To put it simply, at the dawn of the twenty-first century each labor movement is tackling the daunting challenge of organizing the weak, instead of the strong.

The emphasis on workers at the margins reflects a decisive yet paradoxical shift. Rather than question *whether* it is possible to organize more vulnerable segments of the workforce such as immigrants and women, the debate has shifted to exactly *how* and *under what conditions* the powerless can leverage any power at all. This book has sought to address this problematic by comparing concrete cases of labor organizing by marginalized workers in two different countries and situating them in the context of broader shifts in the balance of power among labor, capital, and the state. In doing so, I have outlined two major findings: First, rather than limit the discussion of labor and globalization to transnational capital mobility and free trade agendas, a comparative historical analysis of the South Korean and U.S. labor movements shows that processes of globalization are synonymous with the reconfiguration of local and national hierarchies. This does not refer only to the regulatory role of states in promoting the market-driven practices of neoliberal capital at the expense of public welfare and the common good. It also pertains to the renewed vigor of social movement communities, including within organized labor, toward preserving the dignity and well-being of the poor, excluded, and disenfranchised.

Second, an in-depth inquiry into workers' struggles at the margins reveals that symbolic leverage provides an avenue for the relatively powerless to transform the material circumstances of their jobs and livelihoods. Although differences in the levels of analysis, characteristics of participants, sequence of events, and issues at stake hinder a precise comparative assessment of all the ethnographic cases I examined, these cases demonstrate that workers in even the most atypical forms of employment can attempt to circumvent existing rules and procedures to reconfigure the relations of power and inequality that underpin flexible work arrangements. Key to this process is the ability to reclassify the nature of employer-employee relationships in the eyes of the public, rather than remain in the purview of contractual interpretation. Redirecting the site of struggle from narrowly defined workplace disputes to public contestations over values and meanings also helps revalue the identities and social worth of traditionally disadvantaged workers. Although these efforts might not directly subvert existing hierarchies and inequalities, they generate voice and visibility for previously neglected individuals, infusing demands for redistribution with demands for recognition (Fraser 1995).

While these cases reveal the empirical and theoretical significance of workers' struggles at the margins, it would be naïve and presumptuous to claim that the margins represent some untapped reservoir of power; or that the deeply debilitating dilemmas facing organized labor in the current global economy can be resolved by simply unleashing the power of the excluded and disenfranchised. All the cases reveal that workers at the margins of society and economy do not have power in the conventional sense. Not only is their ability to exercise basic labor rights commonly disputed on legal and contractual grounds, but their location at the lower tiers of labor market hierarchies exposes them to forms of mistreatment and exploitation that are either all too familiar or tucked away from the public eye. The mere fact that marginalized workers face overlapping conditions of economic and social subordination presumes their access to existing structures of power and authority are already constrained. Given these myriad impediments, what, then, can we take away about the broader implications of workers' struggles at the margins?

Symbolic Leverage for What?

One possible implication of the dynamism of marginalized workers' struggles is that *symbolic leverage* has, once again, become a dominant feature of labor politics and organization. Throughout history, workers and their collective organizations have cultivated mutual solidarity between workers and with the broader community as the basis of their power. Mass protests, symbolic actions, morally laden discourses, and vibrant strike communities have all been part of workers' organizational and cultural repertoires, especially during earlier phases of capitalist industrialization in the late nineteenth and early twentieth centuries. The creation of labor law and social welfare frameworks in many industrialized countries since the 1930s channeled contentious worker politics into more contained bureaucratic avenues for redressing workplace grievances. However, as Rick Fantasia (1988, 61–62) reminds us, despite the fact that militant strikes in the United States were largely "driven underground" after World War II, when confronted with employer opposition to adjudicating workers' grievances through existing bureaucratic channels, rank-and-file union members continued to resort to "wildcat strikes" that spilled over from their workplaces into the wider communities.

In the current climate of widespread anti-unionism, it is no surprise that workers in South Korea and the United States have once again resorted to morally driven and publicly escalated tactics as well as broad-based solidarity. Similar to the pre–New Deal era in the United States and state-led authoritarian developmental era in South Korea, workers are confronted with mounting employer (and state) resistance when they attempt to exercise basic forms of associational power. Not only do labor laws fail to protect workers' legally entitled rights to form unions and negotiate collective bargaining agreements in the absence of employer intimidation, but the ambiguous and contradictory features of nonstandard employment arrangements also exclude the growing ranks of low-paid service workers from accessing similar labor protections and benefits as other workers. Thus, when existing institutional channels for adjudicating workers' grievances are blocked or constrained, my cases reveal that workers and their collective organizations have escalated narrow labor disputes into oppositional classification struggles and public dramas to pressure employers and the state to redress their disputes through alternative means.

The proliferation of symbolic leverage on a global scale can also be seen in contemporary examples of international solidarity. In their investigation of women's rights, human rights, and environmental justice campaigns, Margaret Keck and Kathryn Sikkink (1998) found that citizens and movement groups facing resistance from their respective states sought outside assistance from international allies in the form of transnational advocacy networks (TANs). The use of symbolic leverage, as well as other forms of leverage politics, helped TANs exert additional pressure on nonresponsive governments. Once TANs hit on a clear right-or-wrong issue that could easily translate across borders, they employed a variety of strategies such as exchanging massive amounts of information, invoking culturally resonant symbols and stories, and applying targeted moral and political pressure to sway the decisions of nonresponsive governments. Subsequent studies of counterhegemonic globalizations (Evans 2000, 2005), cross-border labor campaigns (Armbruster-Sandoval 2004), and anti-sweatshop campaigns (Armbruster-Sandoval 2005) reveal that soft forms of communicative or symbolic power can also be directed at other institutions such as multinational corporations and public (nonprofit) organizations that are particularly vulnerable to the politics of public shaming on an international scale.

The pervasive exclusion of marginalized workers—as well as other poor and disenfranchised individuals—supports the argument that symbolic leverage has become a prevalent strategy for exercising public power at the national and global scale. However, it also highlights a glaring dilemma: if the emergence and salience of symbolic leverage is tied to a state of institutional exception, especially for traditionally disadvantaged workers, when and how does circumventing existing rules and institutions actually transform their operating logics and practices?

Historical examples, especially in the United States, reveal that state and institutional reforms have been a conventional and effective target of workers' mass-based, symbolic protests. During the New Deal era, the U.S. government institutionalized collective labor rights and social safety net provisions for the poor and unemployed in large part as a response to widespread labor unrest and social upheaval during the Great Depression. However, the transformation of Keynesian welfare states into Schumpeter workfare states (see Jessop 1994) has rendered state intervention an increasingly precarious and detrimental option for workers. Rather than being a universal right and entitlement as in the past, the receipt of welfare in the United States under new policies such as the 1996 Personal Responsibility and Work Act is now tied to labor market participation, which heightens workers' vulnerability to unfair wage bargains. The economic and political orthodoxy of the current world economic system, unlike in the previous Cold War era, is also unlikely to exert external pressures on states to promote the economic welfare of unionized workers. Since the collapse of Communism in the Soviet Union and Eastern Europe in the late 1980s, individual states have emerged as one of the most active agents in promoting the profit-driven interests of transnational corporations and powerful capitalist states.

The unlikely role of the state in promoting labor rights is also clear in countries like South Korea. In response to the social turmoil and worker unrest unleashed during the 1997–1998 Asian debt crisis, the South Korean government passed comprehensive labor law reforms that replaced welfare-based employment standards with market-based logics. What is perhaps most telling about the consequences of state intervention is that the passage of the neoliberal labor policies has occurred in conjunction with the establishment of the first major state welfare policies. Given the unprecedented levels of unemployment and job loss during the financial crisis, the Kim Dae Jung administration (1998–2003) reformed the existing Employment Insurance program and the National Pension Program, created the government-funded Public Works Projects, and instituted the Minimum Living Standard Guarantee. Apart from criticism that these efforts were vastly insufficient to meet the overwhelming needs of the population, Kim Dae Jung's system of social protection was aimed more at enhancing the efficiency and productivity of a globally integrated capitalist economy than shielding its most vulnerable citizens from the vicissitudes of the market (see Song 2006b). Thus, whether in the United States or South Korea, or in many other industrialized countries around the world, state intervention in regulating labor and welfare conditions is more likely to increase, not decrease, workers' vulnerability to insecurity and uncertainty in the workplace.

The negative consequences of state intervention can also be seen in the operating logics of new global regulatory institutions. While there are various institutional arenas in which the welfare of workers as well as other constituent groups can be promoted on an international scale, these arenas also tend to marginalize and disenfranchise less resourceful actors and groups in civil society and privilege more resourceful states and corporations. The "public shaming" of international organizations such as the World Trade Organization (WTO) by global justice movements highlights the persistence of barriers prohibiting the poor and disenfranchised from taking part in key decision-making processes about the regulation of cross-border flows of people, goods, information, and money. According to Walden Bello (2004, 59), one of the most outspoken critics of neoliberal globalization and free trade, the WTO is the most blatant example of an "opaque, unrepresentative and undemocratic organization driven by a free trade ideology which, wherever its recipes—liberalization, privatization, deregulation—have been applied, has generated only greater poverty and inequality."

Given the precariousness of traditional state- and policy-oriented strategies in promoting the interests of the margins, one of the most pressing questions facing social movements, including the labor movement, is not just how to generate symbolic leverage but also "symbolic leverage for what?"[1]

There are multiple ways to answer this question, many of which are outside this book's scope. For example, we could look to the revitalization of socialist political parties in South Africa, India, and Latin America as a vehicle for reasserting the interests of the poor and disadvantaged (see Williams 2008). We could look to the creation of participatory mechanisms at the local governmental level in countries such as Brazil (Baioicchi 2005), India (Agarwala 2007), and even the United States in the form of municipal living wage policies (see Luce 2004). The importance of local political coalitions and support is certainly suggested by the U.S. cases examined in this book, especially for the ongoing struggles of home care workers, and merits additional empirical inquiry into alternative forms and venues for exercising political leverage. We could look to the creation of new international human rights standards, codified in the formal documents of multilateral governance institutions such as the United Nations (UN) and International Labor Organization (ILO), that can hold nation-state's accountable for discriminatory institutional policies against excluded groups such as migrant workers (Soysal 1993). We could also look to the importance of developing an active civil society from the local to transnational scale in holding neoliberal states and employers accountable for prioritizing citizens' welfare needs over market principles (see Voss and Williams 2006).

Empirical attention to specific cases of workers' struggles at the margins have yet to offer a clear answer to the question of how to convert symbolic leverage into more enduring forms of economic, political, and institutional change. The gravity of resolving this question is particularly dire for the subjects of this study: workers at the margins of the economy and society. Without a more decisive shift in the political and ideological climate of unionism, marginalized workers will be perpetually vulnerable to the intensification of cost-cutting labor practices by employers and the state, threatening to deplete the resources, energy, and optimism of their efforts over time. Given the stakes of symbolic leverage, it is crucial, thus, to reflect on the nature of ongoing efforts within both the United States and South Korean labor movements to convert the symbolic leverage of the margins into more lasting forms of change.

Labor at a Crossroads, Again

Resolving the question, "symbolic leverage for what," speaks to the heart of contentious debates occurring in both the U.S. and Korean labor movements. A closer look into the way these debates are playing out reveals that each labor movement is confronting deep internal divides about how to convert the momentum from prior efforts to organize marginal workers into more enduring forms of change. Somewhat ironically, internal divisions within the U.S. labor movement are most fractious among organized labor's elite as they battle over how the crisis-ridden labor movement can turn the tide for the millions of unorganized workers facing declining wages, heightened job insecurity, and increased workloads. By contrast, internal conflicts in the Korean labor movement reflect fierce ideological differences about the autonomy of workers' organizations and the role of the state in mediating power struggles between labor and capital. These dilemmas that highlight attempts to strengthen the leverage of workers at the margins are more suggestive of the kinds of crossroads facing crisis-ridden labor movements at the national level than of the viability of concrete solutions being offered. In other words, the ability of workers' struggles at the margins to expose the stakes of conflicting paths of change speaks to the unique vantage point of its structural position in exposing sedimented power relations within organized labor's ranks. To better understand the explanatory potential of workers at the margins, I present a brief discussion of each labor movement's dilemmas.

United States: Conflicts among Organized Labor's Elite

As I discussed in chapter 4, pressures to steer the U.S. labor movement on a new path of change—one that prioritizes the importance of organizing some of the most vulnerable as opposed to the most powerful workers in the labor market—culminated in the formal establishment of a second national labor federation, Change to Win. At a time when the media ran sparse coverage of union-related news, the split within the House of Labor generated considerable attention, much of which was directed toward SEIU president Andrew Stern and his ambitious plans to implement a "top-to-bottom overhaul" within the U.S. labor movement.[2] When asked about the strident opposition from AFL-CIO leaders about the defection of some of the AFL-CIO's largest affiliates, Stern framed the conflict in moral terms: "For us, the fundamental question...is, Are we going to spend the next four years just worrying about us or worrying about achieving justice for all?"[3] The centerpiece of Stern's "justice for all" approach was the pivotal role of workers at the margins of the economy and society in transforming the U.S. labor movement. Stephen Lerner (2007, 28), the architect of SEIU's Justice for Janitors campaign, highlighted this imperative clearly when he stated: "It is among the most invisible and seemingly powerless workers—whose labor is nonetheless essential to the economic success of the most powerful corporations—that we can build a global movement to reinvigorate trade unions, stop the race to the bottom, and lift workers out of poverty."

Despite the rhetoric of its leaders, one of the most contentious issues surrounding SEIU has been the legitimacy of its approach to strengthening the leverage of "the most invisible and seemingly powerless" workers. Based on its successes among low-paid janitors and home care workers, SEIU's approach to unionism combines strategic research and organizing tactics with the public pressure of mobilized workers and communities. While this approach has enhanced union density among workers in particular industries and geographic areas, it has also tended to favor the calculated decisions made by union leaders over the dynamism of member and community involvement. The internal conflicts generated by this approach can be seen in its unionizing efforts among janitors, including the cases I examined. For example, after the Harvard janitors' campaign ended, the Boston local quickly turned its attention toward organizing a citywide strike in the fall of 2002 that coincided with the expiration of collective bargaining contracts for janitors in the downtown commercial real estate industry. Many student activists who played a leading role in escalating the classification struggle and public drama at Harvard felt sidelined by the union's strategic decision-making process, but some continued to actively support the union's subsequent effort. Because the union had a poor reputation among the city's unionized janitors, the campaign relied heavily on the city's relatively large student population and active community organizations "to portray the strike as a social justice issue and bring community pressure on the building owners and contractors" (DiMaggio 2004, 29).

SEIU's top-down and strategy-centered approach to building union power has also generated fierce internal conflicts within its own ranks. One of the most visible dissenters has been Sal Rosselli, president of one of SEIU's biggest health care locals in California, United Healthcare Workers West. Rather than "justice for all," Rosselli sees Stern's approach as "top-down," "heavy-handed," and "undemocratic."[4] At stake for Rosselli and his supporters is SIEU's commitment to developing members' involvement and participation in union decision-making processes. Stern's "growth at any cost" approach, according to critics, has also alienated union leaders outside SEIU's ranks, including one of its most vocal critics, Rose Ann DeMoro, executive director of the California Nurses Association.[5] While each side has exchanged insults and accusations, whether about the all-too-familiar "union-busting" corporate tactics used by the California Nurses Association or the "business-friendly not worker-friendly" backroom deals made between SIEU leaders and hospital management, each side is also committed to devoting its resources and energy toward organizing the thousands of unorganized health care workers whose pay rates, workloads, and working conditions have worsened under corporate health care practices.

The polarized terrain of organized labor's conflicts touch on a wide range of issues, from union democracy to Big Labor's history of compromising with corporate America to the SEIU's one-sided approach to building global unions. Many of these conflicts are reminiscent of organized labor's past, whether as "junior partners of the power elite" (Aronowitz 2003) or agents of anti-communist agendas in the third world (Scipes 2005). Yet, these conflicts are also taking place in a different historical and political moment. While it is clear than many of SEIU's methods are the subject of fierce contestation, what is most thought-provoking about these debates is not necessarily whether the means justify the ends, but how the moral imperative of organizing the margins is delineating the kinds of crossroads facing the U.S. labor movement: Can the labor movement really change the power imbalance between workers at the margins and global capital without transforming its internal decision-making and power structures?

South Korea: Union Militancy versus Worker Welfare

The renewed drive to organize vulnerable segments of the workforce—namely, irregularly employed workers—has also exposed the key dilemmas plaguing the future of the Korean labor movement. Unlike the nature of the U.S. labor movement's crossroads, the Korean labor movement's dilemmas are not over how much to compromise when it comes to members' involvement or corporate negotiations but over whether any form of compromise is acceptable at all: The justification for building powerful union organizations capable of extracting bottom-line concessions from employers is partly tied to militant labor's disillusionment with the ruling elite. Since the consolidation of neoliberal state regimes in the 1990s the KCTU-led wing of the organized labor movement has experienced repeated disappointments over state labor policies (discussed in chapter 2), including state-sponsored efforts to ameliorate the discrimination and exploitation of irregularly employed workers. While a hard-line union position has resulted in economic concessions for more strategically positioned workers in key sectors of the economy, the refusal of unions to compromise on its bottom line has tended to worsen, not overcome, the material deprivation of irregularly employed workers, especially those who are unable to use their associational power alone to redress their grievances. The Korean Democratic Labor Party, established in 2000, has also attempted to use existing political channels to change the balance of power among labor, capital, and the state, but its radical members are more inclined to support the oppositional struggles of militant unions than work within the established political machinery.

The dilemmas of taking a bottom-line approach to militant union struggles is most clearly exemplified in the case of the E-land union struggle involving hundreds of dismissed cashiers at its Homever and New Core Outlet retail stores. On July 1, 2007, approximately eight hundred E-land unionists occupied

E-land's flagship Homever store in the World Cup Stadium shopping complex and the wealthy Kangnam district's New Core Outlet store in Seoul. The date of the occupation was not a coincidence; it was timed to coincide with the implementation of the Irregular Employment Protection Act (*pijŏngkyujikbohobŏb*). Despite the Act's stated aim of eliminating the ongoing discrimination of irregularly employed workers, labor activists condemned it as an "evil law" (*akbŏb*), a term commonly used to describe repressive labor laws during the authoritarian era, which further legalized employers' use of irregular employment.[6] To expose the law's real consequences, the KCTU-affiliated E-land Trade Union began a militant struggle against the multinational, multibillion-dollar revenue-generating sales, manufacturing, and distribution corporation. Since the E-land group, which specializes in fashion and discount retail stores, began converting its existing workforce into fixed-term and subcontracted employees during the 1998 financial crisis, it had become infamous among its employees and labor activists for taking advantage of legal loopholes to lower wage and compensation levels. E-land's cost-cutting practices were particularly apparent in its hiring and firing practices for cashiers, many of whom were women in their late thirties to fifties making well under the average monthly wage at 800,000 Won ($800 U.S) per month.

The union occupation of E-land–owned stores, which lasted nearly three weeks, mirrored a contentious battle zone. Over three dozen riot police blocked the store's main entrance, refusing to allow anyone entry or exit. Inside the store, unionists used shopping carts to prevent the riot police from easily storming in. Unionists also covered the cash registers, making sure that no revenue flowed into the company coffers. Activities during the occupation were focused on preparing workers—the majority of whom had no prior union experience—for an impending clash with riot police when the latter would use force to drag striking workers out of the store. In addition to giving impassioned speeches and leading workers in rousing chants, union leaders also showed documentary films like "A Single Spark" about labor martyr Chun Tae-Il, who lit himself on fire in the early 1970s to demand that repressive employers and the state abide by the spirit of national labor laws.

Once the riot police violently ended the union occupation, the union immediately escalated their struggle to the broader public arena. Solidarity protests were organized at forty other retail locations and the union issued a call to boycott all E-land products. The E-land struggle also elicited the condemnation of thirty civic organizations over the human rights violation of striking E-land workers as well as many international solidarity appeals, including by UNI (Union Network International), a global union for commerce workers with over fifteen million members and nine hundred affiliate unions. Despite its varied tactics and supporters, however, the E-land Trade Union became mired in a protracted struggle with the company. The union's refusal to compromise on its basic demands—the reinstatement of fired workers as regular employees—emboldened its staunchly anti-union employer; E-land has demonstrated that it would rather absorb millions of dollars in revenue losses than consent to the union's demands. During a 300th-day anniversary of the struggle, E-land union president Kim Gyeong-wook recognized the grim reality facing the union, stating, "The E-land labor dispute will only end if the union dies or the company dies."[7]

In many ways, the E-land struggle resembles previous militant struggles waged by irregular workers, including the over five-hundred-day Korea Telecom Contract Workers' struggle and the KTX "bullet" train attendants' union struggle, which also consisted almost entirely of women workers. Given the costs of waging long, drawn-out union battles, which do not necessarily end well for workers, the Korean Women's Trade Union (KWTU) has adopted a more incremental approach to winning its union struggles, as well as a less antagonistic approach to negotiating with the government. Given what they see as the disproportionate impact on poor women, the KWTU has prioritized "improving the quality of life for women workers" and "empowering women workers to take on the resolution of their own problems" over political or ideological positions (KWWAU 2007). The KWTU's stance toward the Irregular Employment Protection Act is indicative of its extreme conflicts with the ideologically driven positions of KCTU-affiliated unions. According to one KWTU leader, "In terms of the Irregular Employment Protection Act, I think it's the people who are abusing the Act and the spirit of the law, and it's up to labor to fight and stop the abuse of the law. I don't want to think of the Act itself as the problem."[8] Because the Act was the first attempt at addressing the proliferation of abusive forms of irregular employment and the KWTU was not clear how it would impact irregularly employed workers, especially women workers, the KWTU held educational workshops with its members around the country to discuss the pros and cons of the law. The membership decided to try to cooperate with government officials to implement the law, yet its decision was vehemently criticized by many KCTU unionists as the actions of a "yellow union," a venomous insult against many women worker activists who historically fought for the creation of independent, democratic unions and the elimination of government- and employer-controlled unions. Although its one-year assessment highlighted the Act's weaknesses rather than potential benefits, the KWTU continues to prioritize the welfare and livelihood needs of their members in their organizational decisions and strategic planning.

Reconceptualizing the Power of the Margins

The crossroads facing each labor movement highlight important insights about the struggles of workers at the margins. On the one hand, the struggles of low-paid, service workers provide a glimpse into a labor movement that prioritizes grassroots organizing, worker empowerment, symbolic protests, community alliances, and public values as the fulcrum of a revitalized union politics. On the other hand, they reveal the persistence of dominant tendencies within each labor movement to revert to familiar and well-traveled paths rather than adopt new decision-making practices. While the ability to identify pressure points for global corporations and organize strategic transnational protests accordingly has resulted in important victories for the SEIU and other international unions, it relies on the strategic capabilities of organized labor's elite in extracting concessions from conventionally anti-union employers. Building more genuine forms of worker involvement and leadership that dismantle centralized decision-making structures would require a leap of faith that many U.S. union leaders are not prepared or willing to take. By contrast, Korean labor movement leaders are resolute in their defiance of any form of cooperation with employers and the state. As in the past, priority is placed on the capacity of a militant and mobilized rank-and-file union to go head to head with equally combative employers. While there are many costs along the way, especially to the workers who are unable to resume their jobs and lives in the context of protracted and often unresolved struggles, consenting to any form of engagement with the existing ruling elite is viewed as detrimental to the labor movement's long-term struggle of building a worker-led society.

The dilemmas of embarking on alternative paths of change for both the Korean and U.S. labor movements highlight the difficulties of bringing these movements together under a wider umbrella of international solidarity. Although parallel shifts have occurred in different countries around the world regarding the stated importance of marginalized workers to union revitalization and the role of symbolic leverage in strengthening marginalized workers' base of power, there is little agreement regarding how to translate such shifts into the decision-making structures and political values of union leaders at the national, let alone transnational, level. Given the emphasis on strategy over democratic process, U.S. union leaders who recognize the transnational context of labor cost-cutting are more likely to be interested in applying proven strategies to new settings than in considering their role in reproducing power inequities on a global scale. Because of the high-profile and seductive nature of Korean union militancy, particularly to international labor activists, Korean union leaders are also likely to find support for continuing its confrontational and uncompromising approach to unionism, which has the unintended consequence of closing off the possibility of pursuing more varied and creative forms of worker protest. Given the varied histories that have differentiated the struggles of workers and unions in South Korea and the United States as well as other countries around the world, what then, if any, are the possibilities of forging a more unified agenda for labor internationalism when considering the centrality of workers at the margins?

Rather than approach this question from the vantage point of strategy, I conclude by emphasizing the importance of reconceptualizing the power of the margins. One of the most interesting paradoxes of the margins today is that their significance no longer correlates with their size or relative proportion. Unlike the fixed margins on the borders of a page, the margins of the labor movement represent the vast and increasing proportion of unorganized workers. If we think about the empirical centrality of marginal workers in the context of contemporary world capitalism, then we can recognize that attention to their struggles expose the dynamics of existing power relationships at the local, national, and international levels. Chandra Talpade Mohanty (2003, 231–232) puts it most eloquently when she states that attention to the margins "make[s] the workings of power visible" so that one can "read up the ladder of privilege." She adds, "My claim is not that all marginalized locations yield crucial knowledge about power and inequality, but that within a tightly integrated capitalist system, the particular standpoint of poor indigenous and Third World/South women provides the most inclusive viewing of systemic power." Unless the margins are placed in a position to transform the conditions of their institutional subordination, the structural features of their exclusion and the power relations that undergird it remain intact. Without understanding how the margins can more fully participate in determining the conditions that affect their daily lives, the racialized and gendered practices of subordination that are part of the resurgence of market rule under global capitalism remain unchallenged.

Notes

PREFACE

1. In 1997 the Korean government accepted a $58 billion emergency bailout loan from the IMF to prevent banks and non-financial corporations from defaulting on debt payments for short-term foreign loans. See Crotty and Lee (2005) for more detailed discussion.

2. The "Global North" generally represents economically developed and industrialized countries in the northern hemisphere and the "Global South" generally represents economically developing and industrializing countries in the southern hemisphere; however the level of economic development, not geography, is the determining criteria for inclusion. The Global North and Global South have replaced the usage of terms such as the First World and the Third World, respectively, which were heavily criticized for imputing hierarchical values and unequal worth between countries in the industrialized (wealthy Western capitalist nations) versus developing world (impoverished non-Western nations). It is important to note, however, that countries such as South Korea that were part of the cohort of newly industrializing countries (NICs) during the 1960s and 1970s, which also include Brazil, Hong Kong, Singapore, Taiwan, and South Africa, are difficult to categorize according to this binary.

3. "Immigration," AFL-CIO Executive Council statement, February 16, 2000, New Orleans, LA.

4. KCTU New Year's Message by President Dan Byung-ho, "Reject the Inequality and Injustice of 20/80 Society, Build a New Community of Sharing and Equality, Let Us March Together," December 30, 1999, Seoul, Korea, http://www.kctu.org/news/news_991230_newyear.htm (accessed March 5, 2002).

5. The Asian debt crisis, also referred to as the Asian financial crisis and the so-called "IMF crisis," began in July 1997 in Thailand and then spread primarily to South Korea and Indonesia. Affected countries saw the value of their national currencies and stock markets plummet. To prevent the fiscal meltdown in Asian financial markets from spreading around the world, the IMF offered short-term bailout loans to some Asian governments to repay foreign debts.

1. THE SYMBOLIC LEVERAGE OF LABOR

1. According to Ovid's *Fasti*, the ability of the god Janus to "look both ways without moving" gave him the moral authority to determine who could and could not enter the threshold of the "heavenly court," rendering the figure of the janitor a powerful catalyst of transition and change.

2. Studies on U.S. labor revitalization include in-depth analysis of the strategies and tactics used in union organizing campaigns (Bronfenbrenner et al. 1998; Bronfenbrenner and Hickey 2002; Milkman and Wong 2000); the conditions needed to revitalize local bureaucratic unions (Voss and Sherman 2000; Lopez 2004); the development of alternative organizational forms such as community unionism, workers' centers, and labor-community alliances (Fine 2006; Luce 2004); the importance of new frames such as

citizenship, race, and gender in broadening the political underpinnings of the labor movement (Clawson 2003; Johnston 2001); and transnational labor organizing (Armbruster-Sandoval 2004).

3. In his insightful essay on "Everyday Metaphors of Power," Timothy Mitchell (1990) explains that the insistence on treating the material realm and the realm of meaning or culture as separate and distinct reinforces hegemonic forms of domination.

4. While intellectuals in Korea have a relatively more symbolic profile than in the United States, their relevance is also declining.

5. Jeffrey Sallaz and Jane Zavisca (2007, 28) surveyed four major sociology journals between 1980 and 2004 and found that the majority of studies that cite Bourdieu's concept of capital engage mainly with his concepts of cultural and social capital.

2. EMPLOYER AND STATE OFFENSIVES AGAINST UNIONIZED WORKERS

1. U.S. Bureau of Labor Statistics, *Current Population Survey* (CPS). Washington, DC: U.S. Bureau of Labor Statistics, January 28, 2009, http://www.bls.gov/news.release/union2.nr0.htm.

2. In France, 95 percent of workers are covered by union bargaining agreements, which render union membership levels insignificant. See Blanchflower and Bryson 2007.

3. After the GM negotiations, formula wage-setting mechanisms became a norm throughout the industry. By the early 1960s, the COLA principle had been incorporated into approximately 50 percent of all major union contracts, which were crucial in shielding unionized workers from the inflationary years of the late 1960s and 1970s (Ehrenberg, Danzier, and San 1983).

4. Although the amendment to the FLSA was not passed in 1937, President Franklin Delano Roosevelt hoped to include some legislation that prohibited the exchange of "goods produced under conditions which do not meet rudimentary standards of decency... [which] should be regarded as contraband and ought not to be allowed to pollute the channels of interstate trade" (quoted in Nordlund 1997, 47).

5. Despite historic employer concessions to unions between the late 1940s and late 1960s, U.S. employers display a blatant propensity toward anti-unionism. In his account of the development of welfare capitalism in the twentieth century, historian Stanford M. Jacoby (1997, 7) explains, "even the most progressive nonunion employers were willing to spend enormous sums both in the factory and in Congress to stave off unions."

6. A series of articles in *Reader's Digest* included "Wage Madness in the Construction Industry" (Jan. 1971), "The Tyranny of Terrorism in the Building Trades" (June 1973), and "Labor Violence—A National Scandal" (Aug. 1973). In *Fortune,* articles included "The Unchecked Power of the Building Trades" (Dec. 1968), "Breaking the Labor Monopoly" (Oct. 1970), and "The Building Trades versus the People" (Oct. 1970). See Linder 2000.

7. The UAW agreed to $203 million in wage concessions in the first round of concessions in October 1979, another $243 million in January 1980 (after pressure from Congress for additional concessions), and another $156 in 1981 (Katz 1985, 54–55).

8. Editorial Desk, "'Givebacks' and the Comeback." *New York Times,* August 21, 1983.

9. Steven Greenhouse, "Unions Pressed on 'Givebacks,'" *New York Times,* January 11, 1984.

10. Ibid.

11. The National Trade Union and Labor Relations Adjustment Act, which was also passed in the 1950s, guaranteed workers the right to organize unions, engage in collective action, and bargain collectively with employers.

12. The 1953 Labor Standards Act was based on Japan's postwar Constitution in 1946, which included this quote in Article 27. Both Korean and Japanese labor laws were modeled after the U.S. National Labor Relations Act and Fair Labor Standards Act.

13. The LSA states that workers are to be paid a base wage on a specified day of each month (which they can request early in emergency situations such as childbirth, sickness, or accident) as well as several additional forms of compensation such as severance pay and paid monthly and annual leave. If a worker has worked for more than one year, the worker is entitled to receive severance pay in the average amount of a thirty-day period for each year of service. Typically, severance pay is given after resignation, but workers can also request it in advance, corresponding with the number of years worked.

14. For a breakdown by industry in Chŏnp'yŏng, see Cumings 1981, 198 (table 9).

15. Rising real wages of workers in small- and medium-sized, labor-intensive manufacturing firms destabilized the low cost advantage they gained from its "cheap" labor force, and capital began fleeing en masse from Korea's export-processing zones. See H. Kim 1997.

16. KCTU responded by organizing the largest General Strike in the nation's contemporary history. Four hundred thousand workers from 528 different KCTU-affiliated unions participated in the one-month nationwide strike; at its height, participation levels reached one million workers, which represented the first time that KCTU and FKTU went on strike together.

17. Article 31 of the Labor Standards Act, "Dismissals for Managerial Reasons," gave employers the right to lay off workers during periods of economic necessity, and the "Temporary Agency Law" allowed companies to hire temporary workers to reduce labor costs and strengthen firm competitiveness.

18. Kim Dae Jung, "Second Nation Building" *Korea Times,* August 15, 1998.

19. Crotty and Lee (2006, 4) also emphasize that Kim's belief in the market well preceded 1998. "In a 1985 book titled *Mass Participatory Economy: A Democratic Alternative for Korea,* he [Kim] stated that 'maximum reliance on the market is the operating principle of my program' and that world integration is our historic mission."

20. The IMF crisis presented a new situation to the KCTU. During the General Strike, KCTU took the position that there is no alternative for unions except to wage an all-out struggle against the mandates of neoliberal globalization. However, there was another position that acknowledged that it was impossible to retain the gains that organized labor had made over the past ten years and that losses were inevitable, given the current state of global competition. Instead, they called for unions to engage in active negotiation to offset losses in employment and job security. Interview with KCTU labor activist, November 6, 1998, Seoul, Korea.

21. Article 31, "Dismissals for Managerial Reasons," granted employers the right to lay off workers for "economic reasons." However, four conditions granted legal permission for employers to lay off workers: (1) urgent business needs, (2) the exhaustion of all other means before dismissal, (3) selection of dismissed employees is conducted on the basis of fair and reasonable criteria, and (4) management consulted with representatives of employees in good faith before dismissing workers.

3. RECONSTRUCTING THE MARGINALIZED WORKFORCE

1. National Alliance for Fair Employment, "Contingent Workers Fight for Fairness: A Report from the National Alliance for Fair Employment," www.fairjobs.org/report/index.php.

2. Under the 1953 Labor Standards Act, workers are guaranteed one day of paid leave for each month worked as well as ten days of paid leave a year (eight days if total time

worked is 90 percent). If a worker has worked for more than one year, the worker is entitled to receive severance pay in the average amount of a thirty-day period for each year of service. Typically, severance pay is given after resignation, but workers can also request it in advance, corresponding with the number of years worked.

3. Job tenure is extremely important in determining contingent employment status because employment for one year or longer determined eligibility to legal retirement compensation, overtime pay, and bonuses, as stipulated in the Labor Standards Act. Temporary workers, which included those who were employed for less than one year, and daily workers, which included those employed on a day-to-day basis, were not eligible. Since 1999, "fixed term" contracts for less than one year have become prevalent as a way for employers to avoid paying workers their legally entitled benefits. Unpaid workers include self-employed workers and unpaid family workers.

4. In 2001, one U.S. dollar was the equivalent of approximately 1,260 Korean Won.

5. "Women and Men in OECD Countries," report, OECD. 2006. http://www.oecd.org/dataoecd/45/37/37964069.pdf (accessed June 2008).

6. The 1924 immigration law was the last of a series of restrictive legislation that banned the entry of immigrants from the Asia Pacific Region. In 1929, a quota system went into effect that restricted entry by national origin. The total annual limit on immigration was set to 150,000. The annual limit for people from England was 65,631, as opposed to 5,635 from Italy, 308 from Greece, and 100 from all Asian countries. Mexicans were exempted from immigration restrictions due to the pressure from employers who desired a ready and convenient supply of low-cost labor from their neighbor. For full listing per country, see Ngai 2004, 28–29 (table 1.1).

7. Unions did not unconditionally support efforts to restrict immigration. In the late nineteenth century, the Knights of Labor emphasized that it opposed forced immigration but not voluntary immigration. The American Federation of Labor (AFL) also supported this position during the time, stressing that voluntary immigrants could be easily assimilated into U.S. society. The AFL's position changed in the early twentieth century, and it supported efforts by the Immigration Restrictionist League to maintain the racial and cultural superiority of the American people (Higham 1992, 49–50).

8. To promote the United States' international image as a so-called safe haven from Communism, Congress also passed a series of national refugee laws that made provisions for additional admissions beyond quota limits according to foreign policy considerations such as the Refugee Relief Act of 1953, the Refugee Escapee Act of 1957, and the Fair Share Refugee Law of 1960.

9. The 1965 Act equalized annual quota limits for each country (20,000 persons), which allowed for a total of 170,000 from the Eastern Hemisphere and 120,000 from the Western Hemisphere. The figures—170,000 and 120,000—were "simply pulled from the air, and [bore] no relationship to principle at all" (Abrams and Abrams 1975, 3).

10. Under the Clinton administration, $100 million in grants and tax subsides were offered to businesses that committed to creating additional jobs in 11 defined urban empowerment zones (Logan and Molotch 1987, 245–246).

11. The 1987 Employment Equity Act prohibits employment discrimination by employers, supervisors, and fellow coworkers on the basis of gender, pregnancy, or marital status. It also contains provisions that stipulate equal pay for work of equal value and prohibits discrimination in regards to age, personal appearance (height or weight), or other personal attributes that are irrelevant to the performance of the job. However, the lack of enforcement mechanisms, including specific penalties for violating the law, has prevented the law's full implementation.

12. For gendered impact on homeless alleviation and welfare policies during the Asian debt crisis, see Jesook Song 2006a.

13. Yoonsook Moh, "Organizational Strategies of Irregular Women Workers," *Working Women: Newsletter of Korean Women Workers Associations United* 17 (1999).

14. Special Reporting Team, "Not All Workers the Same as Firms Exploit New Rules," May 4, 2004.

4. SOCIAL MOVEMENT LEGACIES AND ORGANIZING THE MARGINALIZED

1. Steven Greenhouse, "Labor Leader Sounds Do-or-Die Warning," *New York Times,* February 19, 2001.

2. The Change to Win Federation's affiliates include the SEIU, the Teamsters, LIUNA (Laborers' International Union of North America), UNITE-HERE, UBC (United Brotherhood of Carpenters and Joiners of America), the UFW (United Farm Workers), and the UFCW (United Food and Commercial Workers).

3. Steven Greenhouse, "4 Major Unions Plan to Boycott A.F.L.-C.I.O. Event," *New York Times,* July 25, 2005.

4. KCTU New Year's Message by President Dan Byung-ho, "Reject the Inequality and Injustice of 20/80 Society, Build a New Community of Sharing and Equality, Let Us March Together," Korean Confederation of Trade Unions (KCTU), December 30, 1999, http://www.kctu.org/news/news_991230_newyear.htm.

5. George Meany, "On Labor's Future," *New York Times Magazine,* December 4, 1955.

6. Ibid.

7. Unless referring to the specific organization, references to the UFW include all its organizational predecessors.

8. The AFL-CIO–affiliated Agricultural Worker Organizing Committee (AWOC) had initiated a strike among Filipino grape workers in 1965, which demanded that growers pay workers the legal minimum wage. Although the NFWA had not planned to begin striking at that time, when the membership approved a proposal to join the AWOC strike, the NFWA joined with AWOC. The formation of the "strike community" served as a model for how a financially strapped union could sustain a strike. The strike community included rank-and-file leaders and members, full-time union activists, community leaders, students and other activists broadened the base of associational power for the NFWA. Tactics such as a "roving picket line," which moved picketing locations to different fields facilitated greater worker participation in pickets and the strategic participation of clergy members, civil rights activists, and student activists who were called to join the strike and engage in acts of civil disobedience (Ganz 2000, 1033–1034).

9. Dick Meister, "*La Huelga* Becomes *La Causa,*" *New York Times Magazine,* November 17, 1968.

10. Ibid.

11. For a full version of the *Port Huron Statement,* see Miller 1994, 329–374 (appendix).

12. ACORN, which organizes poor and disadvantaged communities in major urban areas around the country, is one of the major community organizational forces behind the expansion of living wage movements across the country in the 1990s and 2000s (see Luce 2004).

13. Roy Rogers went on to work with the UFCW to wage historic corporate campaigns against Hormel, and with the Farm Labor Organizing Committee against Campbell's. Michael Locker, a former NACLA leader and the founder of the Corporate Data Exchange served as a key advisor for the Amalgamated Clothing and Textile Workers Union during its corporate campaign against J.P. Stephens. SDS leader Paul Booth, one of the drafters

of the NACLA's manual chapters on researching unions, helped organize two thousand students in support of striking UAW workers in 1970 and later became the organizing director of AFSCME.

14. Power of the Working Class (*nodongja ŭi him*), "Open the New World of Labor Emancipation," Power of the Working Class Preparatory Committee document, 2000, Seoul, Korea.

15. Ibid.

16. According to one of the architects of the New Left, Won J.C., because "bourgeois democracy [has] expanded to all areas including the press, the media, electoral laws and regional self-government," "institutionalized realms including the electoral politics, the media, the schools, and trade unions [are also] important places for formulating and expressing the interests of citizens" (quoted in M. Park 2002, 16–17).

17. Founding members of KWWA included key leaders of democratic unions in the 1970s, including Lee Young-soon and Han Myong-hee of the Control Data Union, Choi Soon-young of the Y.H. trade union, Sol Nan-young of the She-jin electronic trade union, Jang Hyun-ja and Cho Keum-bo of the Bando Sangsa union, Bae Ok-byong of the Soh Tong trade union, Chong In-Sook and Chun Soon-ok of the Chonggye trade union, Lee Soon-keum of the Koh-mi trade unions. Lee Ji-eun, Kim Kyong-ran, Lee Hehran, and Wang In-soon, who were activists in the Women's Committee, were also founding members.

18. 1992 organizational document, *When the Hen Crows…Korea Women Workers Educational Programs*, Hong Kong: Committee for Asian Women and Korean Women Workers Association.

19. "Looking Back over the Women's Movement in the Year 1992," *Working Women* [newsletter of the KWWA], June 1993.

20. Under Article 71 of the Labor Standards Act (LSA), female employees in Korea are entitled to one day of menstruation leave per month. Up until July 2004, female employees received paid leave. However, amendments to the LSA changed this entitlement to unpaid leave.

21. The issue of sexual harassment was thrust to the forefront of both the labor and citizen's movements by the "Committee of 100" (*paekinwŭiwŏnhae*) and their campaign to publicly name male activists accused of sexual harassment.

22. Soon-im Choi, "Establishing the Action Center for Women's Unemployment Prevention Center: A Shield of the Female Unemployed from the IMF," *Working Women*, October 1998.

23. Sang-rim Choi, The Present Situation and Tasks of the Women Workers' Movement," *Working Women*, May 1997.

24. Interview with labor activist, August 8, 2003, San Francisco.

25. Interview with union leader, August 20, 2003, San Jose, CA.

26. Ibid.

27. Interview with union leader, August 20, 2003, Oakland, CA.

28. For example, the number of locals only increased from 300 to 350 during this tremendous growth in union membership.

29. A report commissioned in 1993 entitled "Being Heard," prepared by Greer, Margolis, Mitchell, Burns and Associates, Inc., with Research and Findings by Peter D. Hart Research, March 21, 1994. Cited in Sweeney 1996, 86 n. 20, 164.

30. PICIS Newsletter, 2001.

31. The Seoul Women's Trade Union was created by fifteen members, two of whom were forced to voluntarily resign after getting married (the husband of one of the women also lost his job for protesting the company's actions). In 2003, SWTU had approximately eighty

members from clerical jobs, call centers, and restaurants. The SWTU also organizes unemployed women, which prevented the Seoul city government from granting them legal certification as a union. The SWTU emphasizes the importance of autonomous women worker's activism—distinct from existing trade union bodies and NGOs. The KCTU created the Korean Women's Confederation of Trade Unions. There are eight official branches of the union; however, it has little support within KCTU (see Broadbent 2007; Jinock Lee 2003).

32. Policy and Information Center of Internal Solidarity (PICIS), "The Organizing of Women Workers and Their Struggles, Part 3," 2001.

33. Interview with KWWAU staff, November 12, 2002, Seoul.

34. Interview with KWTU union leader, July 30, 2007, Seoul.

35. "Korean Women's Trade Union Rules and Regulations," internal memorandum. Seoul: Korean Women's Trade Union, December 15, 2008.

36. Representatives of the KCTU and the KFTU sat on the Minimum Wage Commission. However, because the majority of their members received wages that were often twice, if not more, the minimum wage, they did not actively pressure the Commission to increase wage levels in line with the cost of living. In lieu of raising the minimum wage rate, KCTU and FKTU representatives often negotiated other concessions from the state. When the KWTU became aware of the close relationship between the national minimum wage and the wage calculation practices of subcontractors, they immediately initiated plans to raise the national minimum wage.

37. Joint Statement of Co-chairs of the Action Center to Secure the Rights of Non-Standard Women Workers, June 8, 2001.

38. In 2002, a broad-based Minimum Wage Network was created, which included over fifty labor unions and civil society organizations including the FKTU, the KCTU, and the KSPW, to call for a second increase to the minimum wage. The network's efforts, which also included public rallies, press conferences, and a petition drive, helped raise the minimum wage to 2,275 Won per hour or 514,150 Won per month (approximately $436 U.S.), reflecting an 8.3 percent increase from the previous rate.

39. Interview with labor activist, July 13, 2002, Seoul.

40. Interview with KCTU union organizer, October 1, 2001, Seoul.

41. KCTU *Action Alert* 2003.

42. Figures from 2002 report by the Korean Federation of Transportation, Public, and Social Service Union.

43. Contract workers mainly represented two groups of workers: (1) male workers that installed and repaired telephone and Asymmetric Digital Subscriber Line (ADSL) cables and (2) female workers that operated 114 telephone directory assistance (equivalent to 411 directory assistance in the United States).

44. Quoted from Labour News Production feature documentary, "Friends or Foe," directed by Jiyoung Lee, VHS format. Seoul: Labor News Production, 2003.

45. Interview with KT union leader, October 16, 2001, Seoul.

46. Interview with labor activist, August 11, 2003, Oakland, CA.

47. Ibid.

48. Despite intense opposition from labor union and social movement groups, the Irregular Employment Protection Act passed in December 2006 and went into effect on July 1, 2007.

5. ORGANIZING SUBCONTRACTED UNIVERSITY JANITORS

1. For a richer discussion of the implications of flexible employment strategies on increased bifurcation of the labor market, see Houseman and Polivka 2000.

2. To read an elaboration on "public dramas" in janitors' struggles, see Chun 2005.

3. Nik Trendowski, "Officials Announce Custodian Layoffs," *Daily Trojan,* February 2, 1996.

4. Thomas H. Moran, "Changes in Custodial Services," Internal university memorandum, February 1, 1996.

5. Elisa Ung, "Custodians React to Recent Layoffs," *Daily Trojan,* February 9, 1996.

6. Interview with union organizer, June 20, 2003b, Los Angeles.

7. Jin Whang, "Custodians Stage Sick-out Wednesday," *Daily Trojan,* February 23, 1996.

8. Janitors at USC had tried to form a union two previous times with the Teamsters union, which represents shuttle bus drivers on campus. Each of their efforts resulted in lost union elections. However, when the workers heard that they were going to be subcontracted, they contacted the Teamsters again, but this time, the Teamsters said they could not help them. When the workers asked the labor board what union they could go to represent them, they told them "Justice for Janitors."

9. Interview with union organizer, June 20, 2003a, Los Angeles.

10. Interview with union organizer, June 20, 2003b, Los Angeles.

11. Elisa Ung, "Both Local 11 and Local 399 Unions Join Forces to Resist Janitorial Subcontracting." *Daily Trojan,* February 28, 1996.

12. In hindsight, union organizers felt they did not make use of all their potential leverage points, including jeopardizing USC's donor base and its real estate expansion plans, which could be one reason that the campaign lasted over fourteen months.

13. Marcella Bombardieri, "Revitalized Union Determined to Win Better Life for Janitors," *Boston Globe,* September 5, 2002.

14. In addition to Harvard, janitors at Tufts University were also involved in a labor struggle. "In 1993, Tufts became the poster child of how bad this [subcontracting] was for the industry. Tufts decided to bring in UNICCO, the largest cleaning contractor in the industry to Boston....Then, in 1997...they kicked UNICCO out and brought in ONESOURCE....We began to have meetings to try to change the contract....Regardless of whether you are part-time or full-time, every worker should be making the same." The biggest goal they faced was getting members involved in the contract campaigns. Through surveys, the union identified three major issues: (1) equal pay for equal work, regardless of in-house or contracted or part-time, (2) full-time opportunities (many workers wanted full-time employment and had to work two or three jobs to compensate when they only received part-time employment, and (3) living wage and job security. (Interview with union leader, April 30, 2004, Boston.)

15. Interview with union leader, April 30, 2004, Boston.

16. "The Harvard Living Wage Fact Sheet," Harvard Progressive Student Labor Movement, http://www.hcs.harvard.edu/~pslm/livingwage/portal.html.

17. Harvard Workers Center, "Outsourcing, Its Discontents and Some Solutions," report prepared for the Harvard Committee on Employment and Contracting Out Policies (HCECP), October 12, 2001, 28.

18. Interview with student activist, April 22, 2004, Cambridge, MA.

19. Jennifer Heldt Powell, "Activists Raise Living Wage Awareness; Living Wage Movement on Rise in Hub," *Boston Herald,* March 1, 1999.

20. Ibid.

21. In South Korea, the national Labor Standards Act (LSA) guarantees basic labor rights, including freedom of association, but it also outlines detailed rules regarding compensation for regular paid rest during the course of employment and after "resignation" when workers were no longer able to work in waged employment. Chapter 7 discusses at

greater length the relevance of a wage allocation system that calculated wages according to human welfare, not just a competitive price in the labor market.

22. Interview with union leader, October 16, 2002, Incheon, Korea. Sun-ho is a pseudonym.

23. Ibid.

24. Interview with labor activist, August 11, 2003, Oakland, CA.

25. Ibid.

26. Interview with union leader, November 1, 2002, Seoul.

27. Ibid.

28. At the time, the Building Services Industrial Union was still in the planning stages, so the union became affiliated with the KCTU Seoul Regional Center.

29. Interview with labor activist, August 11, 2003, Oakland, CA.

30. The union researcher identified all the dates and times when large numbers of prospective students would be touring the campus during the months of April, May, and June as well as all potential events at which the union could distribute leaflets or stage an action, including meetings at the Academic Senate, informational sessions at the Business School, and social events for the faculty. SEIU Local 399, internal memorandum, April 18, 1996.

31. Letter written by Thomas H. Moran, USC Vice President Business Affairs, addressed to "Parents, Students, Faculty, Staff and Friends," May 8, 1996.

32. Kelly Candaele, "Class Is In," *LA Weekly,* May 10–16, 1996.

33. The injunction required that the union provide twenty-four hour notice when any more than five union members were present within fifty feet of any campus building.

34. Interview with union organizer, October 27, 2003, Los Angeles.

35. During a march on October 24, 1996, geography professor Laura Pulido is quoted as saying, "The workers are the community. We are supposed to be the Trojan family." Kim Santos, "Union Support Labor Complaint," *Daily Trojan,* October 25, 1996.

36. Interview with SEIU union organizer, June 20, 2003, Los Angeles.

37. Interview with SEIU union organizer, October 27, 2003, Los Angeles.

38. Jennifer Lee, "Union Supporters Trick-or-Treat," *Daily Trojan,* October 27, 1997.

39. Nik Trendowski, "Officials Announce Custodian Layoffs," Daily Trojan, February 2, 1996.

40. Elisa Ung, "Local 11 Protests Custodian Layoffs," *Daily Trojan,* February 8, 1996.

41. SEIU internal union memo, "Community, Political and Corporate Strategies; Lessons Learned from the USC Campaign," 1998.

42. Dae Kim, "Custodians Protest Subcontracting," *Daily Trojan,* March 20, 1996.

43. Support for the janitors became the focus of subsequent public debate between students. In response to the petition, Carson Block, a junior majoring in business, publicly challenged the notion that the petition represented the views of the "student body," citing that it contained only 700 of the 10,000 signatures needed to signal a "majority." Block argued, "USC's primary responsibility is to its students." Steve Sidawi, a vocal member of the student support committee, responded less than a month later: "As evidenced by letters printed in the *Daily Trojan,* some people still don't seem to understand what is really going on.... The real issue here is whether USC should be cutting costs on the backs of the workers who already receive the lowest wages and benefits, many of whom have been dedicated university employees for over 20 years." Steve Sidawi, "USC Service Workers are Defended by Support Committee Member," *Daily Trojan,* December 5, 1996.

44. A sister who headed the Esperanza Community Housing Corporation "unabashedly" supported the union, according to organizers. During meetings of the USC Community board, Sister Donahue "was fearless in standing up with the janitors" against the university administration. Interview with union organizer, October 28, 2003, Los Angeles.

45. SEIU internal document, Letter to politicians inviting their participation in community hearing, October 8, 1996.

46. Lee 1997.

47. Jennifer Hamm, "Election to Decide Union's Fate," *Daily Trojan*, May 21, 1997.

48. Jennifer Hamm, "Janitors Vote in Favor of the Union," *Daily Trojan*, May 28, 1997.

49. Interview with union organizer, June 20, 2003a, Los Angeles.

50. Jennifer Kelleher, "Janitors Agree to USC Contract," *Daily Trojan*, February 12, 1998.

51. Amy Offner, "The Numbers Tell a Grim Story," *Harvard Crimson*, April 14, 1999.

52. Diane E. Lewis, "Activist Spirit Drummed Up; Working It Out," *Boston Globe*, November 7, 1999.

53. Interview with union organizer, April 22, 2004, Boston.

54. Interview with union organizer, April 19, 2004, Boston.

55. Harvard Progressive Labor Movement, "Why We Are Sitting In," http://hcs.harvard.edu/~pslm/livingwage/why.html.

56. Amy Offner (2004) explains, "For many people, the highlights of the sit-in were two explosive night-time demonstrations with the campus dining hall workers. The sit-in coincided with the dining hall workers' contract negotiations, and the two developments fed each other. On two nights during the sit-in, the dining hall workers held contract meetings and ended them by marching en masse to the occupied building, where they joined students on the outside and blocked the streets around Harvard Square for hours. The workers brought terrific noisemakers made of laundry detergent bottles with ball bearings inside, making for the loudest, most raucous demonstrations of the sit-in."

57. Also see "Airing out the Living Wage," *Harvard Magazine* 104:65, 2002; "Living Wage: Next Stage" *Harvard Magazine* 104:58.

58. Jules Crittenden, "Harvard, Students End Sit-in with Plan to Form Panel," *Boston Herald*, May 9, 2001.

59. "Harvard Works It Out," *Boston Globe*, editorial, May 9, 2001.

60. HCECP 2001, 3.

61. Interview with union leader, October 15, 2002, Incheon, Korea.

62. Interview with union leader, October 16, 2002, Incheon, Korea.

63. Bourdieu (1989, 21) explains that symbolic struggles over the principles of the social world do not necessarily take on the character of propaganda or purposive, strategic action: "[T]he legitimation of the social world, is not, as some believe the product of deliberate and purposive action of propaganda or symbolic imposition, it results, rather, from the fact that agents apply to the objective structures of the social world structures of perception and appreciation which are issued out of these very structures and which tend to picture the world as evident."

64. Throughout the thirty-five-day struggle, the two dismissed workers continue to show up at work to emphasize their defiance of the company's "unjust" termination of their employment. Their efforts were met with repeated physical confrontations with company security and union leaders.

65. KWTU Incheon branch, internal document, August 2002.

66. Interview with labor activist, August 11, 2003, Oakland, CA.

67. Since many of the workers were older and had never participated in a strike, external activists played a crucial role in boosting workers' morale. One organizer explained, "To prevent workers from getting tired and drained during the struggle, we did a variety of things. We held daily educational sessions/trainings, evaluation/strategy meetings, especially during negotiations, as well as organized picnics and soccer games." Interview with labor activist, August 11, 2003, Oakland, CA.

68. Ibid.

69. Ibid.

70. Interview with student activist, November 14, 2002, Seoul.

71. Interview with labor activist, August 11, 2003, Oakland, CA.

72. Interview with union leader, November 10, 2002, Seoul.

6. WHAT IS A "WORKER"?

1. From 1993 to 1999, seven counties (Alameda, Contra Costa, Los Angeles, Monterey, San Francisco, San Mateo, and Santa Clara) chose to establish public authorities. In 1999, home care unions and consumer advocates successfully lobbied for the passage of state legislation that requires every California county to create a public authority under the independent provider model of assisted services. For detailed analysis of SEIU home care worker campaigns in California, Oregon, New York, and Washington, see Mareschal 2006.

2. Another crucial case of unionism by "specially employed workers" in 1999 involved home-based tutors (*haksŭpchi*) for elementary school students. The most well-known case is the Jaenung Educational Corporation home-based tutors union, which I briefly discussed in chapter 4.

3. While home-based tutors in South Korea—a group of "independently contracted" workers that also successfully unionized during this same period—work in isolated settings like home care workers, they represent a more varied workforce in terms of gender, age, and education. Thus, I excluded them as a comparative case.

4. If we also take into account home health aides, a separate occupational category under the BLS, figures increase from 347,000 to 615,000 between 1992 and 2000, with a projected increase of 291,000 jobs from 2000 to 2010 (U.S. Bureau of Labor Statistics, 2000).

5. The number of home health aides increased from 8,170 in 1990 to 34,500 in 2000. From 2006 to 2016, the number of home health aides is projected to increase from 48,000 to 66,700. The number of personal and home care aides is also projected to increase from 284,200 in 2006 to 361,000 in 2016. "Home Health Aides," "Personal and Home Care Aides," State of California Employment Development Department, http://www.calmis.ca.gov/file/healthcare/hcc-home-health-aides.pdf; http://www.calmis.ca.gov/file/healthcare/hcc-personal-home-care-aides.pdf.

6. Bill Billiter, "In a Stressful State; Budget Deadlock, No Paycheck Put New Pressures on Mother of Disabled Sons," *Los Angeles Times*, August 28, 1992.

7. In the United States, home care workers as a paid category of wage labor did not exist until 1971 when domestic work was finally recognized under the Fair Labor Standards Act (FLSA). Domestic work remained exempt from minimum wage and overtime pay protections, however. (See Klein and Boris 2007, 182.)

8. Although the number of golf courses and the number of individual golfers has been increasing over the past ten years, the number of golf caddies per country club has been decreasing. In 1990, there was an average of 269 golf game assistants per country club. In 2000, this number decreased to an average of 109 golf game assistants per course, and a report by the Korean Contingent Workers Center estimates that this number will further decrease to about 70 to 80 workers per course (Korean Contingent Workers Center 2002, 73).

9. Contradictory decisions between regional courts and the Seoul Supreme Court have also produced conflicting definitions of the employment status of golf caddies. These conflicting interpretations can be traced to different scopes of definition for what a "worker" is under the Trade Union and Adjustment Act, which defines workers more broadly than the Labor Standards Act.

10. "Golf Caddies, Standing for their Rights," *Working Women:* 23 (October): 4–9.

11. Internal union document, Korea Working Women's Network, 2000.

12. Quoted in Steven Greenhouse, "In Biggest Drive since 1937, Union Gains a Victory," *New York Times*, February 26, 1999.

13. Ophelia McFadden brought extensive experience to the home care workers' organizing campaign as both a union and community leader. In a congressional tribute to her in 1999, California House of Representatives member Julian Dixon called her "one of labor's most influential leaders." McFadden has a background in the Los Angeles civil rights movement and joined SEIU Local 434B's staff in 1968. She was also the first African American woman vice-president of SEIU and the AFL–CIO and the first African American woman to serve on the Los Angeles County Federation of Labor board. She has also been active with Coalition of Black Trade Unionists, the Coalition of Labor Union Women, the Los Angeles Branch of the National Association for the Advancement of Colored people (NAACP), and the Praises of Zion Church.

14. Nancy Cleeland and Nicholas Riccardi, "Raise for County Home Care Workers Faces Obstacles," *Los Angeles Times*, May 16, 2000.

15. "SEIU Local 434B Chronology," internal union document, www.seiu434b.org/docUploads/Union%20History%20Dec04.pdf (accessed December 2004).

16. Henry Weinstein, "Union Sues to Make County the Homecare Workers' Boss," *Los Angeles Times*, January 1, 1988.

17. Stu Schneider, "Victories for Home Health Care Workers: Home Care Workers Get Organized," *Dollars and Sense* (September/October 2003): 26.

18. Nancy Cleeland, "California Homecare Workers Press Pay Demands," *Los Angeles Times*, May 16, 2000.

19. Deborah Stone, "Why We Need a Care Movement," *The Nation*, February 25, 2000.

20. One of their first legislative collaborations was a joint campaign to revise IHSS's funding strategy and to reverse the 12 percent cuts to the IHSS budget. In 1992, they were able to secure $800 million in federal funds under Medicaid's "personal care option" and to appoint an advisory group called the IHSS Reorganization Work Group (RWG), consisting of four disabled clients, four elderly clients, six representatives of elder and disabled advocacy groups, two Social Security reps, one IHSS social worker, two home care workers, and one union rep.

21. In a report to the County Board of Supervisors, the IHSS Work Group stated that home care workers suffered from an array of problems under the existing system, such as low wages, high rates of attrition, inadequate referral services, insufficient hours allotted for care, the absence of provisions for emergency services, a lack of help for clients who could not manage workers on their own, and an insufficient number of social workers.

22. Quoted in *SEIU Action*, January/February 2001.

23. Nancy Cleeland, "Home-Care Workers Are Expected to Join Union," *Los Angeles Times*, February 24, 1999.

24. According to Janet Heinritz-Canterbury (2002, 19n8), a "showing of interest" is required to request an NLRB election to represent IHSS workers. "A public authority ordinance or a county resolution stipulates the percentage of workers who are required to indicate that they want to be represented by the union.

25. Nancy Cleeland, "Home-Care Workers Vote for Union," *Los Angeles Times*, February 26, 1999.

26. Ibid.

27. "Struggle against the Retrenchment of Women over 41 Years of Age," *Working Women*, August 1999.

28. Interview with union leader, October 11, 2002, Seoul.

29. Park et al., 2001, 78.

30. During the initial stages, KWWAU researcher Jin Young Park explains, new members joined the union less out of the belief that it would help their labor situation and more because they trusted the individual caddies that recommended the union (Park et al. 2001).

31. *Weekly Human Rights News*, 2000.

32. "88 Tourism Development Assaults a Group of Golf Caddies," *Weekly Human Rights News*, April 27, 2000 (in Korean). The repression by employers at 88CC, however, is typical of the kinds of violence and harassment that women workers faced during collective actions. See incidents at Chung Sungshin Hospital and Lotte Hotel.

33. "Recognize Specially Employed Workers as Workers," *Contingent Worker* [newsletter of the Korean Contingent Worker Center], June 2002.

34. KWTU internal union report, quoted in Park 2001.

35. Despite the legal decision, the company responded by intensifying its anti-union tactics as the strike continued. In addition to setting up a company union to bargain with, management also tried to break the will of workers: They forbade any rest during work hours, cut off the electricity and water in the shower room, and shut down the resting room due to "renovation." But these efforts could not break the strike.

36. Yoon-Ja Shin, "No Achievements Without Struggle," *Working Women*, October 2000.

37. "First Ever Collective Agreement by Golf Caddies (88CC)," *Working Women*, April 2002; "Conclusion of Negotiations and Gain of Accident Insurance for 88CC," *KWTU Newspaper*, September 2002.

38. Korean Contingent Workers Center, 2002.

39. Nancy Cleeland and Nicholas Riccardi, "Raise for County Home Care Workers Faces Obstacles," *Los Angeles Times*, May 16, 2000.

40. Emmett Berg, "County Commits to Raises for Homecare Workers," *City News Service*, September 12, 2000.

41. In October 2002, Local 434B secured wage raises from $6.75 per hour to $7.50 per hour and expanded health care coverage for home care workers (reduced minimum hours necessary to qualify from 112 hours per month to 80 hours). In October 2004, after an aggressive nine-month campaign that mobilized thousands of workers, consumers, and coalition partners against the state's proposed budget cuts, Local 434B won a wage increase from $7.50 to $8.10 per hour.

42. "Local 434B's Membership Helps Kick Off Historical Immigrant Freedom Ride," http://www.seiulocal434b.org/homecarela/freedom_ride_story.cfm (accessed April 10, 2005; Web page now discontinued*).

43. "Launching Poor People's Campaign," http://www.seiu434b.org/homecarela/poorpeoplescampaign.cfm (accessed April 10, 2005; Web page now discontinued).

44. "The Fight Against Poverty Has Begun," Op-Ed by Tyrone Freeman, http://www.seiulocal434b.org/homecarela/fight_against_poverty_has_begun.cfm (accessed April 10, 2005; Web page now discontinued).

45. Joo-Yeon Jeong and Seung-Min Choi, "Neoliberalism through the Eyes of Women," Policy and Information Center of Internal Solidarity (PICIS), November 2001, http://focusweb.org/publications/2001/neoliberalism-through-the-eyes-of-women.html.

46. Ibid.

7. DILEMMAS OF ORGANIZING WORKERS AT THE MARGINS

1. Thanks to Andre Schmidt at the University of Toronto for posing this simple but profound question after a presentation at the Munck Center for International Studies in October 2007.

2. "Can this Man Save Labor?" (cover story), *Business Week,* September 13, 2004; Matt Bai, "The New Boss" (cover story); *New York Times Sunday Magazine* January 30, 2005; Karen Tumulty, "Can Labor Regain Its Clout," *Time,* February 27, 2005; Ruth Milkman "A More Perfect Union" (op-ed), *New York Times,* June 30, 2005; "Nelson Lichtenstein: Can Rebels Revive the Labor Movement?" *Los Angeles Times,* July 26, 2005; Steven Greenhouse, "For Chairwoman of Breakway Labor Coalition, Deep Roots in the Movement," *New York Times,* October 10, 2005; Rik Kirkland, "The New Face of Labor," *Fortune,* October 10, 2006; Lynne Duke, "Love, Labor, Loss," *Washington Post,* January 3, 2006, "Andy Stern: The New Boss," CBS News, May 14, 2006; Steven Greenhouse, "Ambitions Are Fueling a Division of Labor," *New York Times,* July 26, 2006.

3. Steven Greenhouse, "A Union President Presses for Growth amid a New Round of Criticisms," *New York Times,* June 1, 2008.

4. Steven Greenhouse, "Union Grows, But Leader Faces Criticism," *New York Times,* February 29, 2008.

5. Steven Greenhouse, "Conflict Between 2 Unions Intensifies," *New York Times,* April 16, 2008.

6. Under the new law, businesses were legally required to change the employment status of nonregular employees to that of regular employees after two years of employment. However, employers did not have to provide any justification for firing workers within the two-year period, which created a legal loophole for employers to arbitrarily fire workers as a way to avoid converting irregularly employed workers into regularly employed workers with full benefits and access to labor rights. The labor movement's previous experience with laws such as the Dispatch Agency Law (*P'akyŏnbŏb*), which legalized temporary employment agencies, provided evidence that many employers opted to circumvent the law rather than abide by it.

7. "E-land labor union marks 300th day of strike," *The Hankyoreh,* April 17, 2008.

8. Interview with union leader, July 30, 2007, Seoul.

Bibliography

Abrams, E., and F. S. Abrams. 1975. "Immigration Policy—Who Gets In and Why?" *Public Interest* 38 (Winter): 3–29.

Agarwala, Rina. 2007. "From Work to Welfare: A New Class Movement in India." *Critical Asian Studies* 38(4): 419–444.

Ahn, Johyup. 2002a. "Long-Term Trends of Employment and Directions for Labor Market Policies for Sustainable Economic Growth." Paper presented at the International Forum on 1st Northeast Asia Labor Forum, Beijing.

——. 2002b. "What Have We Learned About Alternative Employment Relationships in Korea?" Issue paper, Korea Labour Institute, Seoul.

——. 2006. "Nonstandard Work in Japan and Korea—The Origin of Wage Differentials." Unpublished paper, Korea Labour Institute, Seoul.

Alexander, Jeffrey C. 1988. "Culture and Political Crisis: 'Watergate' and Durkheimian Sociology." In *Durkheimian Sociology: Cultural Studies,* edited by Jeffrey C. Alexander, 187–224. Cambridge: Cambridge University Press.

Alinsky, Saul. 1972. *Rules of Radicals: A Practical Primer for Realistic Radicals.* New York: Vintage Books.

——. 1989. *Reveille for Radicals.* New York: Vintage Books.

Armbruster-Sandoval, Ralph. 2005. *Cross-Border Labor Solidarity in the Americas: The Anti-Sweatshop Movement and the Struggle for Social Justice.* New York: Routledge.

——. 2005. "Workers of the World Unite? The Contemporary Anti-Sweatshop Movement and the Struggle for Social Justice in the Americas." *Work and Occupations* 32:464–485.

Aronowitz, Stanley. 1998. *From the Ashes of the Old: American Labor and America's Future.* Boston: Houghton Mifflin.

——. 2003. "A Mills Revival." *Logos* 2(3/4): 67–93.

Arrighi, Giovanni. 1990. "Marxist Century, American Century: The Making and Remaking of the World Labour Movement." *New Left Review* 179:29–63.

Barrett, Richard E., and Soomi Chin. 1987. "Export-oriented Industrializing States in the Capitalist World System: Similarities and Differences." In *The Political Economy of the New Asian Industrialism,* edited by F. C. Deyo, 23–43. Ithaca, NY: Cornell University Press.

Bello, Walden. 2004. "The Global South." In *A Movement of Movements: Is Another World Possible?,* edited by Tom Mertes, 49–69. London and New York: Verso Press.

Belzer, Michael H. 2000. *Sweatshop on Wheels: Winners and Losers in Trucking Deregulation.* New York: Oxford University Press.

Blanchflower, David G., and Alex Bryson. 2007. *The Wage Impact of Trade Unions in the UK Public and Private Sectors.* 12A Discussion Paper No. 3055.

Blank, Rebecca M. 1998. "Contingent Work in a Changing Labor Market." In *Generating Jobs: How to Increase Demand for Less-Skilled Workers,* edited by Richard B. Freeman and Peter Gottschalk, 258–294. New York: Russell Sage.

Blauner, Bob. 1972. *Racial Oppression in America.* New York: Harper and Row.

Bluestone, Barry, and Bennett Harrison. 1982. *The Deindustrialization of America.* New York: Basic Books.

Bobrow, David B., and James J. Na. 1999. "Korea's Affair with Globalization: Deconstructing Segyehwa." In *Democratization and Globalization in Korea: Assessments and Prospects,* edited by C. I. Moon and J. R. Mo. Seoul: Yonsei University Press.

Bonacich, Edna. 1972. "A Theory of Ethnic Antagonism: The Split Labor Market." *American Sociological Review* 37:547–559.

———. 1976. "Advanced Capitalism and Black/White Race Relations in the United States: A Split Labor Market Interpretation." *American Sociological Review* 41:34–51.

———. 1979. "The Past, Present, and Future of Split Labor Market Theory." In *Research in Race and Ethnic Relations,* edited by H. M. Hunter and R. M. Dennis, 17–64. Greenwich, CT: JAI Press.

———. 1980. "Class Approaches to Ethnicity and Race." *Insurgent Sociologist* 10:9–23.

Bourdieu, Pierre. 1984. *Distinction: A Social Critique of the Judgement of Taste.* Cambridge, MA: Harvard University Press.

———. 1986. "The Forms of Capital." In *Handbook of Theory and Research for the Sociology of Education,* edited by John G. Richardson, 241–258. New York: Greenwood Press.

———. 1989. "Social Space and Symbolic Power." *Sociological Theory* 7:18–26.

———. 1990. *In Other Words: Essays Towards a Reflexive Sociology.* Stanford, CA: Stanford University Press.

———. 1991. *Language and Symbolic Power.* Cambridge: Polity.

———. 2000. *Pascalian Meditations.* Stanford, CA: Stanford University Press.

Bourdieu, Pierre, and Loic J. D. Wacquant. 1992. *An Invitation to Reflexive Sociology.* Chicago: University of Chicago Press.

Broadbent, Kaye. 2007. "Sisters Organising in Japan and Korea: The Development of Women-Only Unions." *Industrial Relations Journal* 38(3): 229–251.

Brody, David. 1993. *Workers In Industrial America: Essays on the Twentieth Century Struggle.* New York: Oxford University Press.

———. 1997. "Labor Elections: Good for Workers?" *Dissent* 71–77.

Bronfenbrenner, Kate, Sheldon Friedman, Richard Hurd, Rudolph Oswald, and Ronald Seeber. 1998. *Organizing to Win: New Research on Union Strategies.* Ithaca, NY: Cornell University Press, ILR Press.

Bronfenbrenner, Kate, and Rob Hickey. 2002. "Changing to Organize: A National Assessment of Union Organizing Strategies." In *Rebuilding Labor: Organizing and Organizers in the New Union Movement,* edited by Ruth Milkman and Kim Voss, 17–61. Ithaca, NY: Cornell University Press, ILR Press.

Burawoy, Michael. 1981. "The Capitalist State in South Africa: Marxist and Sociological Perspectives on Race and Class." *Political Power and Social Theory* 2:279–335.

———. 1991. *Ethnography Unbound: Power and Resistance in the Modern Metropolis.* Berkeley: University of California Press.

———. 2000. *Global Ethnography: Forces, Connections, and Imaginations in a Postmodern World.* Berkeley: University of California Press.

California Employment Development Department. 2000. "Home Health Support Occupations: California Occupational Guide." State of California: Employment Development Department, Labor Market Information Division, Information Services Group.

Chang, Grace. 2000. *Disposable Domestics.* Cambridge, MA: South End Press.

Cho, Soon Kyoung. 1985. "The Labor Process and Capital Mobility: The Limits of the New International Division of Labor." *Politics and Society* 14(2): 185–222.

———. 2000. "Hanbŏbŭl kachanghanwibŏbŭinonri: nonghyŏbŭi sanaepupu usŏn haegowa 'ŭitochŏk ch'apyŏr" [The Logic of Unlawfulness under the Disguise of Lawfulness]. In *Nodong Gwa P'eminichŭm* [Labor and Feminism], edited by Soonkyoung Cho, 138–170. Seoul: Ewha Women's University Press.

Choi, Jang Jip. 1989. *Labor and the Authoritarian State: Labor Unions in South Korean Manufacturing Industries, 1961–1980.* Seoul: Korea University Press.

———. 1993. "Political Cleavages in South Korea." In *State and Society in Contemporary Korea,* edited by Hagen Koo, 13–50. Ithaca, NY: Cornell University Press.

Choi, Sang Rim. 2000. "The Reality of Korean Women Workers and the Activities of the Korean Women's Trade Union." In *Strategies of Organizing Women Workers in the 21st Century: The Experiences of the Women's Trade Union and its Future Tasks.* Seoul: Korean Women's Trade Union.

Chun, Jennifer Jihye. 2001. "Flexible Despotism: The Intensification of Insecurity and Uncertainty in the Lives of Silicon Valley's High-Tech Assembly Workers." In *The Critical Study of Work: Labor, Technology and Global Production,* edited by R. Baldoz, C. Koeber, and P. Kraft, 127–154. Philadelphia: Temple University Press.

———. 2005. "Public Dramas and the Politics of Justice Comparison of Janitors' Union Struggles in South Korea and the United States." *Work and Occupations* 32:486–503.

———. 2008. "The Contested Politics of Gender and Irregular Employment: Revitalizing the South Korean Democratic Labour Movement." In *Labour and the Challenges of Globalization: What Prospects for Transnational Solidarity?,* edited by Andreas Bieler, Ingemar Lindberg, and Devan Pillay, 23–44. London: Pluto Press.

Chun, Soonok. 2004. *They Are Not Machines: Women Workers and Their Fight for Democratic Trade Unions in the 1970s.* London: Ashgate.

Clawson, Dan. 2003. *The Next Upsurge: Labor and the New Social Movements.* Ithaca, NY: Cornell University Press.

Clemens, Elisabeth S. 1993. "Organizational Repertoires and Institutional Change: Women's Groups and the Transformation of U.S. Politics, 1890–1920." *American Journal of Sociology* 98:755–798.

———. 1997. *The People's Lobby: Organizational Innovation and the Rise of Interest Group Politics in the United States, 1890–1925.* Chicago: University of Chicago Press.

Clinton, Angela. 1997. "Flexible Labor: Restructuring the American Work Force. *Monthly Labor Review* (August): 3–27.

Cobb, Rachael. 1999. "Background Memo: Unionizing the Homecare Workers of Los Angeles County." Unpublished paper.

Cobble, Dorothy Sue. 2004. *The Other Women's Movement: Workplace Justice and Social Rights in Modern America.* Princeton: Princeton University Press.

Cobble, Dorothy Sue, and Leah F. Vosko. 2000. "Historical Perspectives on Representing Nonstandard Workers." In *Nonstandard Work: The Nature and Challenges of Changing Employment Relations,* edited by F. Carre, M. A. Ferber, L. Golden, and S. A. Herzenberg, 291–312. Champaign, IL: Industrial Relations Research Association.

Cohany, Sharon R. 1996. "Workers in Alternative Employment Arrangements." *Monthly Labor Review* (October): 31–45.

Comaroff, Jean, and John L. Comaroff. 2000. *Millennial Capitalism and the Culture of Neoliberalism.* Durham, NC: Duke University Press.

Cooper, Frederick. 1987. *On the African Waterfront: Urban Disorder and the Transformation of Work in Colonial Mombasa.* New Haven: Yale University Press.

Cornfield, Daniel B., and Holly J. McCammon, eds. 2003. *Labor Revitalization: Global Perspectives and New Initiatives.* Amsterdam London: JAI Press.

Cranford, Cynthia. 1998. "Gender and Citizenship in the Restructuring of Janitorial Work in Los Angeles." *Gender Issues* 16(4): 25–51.

———. 2000. "Economic Restructuring, Immigration and the New Labor Movement: Latina/o Janitors in Los Angeles." Working Paper, Center for Comparative Immigration Studies, University of California, San Diego.

———. 2007. "It's Time to Leave Machismo Behind!" *Gender & Society.* 21(3): 409–438.

Cranford, Cynthia J., and Leah F. Vosko. 2006. "Conceptualizing Precarious Employment: Mapping Wage Work Across Social Location and Occupational Context." In *Precarious Employment: Understanding Labour Market Insecurity in Canada,* edited by Leah F. Vosko, 43–66. Montreal: McGill–Queens University Press.

Crotty, James, and Kang-Kook Lee. 2006. "The Effects of Neoliberal 'Reforms' on the Post-Crisis Korean Economy." *Review of Radical Political Economics* 38(3): 381–387.

Cumings, Bruce. 1981. *The Origins of the Korean War,* vol. 1. Princeton, NJ: Princeton University Press.

Davis, Mike. 1986. *Prisoners of the American Dream: Politics and Economy in the History of the US Working Class.* London: Verso.

Delp, Linda, and Katie Quan. 2002. "Homecare Worker Organizing in California: An Analysis of a Successful Strategy." *Labor Studies Journal* 27:1–23.

Derickson, Alan. 1994. "Health Security for All? Social Unionism and Universal Health Insurance, 1935–1958." *Journal of American History* 80:1333–1356.

Deyo, Frederic C. 1989. *Beneath the Miracle: Labor Subordination in the New Asian Industrialism.* Berkeley: University of California Press.

DiMaggio, Dan. 2004. "The Justice for Janitors Campaign in 21st century Boston." Unpublished undergraduate thesis, Harvard University, Cambridge, MA.

Dubofsky, Melvyn. 2000. *We Shall Be All: A History of the Industrial Workers of the World.* Urbana: University of Illinois Press.

Durkheim, Emile. 1984 [1933]. *The Division of Labor in Society.* Translated by W. D. Halls. New York: The Free Press.

Ehrenberg, Ronald G., Leif Danzier, and Gee San. 1983. "Cost-of-Living Adjustment Clauses in Union Contracts: A Summary of Results." *Journal of Labor Economics* 1:215–245.

Erickson, Christopher L., Catherine Fisk, Ruth Milkman, Daniel J. B. Mitchell, and Kent Wong. 2002. "California's Revolt at the Bottom of the Wage Scale." In *California Policy Options 2002,* edited by D. J. B. Mitchell, 111–153. Los Angeles: The School of Public Policy and Social Research, University of California, Los Angeles and the UCLA Anderson Forecast.

Evans, Peter. 1997. "The Eclipse of the State? Reflections on Stateness in an Era of Globalization." *World Politics* 50:62–87.

———. 2000. "Fighting Marginalization with Transnational Networks: Counter-Hegemonic Globalization." *Contemporary Sociology* 29:230–241.

———. 2005. "Counter-hegemonic Globalization: Transnational Social Movements in the Contemporary Global Political Economy." In *Handbook of Political Sociology,* edited by Thomas Janoski, Robert R. Alford, Alexander M. Hicks, and Mildred A. Schwartz 655–670, Cambridge: Cambridge University Press.

Fairbrother, Peter, and Charlotte A. B. Yates. 2003. *Trade Unions in Renewal: A Comparative Study.* London: Continuum.

Fantasia, Rick. 1988. *Cultures of Solidarity: Consciousness, Action, and Contemporary American Workers.* Berkeley: University of California Press.

Fantasia, Rick, and Kim Voss. 2004. *Hard Work Remaking the American Labor Movement.* Berkeley: University of California Press.

Farber, Henry S., and Bruce Western. 2000. "Round Up the Usual Suspects: The Decline of Unions in the Private Sector, 1973–1998." Working Paper No. 437, Industrial Relations Section, Princeton University (April): 1–45.

——. 2002. "Ronald Reagan and the Politics of Declining Union Organization." *British Journal of Industrial Relations* 40(3): 385–401.

Fernandez-Kelly, Maria Patricia. 1983. *For We Are Sold, I and My People: Women and Industry in Mexico's Frontier.* Albany: State University of New York Press.

Fine, Janice. 2006. *Workers Centers: Organizing Communities at the Edge of the Dream.* Ithaca, NY: Cornell University Press.

Fraser, Nancy. 1995. "From Redistribution to Recognition? Dilemmas of Justice in a 'Post-Socialist' Age." *New Left Review* 212 (July/August): 68–93.

——. 1996. "Rethinking the Public Sphere: A Contribution to the Critique of Actually Existing Democracy." In *Habermas and the Public Sphere,* edited by C. Calhoun, 109–142. Cambridge, MA: MIT Press.

——. 1997. *Justice Interruptus: Critical Reflections on the "Postsocialist" Condition.* New York: Routledge.

Freeman, Richard. 2001. "Why Not a Living Wage at Harvard?" *Harvard Magazine* 104(2): 69–70.

Fröbel, Folker, Jurgen Heinrichs, and Otto Kreye. 1980. *The New International Division of Labor in the World Economy: Structural Unemployment in Industrialised Countries and Industrialisation in Developing Countries.* Cambridge: Cambridge University Press.

Fuentes, Annette, and Barbara Ehrenreich. 1983. *Women in the Global Factory.* Cambridge, MA: South End Press.

Ganz, Marshall. 2000. "Resources and Resourcefulness: Strategic Capacity in the Unionization of California Agriculture: 1959–1966." *American Journal of Sociology* 105:1003–1062.

Ganz, Marshall, Kim Voss, Teresa Sharpe, Carl Somers, and George Strauss. 2004. "Against the Tide: Projects and Pathways of the New Generation of Union Leaders, 1984–2001." In *Rebuilding Labor: Organizing and Organizers in the New Union Movement,* edited by R. Milkman and K. Voss, 150–195. Ithaca, NY: Cornell University Press.

Gerteis, Joseph. 2007. *Class and the Color Line: Interracial Class Coalition in the Knights of Labor and the Populist Movement.* Durham, NC: Duke University Press.

Gills, Barry K., and Dongsook S. Gills. 2000. "Globalization and Strategic Choice in South Korea: Economic Reform and Labor." In *Korea's Globalization,* edited by S. S. Kim, 29–53. Cambridge: Cambridge University Press.

Glenn, Evelyn Nakano. 1992. "From Servitude to Service Work: Historical Continuities in the Racial Division of Paid Reproductive Labor." *Signs* 18(1): 1–43.

——. 2002. *Unequal Freedom: How Race and Gender Shaped American Citizenship and Labor.* Cambridge, MA: Harvard University Press.

Goldberg, Chad Alan. 2005. "Contesting the Status of Relief Workers during the New Deal." *Social Science History* 29(3): 337–371.

Gonos, George. 1998. "The Interaction between Market Incentives and Government Actions." In *Work: American Employment Relations in Transition,* edited by K. Barker and K. Christensen, 170–191. Ithaca, NY: Cornell University Press.

Griffin, Larry J., Holly J. McCammon, and Christopher Botsko. 1990. "The Unmaking of a Movement? The Crisis of U.S. Trade Unions in Comparative Perspective." In *Change in Societal Institutions,* edited by J. G. Maureen, T. Hallinan, and David Klein, 169–194. New York: Plenum.

Gross, James A. 1995. *Broken Promise: The Subversion of U.S. Labor Relations Policy, 1947–1994.* Philadelphia: Temple University Press.

Gupta, Akhil, and James Ferguson. 1997. "Culture, Power Place: Ethnography at the End of an Era." In *Culture, Power, Place: Explorations in Critical Anthropology,* edited by Akil Gupta and James Ferguson, 1–29. Durham, NC: Duke University Press.

Hardt, Michael, and Antonio Negri. 2000. *Empire.* Cambridge, MA: Harvard University Press.

———. 2004. *Multitude: War and Democracy in the Age of Empire.* New York: Penguin Press.

Hart, Gillian Patricia. 2002. *Disabling Globalization: Places of Power in Post-apartheid South Africa.* Berkeley: University of California Press.

Hartmann, Heidi. 1976. "The Historical Roots of Occupational Segregation: Capitalism, Patriarchy, and Job Segregation by Sex." *Signs* 1(3) Part 2: 137–169.

Harvard Committee on Employment and Contracting Policies (HCECP). 2001. "Final Report: Lower-Paid Workers at Harvard University." Cambridge, MA: Harvard University.

Harvard Workers Center. 2001. "Outsourcing, Its Discontents and Some Solutions." (October 12). Cambridge, MA: Harvard University.

Harvey, David. 1989. *The Condition of Postmodernity: An Enquiry into the Origins of Cultural Change.* New York: Blackwell.

Hatch, Julie, and Angela Clinton. 2000. "Job Growth in the 1990s: A Retrospect." *Monthly Labor Review* 123(12): 3–18.

Heinritz-Canterbury, Janet. 2002. "Collaborating to Improve In-Home Supportive Services: Stakeholder Perspectives on Implementing California's Public Authorities." Report for the Paraprofessional Healthcare Institute and the California Wellness Foundation, New York.

Higham, John. 1992. *Strangers in the Land: Patterns of American Nativism: 1860–1925.* New Brunswick, NJ: Rutgers University Press.

Horwitt, Sanford D. 1989. *Let Them Call Me Rebel: Saul Alinsky, His Life and Legacy.* New York: Knopf.

Houseman, Susan N., and Anne E. Polivka. 1999. "The Implications of Flexible Staffing Arrangements for Job Stability." In *On the Job: Is Long-Term Employment A Thing of the Past?,* edited by D. Neumakr, 427–463. New York: Russell Sage.

Hudson, Kenneth. 1999. "No Shortage of 'Nonstandard Jobs.'" Briefing Paper, Washington, DC.: Economic Policy Institute.

Isaac, Larry W. 1997. "Transforming Localities: Reflections on Time, Causality, and Narrative in Contemporary Historical Sociology." *Historical Methods* 30:4–12.

Jacoby, Sanford M. 1997. *Modern Manors: Welfare Capitalism Since the New Deal.* Princeton, NJ: Princeton University Press.

Jasper, James. 1997. *The Art of Moral Protest: Culture, Biography, and Creativity in Social Movements.* Chicago: University of Chicago Press.

Jeong, Jooyeon. 2005. "Diversity in Union Security among Enterprise Unions: Cases of Korean Metal Firms from a Micro-Socioeconomic Perspective." *Journal of Industrial Relations* 47:43–61.

Jessop, Bob. 1994. "From Keynesian Welfare to the Schumpeterian Workfare State." In *Towards a Post-Fordist Welfare State,* edited by R. Burrows and B. Loader. London: Routledge.

Johnston, Hank, and Bert Klandermas, eds. 1995. Social Movements and Culture. Minneapolis: University of Minnesota Press.

Kalleberg, Arne L., Barbara F. Reskin, and Ken Hudson. 2000. "Bad Jobs in America: Standard and Nonstandard Employment Relations and Job Quality in the United States." *American Sociological Review* 65:256–278.

Kang, Insoon. 2001. *Hankuk Yŏsŏng Nodongcha Undongsa* [Korean Women Workers Movement History]. Seoul: Hanur Academy Publishing.

Katz, Harry Charles. 1985. *Shifting Gears: Changing Labor Relations in the U.S. Automobile Industry.* Cambridge, MA: MIT Press.

Katznelson, Ira, and Aristide R. Zolberg. 1986. *Working-class Formation: Nineteenth-century Patterns in Western Europe and the United States.* Princeton, NJ: Princeton University Press.

KCTU. *See* Korean Confederation of Trade Unions.

Keck, Margaret E., and Kathryn Sikkink. 1998. *Activists Beyond Borders: Advocacy Networks in International Politics.* Ithaca, NY: Cornell University Press.

Kessner, Thomas, and Betty Boyd Caroli. 1981. *Today's Immigrants, Their Stories: A New Look at the Newest Americans.* New York: Oxford University Press.

Kim, Andrew Eungji, and Innwon Park. 2006. "Changing Trends of Work in South Korea." *Asian Survey* 46(3): 437–456.

Kim, Hyun-mee. 1997. "Gender/Sexuality System as a Labor Control Mechanism: Gender Identity of Korean Female Workers in a U.S. Multinational Corporation." *Korea Journal* 37:56–70.

Kim, Iggy. 2000. "South Korean Marxists Regroup." *Green Left Weekly* 395, March 1.

Kim, Marlene. 2000. "Women Paid Low Wages: Who They Are and Where They Work." *Monthly Labor Review* (September): 26–33.

Kim, Seung-kyung. 1996. "Big Companies Don't Hire Us, Married Women": Exploitation and Empowerment among Women Workers in South Korea." *Feminist Studies* 22:555–571.

——. 1997. *Class Struggle or Family Struggle? The Lives of Women Factory Workers in South Korea.* Cambridge, MA: Cambridge University Press.

Kim, Sunhyuk. 2003. "Civil Society in a Democratizing Korea" In *Korea's Democratization,* edited by Samuel S. Kim, 81–106. Cambridge: Cambridge University Press.

Kim, Tae-hyun. 2003. "Post Financial-crisis Challenges and the Korean Labor Movement's New Agenda." Seoul: Korean Confederation of Trade Unions (KCTU).

Klein, Jennifer. 2003. *For All These Rights: Business, Labor, and the Shaping of America's Public-Private Welfare State.* Princeton, NJ: Princeton University Press.

Klein, Jennifer, and Eileen Boris. 2007. "'We Were the Invisible Workforce': Unionizing Home Care." In *The Sex of Class,* edited by Dorothy Sue Cobble, 177–192. Ithaca, NY: Cornell University Press.

Koo, Hagen. 1993. "The State, Minjung, and the Working Class in South Korea." In *State and Society in Contemporary Korea,* edited by Hagen Koo, 131–162. Ithaca, NY: Cornell University Press.

——. 2000. "The Dilemmas of Empowered Labor in Korea: Korean Workers in the Face of Global Capitalism." *Asian Survey* 40:227–250.

——. 2001. *Korean Workers: The Culture and Politics of Class Formation.* Ithaca, NY: Cornell University Press.

——. 2002. "Engendering Civil Society: The Role of the Labor Movement." In *Korean Society Civil Society, Democracy, and the State,* edited by C. K. Armstrong. London: Routledge.

Korea Labor Institute (KLI). 2000. "Analysis of Labor Force Conditions in the First Half of 1999." Seoul: KLI.

Korean Confederation of Trade Unions (KCTU). 1998. "South Korea in the First Half of 1998." Seoul: KCTU.

——. 1999. "Full Steam Ahead for Concerted Action." Seoul: KCTU.

——. 2005. "KCTU Report on Recent Situation of Labour Laws and Industrial Relations." Seoul: KCTU.

———. 2006. "KCTU Counter-Report on the South Korea Government's Report to the UN Human Rights Committee." Seoul: KCTU (October 10).

Korean Contingent Workers Center. 2001. "Special Edition: Temporary, Part-time, Contract and Independent Workers in Korea." *Contingent Worker* 1:23 (in Korean).

———. 2002a. "Recognize Specially Employed Workers as Workers." *Contingent Worker* 6(12): 10–27.

———. 2002b. "Tears Curtained with the Sound of 'Nice Shot': Analysis on the Activities of 88 Country Club Branch of Korean Women's Trade Union." *Contingent Worker.*

Korean National Statistics Office. 1981–2000. "Economically Active Population Survey (EPS)." *Major Statistics of Korean Economy.* Seoul: National Statistics Office.

Korean Women's Trade Union (KWTU). 2000. "Caddies Are Not Flowers! Caddies Are Workers." February 24, http://cast.jinbo.net/news/show.php?docnbr=11995 (in Korean).

———. 2001. "Report of 2001 Struggles." Seoul: KWTU (in Korean).

Korean Women Workers Association (KWWA). 1991. "The Current Labor Situation in South Korea." Report. Seoul: KWWA. July.

Korean Women Workers Associations United (KWWAU). 1994. "Industrial Restructuring in Korea and Consequences for Women Workers." Prepared for Committee for Asian Women. September. Seoul: KWWAU.

———. 1998. "Organizational Strategies of Irregular Women Workers." Report. Seoul: KWWAU.

———. 1999. "Unorganized Women Workers in Korea: Current Conditions and Future Tasks" Open Forum. July 14. Seoul: KWWAU.

———. 2000. "South Korean Women Workers and Globalization." Report. Seoul: KWWAU.

———. 2007. "20 Years of Korean Women Workers Association, Evaluation and Future Tasks." Internal organizational document. Seoul: KWWAU.

Kwon, Du Sup. 2001. "Worker Characteristics of Golf Caddies." *Labor and the World* (September 17).

KWWAU. *See* Korean Women Workers Associations United.

Lee, Byoung-Hoon. 2004. "Solidarity Crisis of Korea's Labor Union Movement." *Journal of Asiatic Studies* 47(4).

Lee, Byoung-Hoon, and Stephen J. Frenckel. 2004. "Divided Workers: Social Relations Between Contract and Regular Workers in a Korean Auto Company." *Work, Employment and Society* 18(3): 507–530.

Lee, Ching Kwan. 2007. *Against the Law: Labor Protests in China's Rustbelt and Sunbelt.* Berkeley: University of California Press.

Lee, Jinock. 2003. "A Study of the Emergence of Women's Trade Unions in South Korea." Paper presented at the Alice Hook 199th Birthday Conference, Institute for Industrial Relations, Cornell University.

Lee, Joohee. 2000. "The Financial Crisis, Search for Flexibility and Changes in Industrial Relations: The South Korean Case." Paper presented at the International Conference on "Transforming Korean Business and Management Culture," Michigan State University, East Lansing, MI.

———. 2003. "Take Gender Seriously: Feminization of Nonstandard Work in Korea and Japan." Paper presented at ILO/UTYO Nobel Peace Prize Social Policy Lectures and Symposium, "New Forms and Meanings of Work in an Increasingly Globalised World." University of Tokyo, Japan. December 1–3.

Lee, Kapyoung. 1998. "Globalisation and Liberalisation: The Challenge for People's Struggle and Solidarity." Seoul: KCTU.

Lee, Kwang-taek. 2000. "Expansion of Basic Rights for Non-Standard Workers: Legal Aspects. Policy Forum, Citizens' Coalition for Economic Justice." Seoul, April 24.

Lee, Namhee. 2001. "Making Minjung Subjectivity: Crisis of Subjectivity and Rewriting History, 1860–1988." PhD diss., University of Chicago.

———. 2005. "Representing the Worker: The Worker-Intellectual Alliance of the 1980s in South Korea." *Journal of Asian Studies* 64(4): 911–937.

———. 2007. *Making of Minjung: Democracy and the Politics of Representation in South Korea.* Ithaca, NY: Cornell University Press.

Lee, Sang Hak. 2001. "The Impact of Neo-Liberal Globalization: Irregular Jobs, Informal Sector Work and Poverty in Asian Workers (with a Focus on the Case of Korea)." Seoul: KCTU.

Lee, Wonduck, and Kang Shik Choi. 1998. "Labor Market and Industrial Relations in Korea: Retrospect on the Past Decade and Policy Directions for the 21st Century." Seoul: Korea Labor Institute (KLI).

Lee, Wonduck, and Joohee Lee. 2002. "Will the Model of Uncoordinated Decentralization Persist? Changes in Korean Industrial Relations after the Financial Crisis." In *The Changing Nature of the Structure of Collective Bargaining: Is "Coordinated Decentralization" the Answer?* Ithaca, NY: Cornell University Press, ILR Press.

Lerner, Stephen. 2007. "Global Corporations, Global Unions." *Contexts* 6(3): 16–22.

Levy, Peter B. 1994. *The New Left and Labor in the 1960s.* Urbana: University of Illinois Press.

Lichtenstein, Nelson. 2002. *State of the Union: A Century of American Labor.* Princeton, NJ: Princeton University Press.

Lie, John. 1998. *Han Unbound: The Political Economy of South Korea.* Stanford, CA: Stanford University Press.

Lim, Linda Y. C. 1983. "Capitalism, Imperialism, and Patriarchy: The Dilemma of Third-World Women Workers in Multinational Factories." In *Women, Men, and the International Division of Labor,* edited by June Nash and Maria Patricia Fernandez-Kelly, 70–91. Albany: State University of New York Press.

Linder, Marc. 2000. *Wars of Attrition: Vietnam, the Business Roundtable, and the Decline of Construction Unions.* Iowa City, IA: Fanpihua Press.

Lingafelter, Teresa. 2003. "Our Voice: A Participatory Action Research Project of SEIU Local 434B." Paper presented at the Annual Graduate Student Conference of the UC Institute for Labor and Employment. Santa Cruz, CA.

Logan, John R., and Harvey Luskin Molotch. 1987. *Urban Fortunes: The Political Economy of Place.* Berkeley: University of California Press.

Lopez, David, and Cynthia Feliciano. 2000. "Who Does What? California's Emerging Plural Workforce." In *Organizing Immigrants: The Challenge for Unions in Contemporary California,* edited by Ruth Milkman, 25–48. Ithaca, NY: Cornell University Press.

Lopez, Steven Henry. 2004. *Reorganizing the Rust Belt: An Inside Study of the American Labor Movement.* Berkeley: University of California Press.

Lovell, Vicky, Heidi Hartmann, and Misha Werschkul. 2007. "More than Raising the Floor: The Persistence of Gender Inequalities in the Low-Wage Labor Market." In *The Sex of Class: Women Transforming American Labor,* edited by Dorothy Sue Cobble, 35–57. Ithaca, NY: Cornell University Press.

Luce, Stephanie. 2004. *Fighting for a Living Wage.* Ithaca, NY: Cornell University Press.

MacLean, Nancy. 2006. *Freedom Is Not Enough: The Opening of the American Workplace.* New York and Cambridge, MA: Russell Sage Foundation and Harvard University Press.

McCall, Leslie. 2001. "Sources of Racial Wage Inequality in Metropolitan Labor Markets: Racial, Ethnic, and Gender Differences." *American Sociological Review* 66(4): 520–541.

McCarthy, John, and Mayer N. Zald. 1977. "Resource Mobilization and Social Movements: A Partial Theory." *American Journal of Sociology* 82: 1212–1241.

McMichael, Philip. 2005. "Globalization." In *The Handbook of Political Sociology: States, Civil Societies, and Globalization*, edited by Janoski et al., 587–606. Cambridge: Cambridge University Press.

Manheim, Jarol B. 2000. *The Death of a Thousand Cuts: Corporate Campaigns and the Contemporary Attack on the Corporation*. Mahwah, NJ: Lawrence Erlbaum Associates Publishers.

Mareschal, Patrice M. 2006. "Innovation and Adaptation: Contrasting Efforts to Organize Home Care Workers in Four States." *Labor Studies Journal* 31:25–49.

Marshall, T. H. 1964. "Citizenship and Social Class." In *Class, Citizenship, and Social Development*. New York: Doubleday.

Massey, Doreen B. 1994. *Space, Place, and Gender*. Minneapolis: University of Minnesota Press.

Massey, Douglas S., Jorge Durand, and Nolan J. Malone. 2002. *Beyond Smoke and Mirrors: Mexican Immigration in an Era of Economic Integration*. New York: Russell Sage Foundation.

Matthiessen, Peter. 1969. *Sal Si Puedes: Cesar Chavez and the New American Revolution*. New York: Random House.

Meyerson, Harold. 1998. "A Second Change: The New AFL-CIO and the Perspective Revival of American Labor." In *Not Your Father's Union Movement: Inside the AFL-CIO*, edited by J.-A. Mort. New York: Verso Press.

Milkman, Ruth. 1997. *Farewell to the Factory: Auto Workers in the Late Twentieth Century*. Berkeley: University of California Press.

——. 2000. "Introduction." In *Organizing Immigrants: The Challenge for Unions in Contemporary California*, edited by R. Milkman, 1–24. Ithaca, NY: Cornell University Press.

——. 2006. *L.A. Story: Immigrant Workers and the Future of the U.S. Labor Movement*. New York: Russell Sage Foundation.

——. 2007. "Two Worlds of Unionism: Women and the New Labor Movement." In *The Sex of Class: Women Transforming American Labor*, edited by Dorothy Sue Cobble, 63–80. Ithaca, NY: Cornell University Press.

Milkman, Ruth, and Kim Voss, eds. 2004. *Rebuilding Labor: Organizing and Organizers in the New Union Movement*. Ithaca, NY: Cornell University Press.

Milkman, Ruth, and Kent Wong. 2000. "Organizing the Wicked City: The 1992 Southern California Drywall Strike." In *Organizing Immigrants*, edited by R. Milkman, 169–198. Ithaca, NY: Cornell University Press.

Miller, James. 1994. *Democracy Is in the Streets: From Port Huron to the Siege of Chicago*. Cambridge, MA: Harvard University Press.

Mishel, Lawrence, Jared Bernstein, and Heather Boushey. 2003. *The State of Working America 2002/2003*. Ithaca, NY: Cornell University Press.

Mitchell, Timothy. 1990. "Everyday Metaphors of Power." *Theory and Society* 19(5): 545–577.

Mohanty, Chandra Talpade. 1997. "Women Workers and Capitalist Scripts: Ideologies of Domination, Common Interests and the Politics of Solidarity." In *Feminist Geneologies, Colonial Legacies, Democratic Futures*, edited by M. J. Alexander and C. T. Mohanty. New York: Routledge.

——. 2003. *Feminism Without Borders: Decolonizing Theory, Practicing Solidarity*. Durham, NC: Duke University Press.

Moody, Kim. 1997. *Workers in a Lean World: Unions in the International Economy.* London: Verso.

Moon, Kyoung-Hee. 2006. "Gender Impact of Employment Adjustment in Post-1997 Korea: Cases of Hyundai Motor Company and the Commercial Banking Industry." Australian National University. http://www.gu.edu.au/centre/gapc/activitiespast/kyoung-hee01.html (accessed December 2006).

Morris, Aldon. 1983. "Black Southern Student Sit-in Movement: An Analysis of Internal Organization." *American Sociological Review* 46(6): 744–767.

Morris, Aldon, and Naomi Braine. 2001. "Social Movements and Oppositional Consciousness." In *Oppositional Consciousness: The Subjective Roots of Social Protest,* edited by Jane J. Mansbridge and Aldon D. Morris. Chicago: University of Chicago Press.

Morris, Aldon, and C. M. Mueller, eds. 1992. *Frontiers in Social Movement Theory.* New Haven, CT: Yale University Press.

Munck, Ronaldo, and Peter Waterman. 1999. *Labour Worldwide in the Era of Globalization Alternative Union Models in the New World Order.* New York: Palgrave Macmillan.

Nam, Jeong-Lim. 2000. "Gender Politics in the Korean Transition to Democracy." *Korean Studies* 24:94–112.

Nam, Sunghee. 1991. "Determinants of Female Labor Force Participation: A Study of Seoul, South Korea, 1970–1980" *Sociological Forum* 6(4): 641–659.

Ngai, Mai M. 2004. *Impossible Subjects: Illegal Aliens and the Making of Modern America.* Princeton, NJ: Princeton University Press.

Nordlund, Willis J. 1997. *The Quest for a Living Wage: The History of the Federal Minimum Wage Program.* Westport, CT: Greenwood Press.

North American Congress on Latin America (NACLA). 1970. NACLA Research Methodology Guide. New York: NACLA.

Offner, Amy. 2004. "Harvard Sit-in." Unpublished draft. Boston.

Ogle, George E. 1990. *South Korea's Dissent Within the Economic Miracle.* London: Zed Press.

Ohmae, Kenichi. 1995. *The End of the Nation State-How Region States Harness the Prosperity of the Global Economy.* New York: Free Press.

Ong, Aihwa. 1999. *Flexible Citizenship: The Cultural Logics of Transnationality.* Durham, NC: Duke University Press.

——. 2006. *Neoliberalism as Exception: Mutations in Citizenship and Sovereignty.* Durham, NC: Duke University Press.

Park, Chung Hee. 1970. *Our Nation's Path: Ideology of Social Reconstruction.* Seoul: Hollym Corporation Publishers.

Park, Hyun Ok. 2008. "For the Rights of "Colonial Returnees": Korean Chinese, Decolonization, Neoliberal Democracy in South Korea," Paper presented at the Neoliberalism in South Korea Workshop, University of Toronto. February 2.

Park, Jin Young. 2000. "Women's Strategies to Challenge Globalization." Paper presented at Globalisation and Informalisation: An International Women Workers Workshop. Organized by Korean Women Workers Associations United (KWWAU), the Committee for Asian Women and Women Working Worldwide, Seoul, Korea.

——. 2001. "Urgent Measures Needed to Adjust Minimum Wages to a Realistic Level." *Working Women. Newsletter of Korean Women Workers Associations United* 26:3–10.

Park, Jin Young, Seung Hee Han, Myoung Suk Kim, and Ju Hwan Lee. 2001. "Women's Organizing Model for Women's Empowerment." Research report presented at Second Anniversary of the Korean Women's Trade Union, Seoul, Korea.

Park, Mi. 2002. "Ideology and Lived Experience: Revolutionary Movements in South Korea." Unpublished paper. London School of Economics.

Park, Min-na. 2005. *Birth of Resistance: Stories of Eight Women Worker Activists.* Translated by Sarah Eunkyung Chee. Seoul: Korea Democracy Foundation.

Park, Namhee. 2006. Korean Women Workers' Activism. *Peace Review: A Journal of Social Justice* 18:491–498.

Peck, Jamie, and Nik Theodore. 2009. "Labor Markets from the Bottom Up." In *Handbook of Employment and Society: Working Space,* edited by S. McGrath-Champ, A. Herod, and A. Rannie. London: Edward Elgar.

Perry, Charles R. 1987. *Union Corporate Campaigns.* Philadelphia: Industrial Research Unit, Wharton School, University of Pennsylvania.

Piven, Francis Fox, and Richard A. Cloward. 1977. *Poor People's Movements: Why They Succeed, How They Fail.* New York: Pantheon Books.

Polanyi, Karl. 1944. *The Great Transformation: The Political and Economic Origins of our Time.* Boston: Beacon Press.

Pollin Robert, and Stephanie Luce. 1998. *The Living Wage: Building a Fair Economy.* New York: New Press.

Pred, Allan Richard, and Michael Watts. 1992. *Reworking Modernity: Capitalisms and Symbolic Discontent.* New Brunswick, NJ: Rutgers University Press.

Prezeworski, Adam. 1985. *Capitalism and Social Democracy.* Cambridge: Cambridge University Press.

Reich, Michael, David M. Gordon, and Richard C. Edwards. 1973. "A Theory of Labor Market Segmentation." *American Economic Review* 63(2): 359–363.

Reimers, David M. 1998. *Unwelcome Strangers: American identity and the Turn against Immigration.* New York: Columbia University Press.

Reubens, Beatrice G. 1949. "Social Legislation in Japan." *Far Eastern Survey* 18:269–275.

Rivas, Lynn. 2005. "A Significant Alliance: The Independent Living Movement, the Service Employees International Union, and the Establishment of the First Public Authorities in California." Unpublished paper. University of California, Berkeley.

Rooks, Daisy. 2004. "Sticking It Out or Packing It In? Organizing Retention in the New Labor Movement." In *Rebuilding Labor: Organizing and Organizers in the New Union Movement,* edited by Ruth Milkman and Kim Voss, 195–224. Ithaca, NY: Cornell University Press.

Rose, Sonya O. 1999. "Cultural Analysis and Moral Discourse: Episodes, Continuities, and Transformations." In *Beyond the Cultural Turn: New Directions in the Study of Society and Culture,* edited by Victoria E. Bonnell and Lynn Hunt, 217–238. Berkeley: University of California Press.

Roseman, Curtis C., and Gregg A. Wassmansdorf. 1994. "The Social Geography of an Urban University Community." Working paper No. 54, Los Angeles Project: Research on the Peoples of Los Angeles, Los Angeles.

Rothenbuhler, Eric W. 1988. "The Liminal Fight: Mass Strikes as Ritual and Interpretation." In *Durkheimian Sociology: Cultural Studies,* edited by Jeffrey C. Alexander, 66–89. Cambridge: Cambridge University Press.

Rudy, Preston. 2004. "'Justice for Janitors,' Not 'Compensation for Custodians': The Political Context and Organizing in San Jose and Sacremento." In *Rebuilding Labor: Organizing and Organizers in the New Union Movement,* edited by R. Milkman and K. Voss, 133–149. Ithaca, NY: Cornell University Press.

Rumbaut, Ruben G. 1994. "Origins and Destinies: Immigration to the United States Since World War II." *Sociological Forum* 9(4): 583–621.

Sallaz, Jeffrey J., and Jane Zavisca. 2007. "Bourdieu in American Sociology, 1980–2004." *Annual Review of Sociology* 33:21–41.

Salzinger, Leslie. 2003. *Genders in Production: Making Workers in Mexico's Global Factories.* Berkeley: University of California Press.

Sassen, Saskia. 1988. *The Mobility of Labor and Capital: A Study in International Investment and Labor Flow.* Cambridge: Cambridge University Press.

———. 1996. *Losing Control?: Sovereignty in an Age of Globalization.* New York: Columbia University Press.

———. 1998. *Globalization and Its Discontents.* New York: New Press.

———. 2000. *Cities in a World Economy.* Thousand Oaks, CA: Pine Forge Press.

Savage, Lydia. 1998. "Justice for Janitors: Geographies of Organizing." In *Organizing the Landscape: Geographical Perspectives on Labor Unionism,* edited by A. Herod, 225–253. Minneapolis: University of Minnesota Press.

Scipes, Kim. 2000. "It's Time to Come Clean: Open the AFL-CIO Archives on International Labor Operations." *Labor Studies Journal* 25(2): 4–25.

Scott, Joan Wallach. 1988. *Gender and the Politics of History.* New York: Columbia University Press.

Seidman, Gay. 1994. *Manufacturing Militance: Workers' Movements in Brazil and South Africa, 1970–1985.* Berkeley: University of California Press.

Seo, Yongju. 2004. "Industrialization, Globalization, and Women Workers in South Korea, 1960–2003." MA thesis, University of Massachusetts, Lowell.

Silver, Beverly J. 2003. *Forces of Labor: Workers' Movements and Globalization since 1870.* Cambridge: Cambridge University Press.

Smith, Jackie, and Hank Johnston. 2002. *Globalizing Resistance: Transnational Dimensions of Social Movements.* Boulder, CO: Rowman and Littlefield.

Snow, David A., and Robert D. Benford. 1992. "Ideology, Frame Resonance, and Participant Mobilization." *International Social Movement Research* 1:197–217.

Snow, David A., E. Burke Rochford, Jr., Steven K. Worden, and Robert D. Benford. 1986. "Frame Alignment Processes, Micromobilization, and Movement Participants." *American Journal of Sociology* 51:464–91.

Song, Jesook. 2006a. "Family Breakdown and Homeless Women: Neoliberal Governance during the Asian Debt Crisis in South Korea, 1997–2001." *Positions* 14(1): 37–65.

———. 2006b. "Historicization of Homeless Spaces: The Seoul Train Station Square and the House of Freedom." *Anthropological Quarterly* 79(2): 193–223.

Soysal, Yasemin. 1993. *Limits of Citizenship: Migrants and Postnational Membership in Europe.* Chicago: University of Chicago Press.

Standing, Guy. 1999. "Global Feminization Through Flexible Labor: A Theme Revisited." *World Development* 27:583–602.

Suh, Doowon. 2003. "Korean White-Collar Unions' Journey to Labor Solidarity: The Historic Path from Enterprise to Industrial Unionism." In *Labor Revitalization: Global Perspectives and New Initiatives, Research in the Sociology of Work,* edited by Daniel B. Cornfield and Holly J. McCammon, 153–180. Oxford: Elsevier JAI.

Sweeney, John J. 1996. *America Needs a Raise: Fighting for Economic Security and Social Justice.* Boston: Houghton Mifflin.

Swidler, Ann. 1995. "Cultural Power and Social Movements." In *Social Movements and Culture,* edited by Hank Johnson and Bert Klandermas, 25–40. Minneapolis: University of Minnesota Press.

Tarrow, Sydney. 1998. *Power in Movement: Social Movements, Collective Action, and Politics.* Cambridge: Cambridge University Press.

Thompson, E. P. 1966. *The Making of the English Working Class*. New York: Vintage.

Tilly, Charles. 1995. "Globalization Threatens Labor's Rights." *International Journal of Working-Class History* 47:1–23.

Turner, Lowell. 2005. "From Transformation to Revitalization." *Work and Occupations* 32:383–399.

Turner, Lowell, and Richard W. Hurd. 2001. "Building Social-Movement Unionism: The Transformation of The American Labor Movement." In *Rekindling The Movement: Labor's Quest for Relevance in the Twenty-First Century*, edited by L. Turner, H. C. Katz, and R. W. Hurd, 9–26. Ithaca, NY: Cornell University Press, ILR Press.

Turner, Victor. 1974. *Dramas, Fields, and Metaphors: Symbolic Action in Human Society*. Ithaca, NY: Cornell University Press.

U.S. Bureau of the Census. Selected years (1979–1990). Statistical Abstract of the United States. Washington, DC: Government Printing Office.

U.S. Bureau of Labor Statistics. 1969–1987. *Directory of National and International Labor Unions*. Washington, DC: Government Printing Office.

——. 1983–2002. "Union Affiliation of Employed Wage and Salary Workers by Occupation and Industry." Current Population Survey, aggregated data. Washington, DC: Government Printing Office.

——. 2005. "Contingent and Alternative Employment Relationships," February. Washington, DC: Department of Labor.

——. 1999. "MLR: The Editor's Desk," December 22. Washington, DC: Government Printing Office.

——. Selected years. Household Data Annual Averages. 42. Union affiliation of employed wage and salary workers by occupation and industry. Washington, DC: Government Printing Office.

——. 2000a. Establishment Data Historical Employment. B-1. "Employees on nonfarm payrolls by major industry sector, 1954 to date." Washington, DC: Government Printing Office.

——. 2000b. "Personal and Homecare Aides; Service Occupations." *Occupational Outlook Handbook for 2000*, 335–336. Washington, DC: Government Printing Office.

Van Der Werf, Martin. 2000. "How the U. of Pennsylvania Learned that Outsourcing Is No Panacea." *Chronicle of Higher Education* 46(31): 38–39.

Vosko, Leah F., and Dorothy Sue Cobble. 2000. "Historical Perspectives on Representing Nonstandard Workers." In *Nonstandard Work: The Nature and Challenges of Changing Employment Arrangements*, edited by F. Carre, 291–312. Champaign: Industrial Relations Research Association, University of Illinois at Urbana-Champaign.

Vosko, Leah H., N. Zukewich, and Cynthia Cranford. 2003. "Precarious Jobs: A New Typology of Employment." *Perspectives on Labour and Income* 15:39–49.

Voss, Kim. 1993. *The Making of American Exceptionalism: The Knights of Labor and Class Formation in the Nineteenth Century*. Ithaca, NY: Cornell University Press.

Voss, Kim, and Rachel Sherman. 2000. "Breaking the Iron Law of Oligarchy: Union Revitalization in the American Labor Movement." *American Journal of Sociology* 106:303–349.

Voss, Kim, and Michelle Williams. 2006. "The Local in the Global: Rethinking Social Movements in the New Millennium." Paper presented at the RC44 Labor and Labour Movements Section of the ISA—XVI ISA World Congress of Sociology. July 2006. Durban, South Africa.

Waldinger, Roger, C. Erickson, Ruth Milkman, Daniel Mitchell, Abel Valenzuela, Kent Wong, and Maurice Zeitlin. 1998. "Helots No More: A Case Study of the Justice for Janitors Campaign in Los Angeles." In *Organizing to Win: New Research on Union Strategies,* edited by K. Bronfenbrenner, S. Friedman, R. Hurd, R. Oswald, and R. Seeber, 102–119. Ithaca, NY: Cornell University Press.

Waldinger, Roger, and Jennifer Lee. 2001. "New Immigrants in Urban America." In *Strangers at the Gate: New Immigrants in Urban America,* edited by Roger Waldinger 30–79. Berkeley: University of California Press.

Walsh, Jess. 2001. "Creating Unions, Creating Employers: A Los Angeles Home-Care Campaign." In *Care Work: The Quest for Security,* edited by M. Daly, 219–232. Geneva: International Labour Office.

——. 2002. "Building Unionism in Non-Standard Service Industries: The Case of Homecare Organising in Australia and the United States." Paper presented at XV World Congress of Sociology. Brisbane, Australia.

Warner, Michael. 2002. *Publics and Counterpublics.* New York: Zone Books.

Webster, Edward, and Sakhela Buhlungu. 2004. "Between Marginalisation and Revitalisation? The State of Trade Unionism in South Africa." *Review of African Political Economy* 100:229–245.

Western, Bruce. 1997. *Between Class and Market: Postwar Unionization in the Capitalist Democracies.* Princeton, NJ: Princeton University Press.

Williams, Michelle. 2008. *Roots of Participatory Democracy: Democratic Communists in South Africa and Kerala, India.* London: Palgrave.

Williams, Rhys H. 1995. "Constructing the Public Good: Social Movements and Cultural Resources." *Social Problems* 42(1): 124–144.

——. 2004. "The Cultural Contexts of Symbolic Action: Constraints, Opportunities, and the Symbolic Life of Social Movements." In *Blackwell Companion to Social Movements,* edited by David A. Snow, Sarah A. Soule, and Hanspeter Kriesi, 91–115. Malden, MA: Blackwell.

Wilton, Robert D, and Cynthia Cranford. 2002. "Toward an Understanding of the Spatiality of Social Movements: Labor Organizing at a Private University in Los Angeles." *Social Problems* 49:374–394.

Wright, Erik Olin. 2000. "Workers Power, Capitalist Interests, and Class Compromise." *American Journal of Sociology* 105:1559–1571.

Wright, Erik Olin, and Rachel Dwyer. 2000. "The American Jobs Machine: Patterns of Job Growth in the 1960s and the 1990s." *Boston Review* 25(6): 21–26.

Zald, Mayer N., and John D. McCarthy. 1980. "Social Movement Industries: Competition and Cooperation Among Social Movement Organizations." *Research in Social Movement, Conflict, and Change* 3:1–20.

Zieger, Robert H. 1995. *American Workers, American Unions.* Baltimore, MD: Johns Hopkins University Press.

Zieger, Robert H., and Gilbert J. Gall. 2002. *American Workers, American Unions.* 2nd ed. Baltimore, MD: Johns Hopkins University Press.

Index

Note: Page numbers with an *f* indicate figures; those with a *t* indicate tables.